"Women perform very well at school but lose ground as soon as they start working. *The Broken Rung* shares deep research, lessons, and advice to raise awareness and help women succeed in their careers. Very good insights for men, too!"

    —**ANA BOTÍN**, Executive Chairman, Banco Santander

"Most people say they support women's success. If you really do, read and apply this book. And then give it to everyone you know. When women succeed, we all do."

    —**REID HOFFMAN**, cofounder, LinkedIn and Inflection AI; partner, Greylock Partners

"Around the world, women still face many barriers to advancement. The authors of this book aren't just committed to building fairer workplaces, they're working to help women navigate unfairness. *The Broken Rung* is a timely resource for women to take their careers into their own hands."

    —**ADAM GRANT**, #1 *New York Times* bestselling author, *Hidden Potential* and *Think Again*; podcast host, *Re:Thinking*

"A powerful guide for women aiming to succeed in their careers . . . *The Broken Rung* not only reflects on the systemic challenges that women face in the workplace but also shares many real-life, personal stories that are very relatable, actionable, and inspiring."

    —**JESSICA TAN**, President, Sun Life Canada; former Co-CEO, Ping An Insurance

"*The Broken Rung* identifies one of the world's toughest challenges for women and their careers, and it offers insightful, powerful, and practical help for them to overcome it through gaining and leveraging experience capital."

    —**PAUL POLMAN**, former CEO, Unilever; coauthor, *Net Positive*

"*The Broken Rung* explains why so many women fail to reach the highest levels of business and what we can do to give ourselves an essential leg up on the slippery corporate ladder. A great guide for professional women with ambition."

—**SALLY SUSMAN**, Executive Vice President and
Chief Corporate Affairs Officer, Pfizer;
author, *Breaking Through*

"*The Broken Rung* paints a vivid picture of the systemic, often hidden barriers women face in the workplace. With data-driven insights and inspiring stories, it's an essential guide for overcoming career obstacles."

—**MARC BENIOFF**, cofounder, Chairman, and CEO, Salesforce

THE BROKEN RUNG

THE BROKEN RUNG

When the Career Ladder Breaks
for Women—and How They
Can Succeed in Spite of It

KWEILIN ELLINGRUD
LAREINA YEE
MARÍA DEL MAR MARTÍNEZ

HARVARD BUSINESS REVIEW PRESS
BOSTON, MASSACHUSETTS

Copyright 2025 McKinsey & Company, Inc. United States

All rights reserved

Printed in the United States of America

10 9 8 7 6 5 4 3 2 1

No part of this publication may be reproduced, stored in or introduced into a retrieval system, or transmitted, in any form, or by any means (electronic, mechanical, photocopying, recording, or otherwise), without the prior permission of the publisher. Requests for permission should be directed to permissions@harvardbusiness.org, or mailed to Permissions, Harvard Business School Publishing, 60 Harvard Way, Boston, Massachusetts 02163.

The web addresses referenced in this book were live and correct at the time of the book's publication but may be subject to change.

Cataloging-in-Publication data is forthcoming.

ISBN: 978-1-64782-718-2
eISBN: 978-1-64782-719-9

The paper used in this publication meets the requirements of the American National Standard for Permanence of Paper for Publications and Documents in Libraries and Archives Z39.48-1992.

This is a book to help women harness their power and reach their full potential. We dedicate it with gratitude to those who supported us on our own journeys and inspired us to pay it forward.

CONTENTS

PART FOUR

PREPARE FOR THE INEVITABLE

THE
BROKEN
RUNG

The Broken Rung Effect

Women are doing everything they can to prepare themselves for successful careers, especially when it comes to their educations. As early as kindergarten, girls on average outperform boys across all disciplines, including math. The trend continues into high school, college, and beyond. In almost all developed countries, women on average earn undergraduate and graduate degrees at higher rates than men and attain better grade point averages. By the time they accept their well-earned diplomas, many bright, motivated women are ready to take the job market by storm.

And yet, a strange thing happens as soon as they cross the graduation threshold. Women, who make up 59 percent of college graduates in the United States, immediately lose ground, representing only 48 percent of those entering the corporate workforce.* At the pivotal moment when the first promotions to become a manager happen, the odds of advancement are lower for women. For every one hundred men, only 81 women

---

* We recognize and acknowledge that not everyone fits into the gender binary. Most research, however, is broken down this way, given the lack of data that's split beyond male and female groups. We firmly believe that intersectionality is critical to understanding gender inequality and look forward to a day when we have better data available. Regardless of how you identify, we hope you will find this book inspiring and valuable.

receive that same promotion opportunity. By race, promotion rates differ quite a bit: for every 100 men who receive that first promotion to manager, 89 white women, 99 Asian women, 65 Latina women, and 54 Black women do—the blended average is 81 women overall (see figure I-1).[1] This disparity continues at each step up the corporate ladder. We call this phenomenon the *broken rung*, which cuts short women's progress up the career ladder. The broken rung is the most significant obstacle women encounter on the path to senior leadership, as their odds of being promoted in their early careers to managerial positions are much lower than men's. This advancement gap persists and compounds over women's careers, and causes lower and lower female representation on every step of the corporate leadership ladder.

For instance, consider two peers: Patricia and James. They both graduated with good grades and the same degree from the same university, and Patricia was class valedictorian. After graduation, they ended up at the same *Fortune* 500 company, both in entry-level positions with equal starting salaries.

From there, however, their paths quickly began to diverge. After just two years on the job, James was promoted and received a fairly significant pay raise, while Patricia got a small cost-of-living bump. Then James moved to another company and received another promotion. Five years into his career, he had doubled his starting salary, while Patricia had seen only incremental raises. Despite hard work and consistently strong performance reviews, she hadn't been given many new responsibilities or received a promotion.

Finally, Patricia landed a job at a new company, which came with a healthy pay increase that meant she started earning six figures. She was excited until she realized that she was making eighty cents on the dollar compared with her male counterparts in the same role. Further, her new employer didn't offer much in the way of training or advancement.

Imagine Patricia looking over at James as they ascend their career ladders. She sees that he is several rungs ahead of her, well on his way to senior leadership, and she views his professional success with confusion and frustration. They started on equal footing, and as far as she can tell,

FIGURE I-1

The broken rung: For every 100 men who were promoted to the first-level manager role, only 81 women overall, 86 white women, 99 Asian women, 65 Latina women, and 54 black women were

Men, women overall, white women

| For every 100 men promoted to manager | 81 women overall are promoted | 86 white women are promoted | 99 Asian women are promoted | 65 Latina women are promoted | 54 Black women are promoted |

Latina women, Black women

Source: Alexis Krivkovich, Rachel Thomas, and Lareina Yee et al., "Women in the Workplace Report 2024: The 10th-Anniversary Report," McKinsey & Company and Leanln.org, 2024.

she's done everything right. Yet their careers have played out so differently. What happened?

Unfortunately, this story is not extreme or rare. The truth is that there are more Patricias out there than we can possibly count. They are talented, educated, and hardworking, and several years into their careers they are caught completely off guard when they feel they have gotten short shrift, yet they can't put a finger on exactly how or why. We wrote this book to break that cycle.

As Patricia's story shows, the first broken rung of the corporate ladder opens up a gender gap that widens further at every subsequent rung, with women stagnating in their roles rather than being promoted, and it continues from entry level all the way to senior leadership. *Every rung on the corporate ladder is broken.* It is that first broken rung, however, that affects everything else beyond the entry level.

Despite many initiatives to improve gender parity in the corporate ranks over the last decade, we have only seen modest gains. The largest improvement has been in the C-suite, where women moved from being one in five top executives to just over one in four reporting to the CEO. But 29 percent at the top is still far from gender parity. And that C-suite representation is one out of fourteen people (7 percent) for women of color, which breaks down as follows: 2.8 percent Black, 2.5 percent Asian, 1.4 percent Latina, 0.4 percent multiracial, and <0.1 Indigenous. The overall pipeline shows that women lose ground at every level. Women start the talent pipeline below their population parity and college graduation rates at 48 percent, then managers are 39 percent; directors, 37 percent; vice presidents, 34 percent; and senior vice presidents, 29 percent. By the time we get to the top, it's no surprise that gender parity seems elusive.[2]

This outcome is not due to a lack of ambition. For the past decade through McKinsey's Women in the Workplace report and other global surveys, women have consistently expressed the same or greater intensity as men in their desire to be promoted and hold leadership positions. The level of ambition to be a leader, be promoted, or hold the top job is even higher among women under thirty and women of color. Yet year after year the data shows us that this ambition is met with tough odds of success. Why?

After analyzing four million job profiles posted online across numerous countries and using longitudinal data to trace actual career trajectories, we made an intriguing discovery: On average, for men and women across the globe, half of their lifetime earnings stem from the value of what they bring to the table when they start their careers, including their natural talents and formal educations. The other half of their earnings stem from the value of the skills and experiences gained on the job, or what we call *experience capital*.[3]

As we reviewed the patterns in the career trajectories of both men and women in the United States, it became clear that women are not building the same levels of experience capital as men. In other words, they are not amassing the specific skills and experiences on the job that they need to be promoted at equal rates and to maximize their earning potential. Job moves can be made at the same company by taking a new role or by changing companies. While skills can be built within the same role, they are developed the most—and are most recognized by the talent market—when individuals are promoted to a new role. This gender gap in job moves or promotions is a long-hidden driver of the gap between women's and men's incomes over the course of their careers and is holding women back in the workplace.

Make no mistake: Women's struggles to be promoted and build experience capital at equal rates are not their fault, and we are not implying that they need to fix this problem themselves. There are multiple systemic issues at play, and we need to see more progress in policies, programs, and actions by governments, companies, leaders, and individual workers to accelerate the pace of change. That said, we believe the insights in this book will help women steer their careers and maximize success while navigating an imperfect system. It's a collective challenge that we all need to own.

There is a lot that women can do to counter the broken rung effect and build experience capital in the face of these structural barriers. In many ways, focusing on building experience capital can act as an antidote to the broken rung. It isn't a substitute for structural reform, but it represents a source of real empowerment. That's what this book is about.

The insights from our research, combined with the stories of women who have navigated multiple broken rungs, show how to most effectively build experience capital—the best way to avoid being held back and instead fast-track your career. This book is for every woman who wants to accelerate her path at work, who feels there is still a gap between her current position and her greatest aspirations.

Who We Are

Together and separately, the three of us have been researching these phenomena that affect women's careers for decades. And starting in 2018, the three of us have served as McKinsey & Company's first and successive chief diversity and inclusion officers, so we have been applying those findings to our own company. As we sat together at a conference, listening to the incredible stories of women who had achieved great things, we were struck by how much even they had struggled. Many shared the missteps, lonely moments, and obstacles they had faced along the way. And while the three of us may have crossed the chasm to becoming senior leaders in our own careers, it was not without moments when we, too, wondered why the curve felt so steep. We imagined what it would be like if women could just skip that part and experience a smoother path from the beginning. We wrote this book to do our part to help make that happen and to share the unwritten rules that we wish we'd had access to earlier in our careers.

Let us introduce ourselves a bit more and how we came to write this book. In addition to being senior partners in McKinsey & Company's consulting practices and serving as McKinsey's chief diversity and inclusion officers, we are also all working moms. We each have three kids and live in different parts of the world.

Kweilin Ellingrud's international childhood across China, Japan, Ecuador, France, and the United States gave her a window into the ways in which women's lives and careers vary in different societies, fueling her personal passion for women's equity. As director of the McKinsey Global Institute, the research think tank of McKinsey & Company, she has explored the topics of gender equality, the future of work, human capital, and productivity, which has informed much of the data we share in this book. Kweilin is also McKinsey's current chief diversity and inclusion officer, shaping initiatives globally to improve attraction, retention, and inclusion for individuals from diverse backgrounds broadly defined.

Lareina Yee, a senior partner at McKinsey, is the global head of alliances and ecosystems and a director of technology research in McKinsey's Global Institute, who spearheads the firm's gender and diversity research. Throughout her career, she too often found that she was the only woman in the room. Over a decade ago, she took action and cofounded Women in the Workplace, which, in partnership with LeanIn.org, is the largest annual study of women in corporate America. The study's data insights and strategies for companies and individuals to create more inclusive workplaces are the basis for much of this book. Lareina's focus has been to shine a light on the facts and give companies the tools to bridge the gap between their positive intent and results. She served as McKinsey's first chief diversity and inclusion officer, setting the organization on a different course.

María del Mar Martínez was lucky enough to grow up in an egalitarian context and was not prepared for the fact that the curve of her career would be any different from a man's. But as she progressed, she realized that fewer and fewer women were getting promoted at the same pace as men in many European organizations. In fact, she was the first woman elected partner and senior partner in her office, so she committed to making a difference. María del Mar felt there were not enough global insights on the drivers behind this persistent worldwide phenomenon, so she led diversity research in Spain, Europe, and globally. She has delivered on her commitment to diversity as a senior partner and leader in McKinsey's Global Banking Practice, the global leader of the Risk and Resilience Practice, and the chair of the global senior partner nomination committee. She also served as McKinsey's chief diversity and inclusion officer, where she brought new rigor and accountability to diversity efforts internally and with clients.

About This Book

Thankfully, just as data makes clear the problems at the core of workplace inequality, it also reveals the solutions. The insights shared in this book build on nearly two decades of gender and leadership research that McKinsey has invested in, starting with the Women Matter series, the Power of Parity reports, the Centered Leadership initiative, and more. While we have brought together the best of the latest global research, this book is deeply grounded in two specific research reports: Human Capital, which looks at how people navigate their careers, and Women in the Workplace, which focuses on women at work and how they progress.

The Human Capital research is done by the McKinsey Global Institute and is based on millions of professional profiles across four countries, and then a deeper-dive cut by gender in the United States. Meanwhile, Women in the Workplace has been a ten-year partnership with LeanIn .org to publish the broadest and deepest benchmarks by gender and race across large US companies. Each year, Women in the Workplace tracks data within and across roughly three hundred large North American companies and outlines the talent pipelines as well as the policies in place.

These areas of research and others form the backbone of this book's information on how women can best navigate their careers, and we are excited to provide you with strategies that will enable you to live up to your professional potential. Bear in mind, we're not encouraging you to be driven exclusively by money or to sacrifice personal fulfillment for a higher salary. One of the most exciting takeaways is that your career is about so much more than just a job, a title, or a salary. We want to empower you to make any necessary trade-offs consciously and in the ways that work best for you.

We also believe that gaining equal access to promotions and experience capital is essential—it's how you can put yourself in a position to choose, whether that's to work for an organization that is aligned with your personal purpose, to leave a job for a better opportunity, to shoot for the C-suite, to prioritize flexibility, or to maximize your earnings. Every woman is on a unique path. Whatever your priorities, this book will help you understand the barriers you will face, provide tactics to overcome them, and guide you in building a road map for achieving all that you can.

In part one, we will take a thorough look at the problem of the broken rung and how its impact compounds over the course of a woman's career. We'll also explore the potential of experience capital to help women gain traction and counter this effect. In part two, we will start to get tactical and show you how to maximize your experience capital in a variety of ways. Here, we'll focus on the experiences that matter most, including choosing the right company and roles and making the right job moves at the right time. In part three, we'll move on to skill-building, sharing which skills (including technological, social, emotional, and entrepreneurial skills) will enhance your experience capital the most and make you even more valuable in the future. We'll also look at how best to build and signal these skills.

In part four, we will help you avoid some of the most common potential interruptions in your acquisition of experience capital. These include the biases that women too often face in the workplace, health and financial problems, and the decision of whether to become a mother. In each case, we will provide tactics to help prevent career disruption and to continue building your experience capital without letting these life experiences slow you down.

To bring the data to life and show you firsthand what is possible for you, we interviewed dozens of inspiring women from around the globe, spanning different racial and ethnic backgrounds as well as different industries and functions. Among many others, you'll learn from the lived experience of women like Stephanie Carullo, who left Australia to attend a seminal training program that invested in her as a leader, and who brought the skills she gained there all the way to the C-suite. You'll meet Noorain Khan, who made a risky jump from a prestigious law firm to the public sector to follow her purpose, and who is now the senior adviser to the president of the Ford Foundation. And you'll meet Karlie Kloss, the supermodel who transformed her career—and the careers of many others—by learning how to code.

Just like the women we profile, you have always been in the driver's seat of your career. By the end of this book, our greatest hope is that you will have all of the tools and insights you need to accelerate your progress. Your opportunity to find fulfillment, impact, and success on your terms is all within your reach—let's make it happen.

PART ONE

THE ROOTS OF
THE PROBLEM

CHAPTER 1

The Broken Rung

Alexa Johnson is the first person to point out that she has been very lucky. She grew up in an affluent suburb of New York City with parents who both had full-time, robust careers, and she received a great education at Duke University, where she studied hard, held prestigious internships each summer, and graduated at the top of her class.

Yet despite all of her advantages, Alexa's career path so far has not been smooth. After she did a brief stint of consumer marketing for a magazine publisher, her team began experiencing layoffs. She knew that in this shrinking industry, it was only a matter of time before her role would also be eliminated. A fellow alum of Duke introduced Alexa to the hiring manager at a global investment management company, and she was offered an entry-level role as an analyst.

This was Alexa's first lateral pivot, and she was excited about her new job and professional prospects. She did notice that women accounted for less than 25 percent of the senior leadership team, but among her peer group she saw a more even split between men and women. She figured that the next generation of leadership would be more diverse.

Compared with people from her graduating class who hadn't switched career tracks already, Alexa knew she needed to work hard to make up for time spent in a very different profession. The hiring manager at her new job didn't seem to value the experiences Alexa was bringing to the table from her previous role, but she assured Alexa that as long as her performance was satisfactory, she would receive a significant increase in salary and title at the end of her first year; this would essentially put her back on the same level as her peers from her graduating class. Alexa felt reassured, knowing that her performance was within her control. She was ready to roll up her sleeves.

Alexa did indeed work hard, and for the most part she enjoyed her job despite the long hours. There were nights when she worked so late that she ended up sleeping on the floor at the office. She experienced quite a few wins, and at the end of the year she received a glowing review from her manager. So she was incredibly confused and frustrated when she was told that she would not be receiving a promotion or a pay increase as promised.

When she pushed to find out why, the explanation she received was far from satisfying. Alexa's manager and the human resources team all seemed to feel that she deserved to be promoted, but they told her that it just wasn't possible to make a change in her compensation at that time. Even worse, while Alexa was working on her first promotion, men around her who had only started a few years earlier than she had were landing their second and third promotions.

She was feeling completely defeated. Alexa felt she had done everything right. She'd gone to a top school, earned good grades, and worked incredibly hard, and everyone agreed that she'd exhibited a stellar performance. With all of that, how had she already fallen behind so quickly? Would she ever make up the lost ground?

The Glass Ceiling Meets the Broken Rung

In 1978, more than a decade before Alexa was born, a human resources executive named Marilyn Loden participated in a panel discussion at the Women's Exposition in New York City about women's career ambitions. While much of the conversation revolved around the behavioral changes that women should make in order to succeed, Marilyn argued instead that the real issue was the structural barriers keeping them from the top. She stated that there was an "invisible glass ceiling" standing in the way of their aspirations and opportunities.[1] Since then, that image of a glass ceiling sitting at the top of the corporate ladder has become a pervasive symbol of the obstacles that women face when reaching for the top rungs of leadership.

Fast-forward from Marilyn Loden's era to the 1990s, when more women were joining the workforce than ever before. The US Congress responded by forming the Glass Ceiling Commission to study issues in women's advancement, with the group reporting that women represented only 3 to 5 percent of senior leaders at *Fortune* 500 companies. This finding led many organizations to begin focusing on increasing the number of women in these high-level positions.[2]

Progress has been slow but steady. In the roughly thirty years since the Glass Ceiling Commission released its report, women have gone from representing 3 to 5 percent to 29 percent of the C-suite. This is still hardly equitable, but women have made some gains. In the United States in the decade between 2012 and 2022, women's representation in the C-suite increased by 10 percentage points, which is roughly one additional direct report to a CEO out of a ten-person team. The true top is still not diverse, though: in 2023 women made up just over 10 percent of *Fortune* 500 CEOs, 9 percent of the FTSE CEOs, and 5.4 percent of CEOs of the S&P Global Broad Market Index.[3]

One important and often overlooked step in helping more women like Alexa get ahead is addressing the obstacle that affects them—not as they approach the glass ceiling, but actually at the beginning of their careers: the broken rung. The glass ceiling does persist, despite a few small cracks in its surface, but many women begin to fall behind their male counterparts long before they are anywhere near that level.

In our research, we found that women who are just starting out have significantly lower odds of reaching that first manager role than their male peers. And when they typically do reach that first manager role, it is later on in their careers. In the United States, for every one hundred men who get that very first push up the corporate ladder to manager, eighty-one women will receive the same opportunity.[4] The gap has been stubbornly persistent for the last decade, as we have seen a paltry improvement.

The broken rung phenomenon often persists through the manager and director levels and shows that too often women are never able to catch up. Across over one thousand US companies surveyed over the last ten years, women averaged 48 percent of entry-level positions but only 37 percent at the director level, a middle level of seniority. That is a lot of women getting stalled or falling out of the corporate workforce. At the senior levels, women hover at 29 percent, a far cry from the parity they experienced in college or on their first day on the job. Between the entry level and the C-suite, women's representation is nearly cut in half (see figure 1-1).[5]

We see similar trends globally. On the top end of the range are Norway, Australia, and Sweden, with 29 percent to 35 percent of their senior leadership teams made up of women. In the middle we have the United Kingdom at 25 percent, France at 20 percent, and Italy, Brazil, and Germany at 15 percent. On the bottom end of the range, we have Mexico with 12 percent and India and Japan with 7 and 6 percent respectively (see figure 1-2).[6]

Every rung on the ladder is broken, as women, particularly women of color, try to move up the corporate pipeline. But it's that first rung that

FIGURE 1-1

Representation of women falls across the pipeline (% of employees by level as of year-end 2023; US and Canada)

	Entry-level	Manager	Senior manager/ director	Vice president	Senior vice president	C-suite
White men	33	41	46	52	58	56
Men of color	18	18	15	13	13	14
White women	28	27	28	26	22	22
Women of color	19	13	10	8	6	7
Total % of women by level, 2024	48	39	37	34	29	29

Note: The race pipeline does not include employees with unreported race data, so totals may not sum to the overall corporate pipeline totals. Some percentages may sum to 99 percent or 101 percent due to rounding.

Source: Alexis Krivkovich, Rachel Thomas, and Lareina Yee et al., "Women in the Workplace 2024: The 10th-Anniversary Report," McKinsey & Company and LeanIn.org, September 17, 2024.

FIGURE 1-2

Globally, women are underrepresented on executive teams

	Women on executive team (% of total)	Companies with at least one woman executive (%)	Women's labor force participation (%)
Norway	35	100	62
Australia	30	95	62
Sweden	29	97	63
New Zealand	28	92	68
United States	29	93	57
United Kingdom	25	92	58
Singapore	24	96	62
Canada	23	92	61
Colombia	22	83	51
Israel	21	85	61
South Africa	21	79	52
France	20	76	53
Malaysia	19	81	52
Denmark	19	77	59
Spain	16	78	53
Italy	15	82	41
Brazil	15	62	53
Germany	15	62	56
Mexico	12	55	47
India	7	50	33
Japan	6	57	55
Average	20	80	47

Source: McKinsey analysis: Diversity Matters 2022 data set (*n* = 1,265 companies); World Bank labor force participation rate, female (% of female population age 15+), 2023. Alexis Krivkovich et al., "Women in the Workplace 2024: The 10th-Anniversary Report," McKinsey & Company and LeanIn.org, September 17, 2024.

has the greatest impact, both on individual women and on organizations. For every 100 men promoted to manager, there are 81 women overall promoted and 77 women of color. After a nineteen percentage point drop so early in the talent pipeline, it is nearly impossible to close that gap. The impact compounds all the way up the ladder.

Missing the first promotion to manager affects someone's entire career trajectory, especially when it comes to gaining valuable skills and experiences. And with a decrease in female representation at every rung, there are fewer and fewer women to promote at each subsequent level. This leaves very few women with a chance of getting close enough to even tap the glass ceiling.

Making matters worse, the broken rung is often a blind spot of leaders. Many CEOs, managers, and human resources executives have positive intentions about supporting women, but gaps remain in execution. More than half of HR leaders believe that their organization will reach gender parity within the next 10 years.[7] But according to the United Nations, at the current rate of improvement, it will be 176 years until we achieve equal representation in management positions around the world.[8]

To take an optimistic view, however, the problem and solution are opposite sides of the same coin. If we began promoting women and men to manager at the same rates, it would create a powerful domino effect, leading to an increase in representation across the entire pipeline. There would be more women to promote and hire at each subsequent rung.

It would still take time to achieve equality, but if we fixed that first broken rung, women could reach near parity all the way up the ladder within a generation. This shift would also help companies retain ambitious, talented women and create mentors and leaders at all levels for young women to learn from, look up to, and follow.

In other words, we must tackle parity in leadership from the bottom up, rather than only from the top down.

The Double Broken Rung on the Front Lines

Bear in mind, broken rungs aren't just a problem in corporate offices. There is also a double broken rung phenomenon for frontline workers. We define frontline workers as those who work directly with customers or are directly involved in making a product or providing a service. They can be hourly employees, such as baristas, retail associates, and cashiers, or salaried ones, such as facilities managers.

All told, approximately 70 percent of the workforce in the United States holds frontline jobs. These workers face their own obstacles to advancement. A full 70 percent of frontline workers say that they want to advance in their careers.[9] But as in the corporate world, women are held back by broken rungs.

First, there is the earliest promotion within the front line—for example, from retail salesperson to manager or from hourly to salaried worker. Second, there is a broken rung when making the leap to an entry-level corporate role; on average, US companies only promote 4 percent of frontline workers to corporate jobs.[10] Career paths for this transition are rare at best. Companies look at alternative candidate pools to fill corporate roles and often do not offer training and development programs for frontline workers, leaving them with few opportunities to gain the skills they need to advance. As with corporate roles, the broken rungs on the front lines disproportionately affect women of color. Over 70 percent of Black and Latina workers are in frontline roles, and the challenges that women of color face in overcoming both broken rungs further contribute to their low representation in frontline managerial roles and in corporate entry-level positions.

Valentina Lopez, a frontline worker in retail who identifies as Hispanic, is a good example of this. She has been a salesperson at a popular home decor store for two years and wants to move up in the company. In fact, she says that she goes out of her way to try to advance, but she has not had an opportunity to do so. Meanwhile, she has seen several of her male peers be promoted while she remains on the front lines. "They tend to get more support from the higher-ups, especially from the male higher-ups," she says.

Importantly, the broken rung is not a "women's issue." It is an issue for our whole society and the global economy. Like Alexa, Valentina feels unsupported by her company and somewhat demoralized. As she puts it, "It's a lot of lonely work to push yourself upwards."

Across the board, women like Alexa and Valentina are not missing out on promotions because of a lack of ambition. In fact, there is a crowded pool of talented, hardworking women to draw from for these early promotions. Seventy percent of men and women say they are interested in being promoted to the next level. Younger women are even more ambitious, with 80 percent interested in being promoted.[11]

These ambitious women do not anticipate tripping over a broken rung and falling behind so early. Like Alexa or Valentina, many women start their careers believing that inequality won't affect them until much later, as they approach the glass ceiling. Others are not even aware when it is happening to them. It is only when they reach middle management that they realize they have fallen behind their male peers and begin to question whether they will ever be able to reach senior levels of leadership. Indeed, they are now fighting an uphill battle, as their career trajectories have flattened dramatically compared with their peers'.

Therefore, it is especially important for early-career women to have awareness of the broken rung as they enter the workforce and approach their first promotions. Applying tactics to overcome the broken rung can have a strong positive effect on their trajectories.

The Broken Rung's Ripple Effects

The broken rung is not simply a case of missing a single promotion. It's the beginning of a cycle of women receiving "less than," and this compounds to have a long-term impact on multiple dimensions of their careers.

To start, stumbling on a broken rung directly impairs a woman's ability to maximize her experience capital, which has a lasting effect on her lifetime earning potential. As she stagnates in the same role longer than her peers, she is not gaining new experiences or acquiring new skills at the same rate as someone who has moved up to a new position. This, of course, flattens the curve of her career trajectory and therefore her experience capital. The problem may be especially important when it comes to moving into a manager position. Whether or not someone gains leadership skills as a manager will directly impact her ability to be considered for a more senior leadership position down the road.

Even if a woman misses only one promotion, the lack of skill-building will compound over time. Many women who experience it feel that they are constantly playing catch-up. In order to accumulate the same skills over the course of their careers, they have to somehow make up time by accelerating their advancement later on.

In essence, the broken rungs push the glass ceiling even further away. Compared with the more pervasive problems that women face widely in early and midcareer, the glass ceiling is an issue that affects relatively fewer people. After all, a woman who has not been promoted in step with her peers simply has less time to make that final jump to a senior leadership role. This leaves the final rung of the ladder—when someone would encounter the glass ceiling—unreachable for far too many women.

The broken rung also, of course, comes with a direct loss of earnings. At first, the financial impact of missing one promotion may seem insignificant, but this, too, compounds over time. We estimate that over a fifteen-year period, women who are delayed when it comes to their first promotion or miss that first promotion altogether may earn up to 25 percent less than those who did not.[12]

Being passed over, especially more than once, also can have implications on a woman's confidence. It is difficult to stay motivated and positive at work when you feel that you are not getting the opportunities you've earned. Working in a meritocratic environment matters. Research shows that women and men who perceive they work in a fair environment are three times more likely to say they are happy, three times more likely to want to advance, and three times more likely to recommend their company to a friend.[13]

Many women who trip over one or more broken rungs are aware of the fact that it gives them fewer opportunities to make an impact. The more junior someone is, the less of a chance she has to make decisions that help shape her organization in areas from business strategy, to work-life balance, to diversity and inclusion initiatives, to the very hiring and promotion decisions that could help fix the broken rungs for others.

When Women Don't Thrive, Companies Lose

After Alexa did not receive the raise and promotion that she felt she deserved, she realized that putting in hard work and long hours wasn't enough. Something had to change.

The first thing Alexa did was to start taking every opportunity to advocate for herself by sharing a snapshot of her accomplishments with mentors and managers, raising her hand for high-profile projects, and sharing her longer-term aspirations with managers. It didn't come naturally to her at first, but she tried to make sure that her boss knew about every win she experienced, no matter how big or small. She also tracked all of the data related to those wins so she would have the most powerful argument for a promotion possible at her next review.

Alexa also realized that she had to go out of her way to be trusted with new opportunities, which came down to building relationships. She began blocking time on her calendar every Friday for networking with people both inside and outside of her company and always mentioned to them that she wanted to take on more senior-level work. When she was offered these opportunities, she ran with them.

Before the year was up, Alexa finally got the promotion she'd been waiting for. She is now equal to her peers from a title perspective and is getting closer when it comes to her compensation. However, she feels that her future at the company is still uncertain. Alexa says that it's incredibly tiring to feel that she has to fight so hard to be treated fairly. Plus, after her initial experience, she does not trust that her company will do right by her going forward. But with a few changes to her performance, she has been able to make up time as she works her way toward a more senior leadership position, which will serve her well no matter what she chooses to do next.

When ambitious women like Alexa experience stalls in their careers, they will not hesitate to evaluate other opportunities. The broken rungs can cost organizations when it comes to attrition and the cost of talent development. In 2022 and 2023, after Covid, women in the United States voted with their feet and began switching jobs at the highest rates in the last decade, and at higher rates than men. Over 10 percent of women leaders left their jobs, and for every woman director who was promoted to the next level, two chose to leave their companies.[14] Every hourly worker who quits costs the company roughly 16 percent of their salary (based on recruiting and retraining), while highly skilled workers cost approximately two times their annual salary.[15]

How Organizations Can Repair the Broken Rungs

As Marilyn Loden said when she coined the phrase "glass ceiling," the pressure shouldn't be all on women to make behavioral changes when there are structural barriers that keep them from advancing. We wholeheartedly agree. And while our aim in this book is to make sure that you as an individual have all of the tools you need to successfully navigate your career and reach your potential, it is just as important, if not more so, for organizations to do their part.

Many companies have stepped up and made significant efforts to hire and promote senior women without extending these efforts to entry-level women or frontline workers.[a] As we have shown in this chapter, this only perpetuates the problem throughout the pipeline. In order to achieve parity, organizations must ensure that initiatives are implemented at every level, starting at the entry level, which in most organizations includes 70 percent of the total workers.

We have identified the following steps that organizations can take to fix their broken rungs. You can look for these tactics when choosing a company to work for, as the companies that have implemented them will have more room for you to grow. And when you are in a position to do so, pushing to create these changes in your organization will have a powerful impact on the women coming up behind you.

Set goals at the first rung. Only about a third of companies set expectations for women's representation at the manager level, and even fewer do so for frontline workers. Setting, transparently sharing, tracking, and holding leaders accountable for meeting these expectations would go a long way toward repairing the initial broken rung and creating a cascade of talented women throughout the pipeline.

(continued)

Balance the candidate pool. Similarly, companies are more likely to require diverse candidate slates for promotions at senior levels than at lower levels. But research has shown that having a diverse slate dramatically increases the likelihood that a woman or a woman of color is hired or promoted, so requiring diverse slates at all levels could have a profound effect.

For instance, a study featured in *Harvard Business Review* reported that when there are two women in a finalist pool, the odds that a woman is hired or promoted are seventy-nine times greater, regardless of the size of the pool.[b] That increase is too large to be due to chance. The effect is even more dramatic for race: when there is more than one person from a racial minority in the pool, the odds that one of them will be hired or promoted are 193 times greater.

De-bias the process. Companies are more likely to put employees who participate in senior-level reviews through bias training than those who participate in entry-level reviews. But unconscious biases play a role in determining who receives a promotion at every level. Junior employees haven't had as much time to prove themselves and drive quantifiable results, so promotions and hiring decisions about them, too, can be subjective. It is essential to make sure that biases don't affect who is given opportunities to advance.[c]

Organizations should establish clear evaluation criteria to make reviews more objective. For hiring decisions, they should make sure that candidates for the same role are being evaluated using the same objective criteria. For performance reviews and promotions, they should focus on goals that can be measured and tracked. If the deliverables cannot be measured, decision-makers should agree beforehand on what factors will determine an employee's success and on the need for concrete examples of what that looks like in practice.

Support women starting their careers. It is essential for organizations to help women maximize their experience capital early on, so they are ready to move up the ladder. Best practices here include offering career development (particularly robust training programs for frontline managers), leadership training, targeted sponsorship programs, and support for work-life balance. Currently, for example, many frontline and entry-level workers do not have access to the same childcare benefits as more senior leaders—yet this stage of their careers is actually when they need those benefits the most, financially speaking. The lack of childcare benefits can keep them from advancing in their careers and maximizing their experience capital.

Notes

a. Alexis Krivkovich, Rachel Thomas, Lareina Yee et al., "Women in the Workplace Report 2022," McKinsey & Company and LeanIn.org, 2022.

b. Stefanie K. Johnson et al., "If There's Only One Woman in Your Candidate Pool, There's Statistically No Chance She'll Be Hired," hbr.org, April 26, 2016.

c. Rebecca Knight, "7 Practical Ways to Reduce Bias in Your Hiring Process," hbr.org, June 12, 2017.

Companies are now struggling to hold on to the women leaders they have. In fact, only 46 percent of 331 large companies in the United States and the United Kingdom that we have been tracking since 2014 made significant progress on gender diversity over the 2014–2022 period. The others simply tried to replace the diversity they lost over time.[16] And when organizations look at their ranks to fill those roles, they find that they haven't cultivated the next generation of women leaders. There simply aren't enough women in the pipeline for them to promote. But when workers feel that they have equal opportunities and their workplaces are fair, they are two times less likely to consider leaving their companies.[17]

Attrition of women leaders comes at a cost to the overall economy as well. According to Gallup's 2022 State of the Global Workplace report, low engagement *alone* costs the global economy $7.8 trillion in lost productivity. That amount accounts for 11 percent of global gross domestic product.[18]

Attrition also comes with indirect costs. A 2022 study from Ken Moon of the University of Pennsylvania's Wharton School showed that in a smartphone factory, product failure was over 10 percent more common if that product was made during weeks with high employee turnover. The costs associated with these product failures amounted to hundreds of millions of dollars.[19]

The good news is that the broken rungs are fixable—it requires awareness and commitment from organizations to implement unbiased processes throughout the pipeline. But, like Alexa, you don't have to wait for the system to fix itself to start taking the necessary steps to avoid tripping over these obstacles.

If you have begun to fall behind your peers, rest assured that it's not too late to catch up and achieve your aspirations. Missing the first rung is an early marker that you're not on the path to maximizing your experience capital. It's an important feedback signal, and it's one that you can use to shift gears and start to better position yourself moving forward. So, let's take a look at the value of experience capital over time and how it can help counteract the broken rung.

CHAPTER 2

Experience Capital: Getting Past the Broken Rung

When Rachel Robboy was in high school, she participated in a study abroad program in Honduras. Her mother taught Spanish, and both of her parents had spent time abroad, so it felt like a logical choice for Rachel. At first this program seemed like just a fun adventure and an important step in building her fluency in Spanish. Once she was there, though, Rachel fell in love with Latin American culture, and her time in Honduras proved to be life-changing.

Later on, as an undergraduate at Georgetown University, Rachel studied Spanish and international affairs, and then enrolled in graduate school at George Washington University, where she earned a joint MBA and master's degree in international affairs.

While she was in graduate school, Rachel held several internships that allowed her to gain work experience at a few different places, including the US State Department. But as she looked ahead at her career, Rachel was driven by a desire to help developing countries like Honduras.

Before she graduated, Rachel took a job at a satellite office in Washington, DC, for a *Fortune* 500 company. As fate would have it, shortly after she joined, the firm bought three Latin American power assets out of bankruptcy. This was a brand-new venture, and the team was learning together as they went.

Part of the small team, Rachel gained a tremendous amount of knowledge about infrastructure, energy, political risk insurance, lobbying governments, and managing distressed companies. Looking back, she feels this hands-on experience in emerging markets in Latin America and infrastructure development proved an important fit for her academic background, and ended up playing a big role in shaping her career.

After completing graduate school, Rachel joined the Inter-American Development Bank (IDB), a regional bank that supports the economic and social development of Latin America and the Caribbean. IDB's private-sector area focused on financing for private companies working to develop infrastructure, access to finance, and corporate expansion. Rachel was eager to learn on the job and jumped into everything from doing financial analysis to drafting letters of interest, organizing due diligence trips, and negotiating term sheets.

She enjoyed the analyst role, and although she was learning and growing her skills and network, she knew that in order to build a career, it was important to improve her skills in other areas of the business. It was important to her to maximize her contributions and generate results that were in line with IDB's mission to improve lives. Yet, rotating between jobs was not the norm at the company.

Rachel regularly participated in technical and leadership trainings and workshops to build new skills and managerial expertise. While her career growth continued through promotions, she also decided that she would do her best to move around the organization in sideways or diagonal moves. This turned out to be one of the best decisions she's ever made.

From her role as an analyst, Rachel became an investment officer and then a senior investment officer, managing some of the earliest distressed debt cases in the portfolio. Later, when the company hired a new leader for private-sector operations, Rachel made another unexpected move. Inspired by the vision put forward by the new head, Rachel applied for and was selected for a role as his adviser, which meant she was now supporting investment decision-making, reforming processes, building the customer frameworks for the private sector, and revising lending policies.

After a few more years, Rachel made another lateral move, this time returning to the business side of the organization as a senior, and later principal, investment officer. She loved doing deals, and she felt that she could make the greatest personal impact by financing specific projects that contributed to the economic growth of Latin America and the Caribbean. Projects such as these were incredibly meaningful to Rachel, and for her, the hardest part of the job was letting go and allowing others to take over after she put together the deals. At that point in her career she wanted a new challenge, and she moved on to become the head of the portfolio management unit, leading the team that oversaw transaction implementation from the financial and development impact perspectives. After all, projects in this space did not manage themselves, and proactive portfolio supervision proved key to ensuring a successful implementation and to maximizing impact.

This position was a great opportunity for Rachel to further develop her managerial skills, her technical skills, and even her process skills by building expertise and efficiencies within the team to manage an ever-growing and more complex portfolio. She invested in team building, worked to improve systems and standardize processes and reporting, and built an analytics team. She also started a back office for loan administration in Costa Rica to support the portfolio management officers. Rachel thrived in this role and eventually moved up to manage a bigger portfolio while chairing credit and portfolio committees for the bank.

Then came a twist that she didn't anticipate. Several of her mentors had suggested that Rachel pursue a leadership role in risk management, following her work in origination, portfolio supervision, management advisory, and special assets. She felt that a position like that could come at a later point in her career; however, the opportunity presented itself earlier than anticipated. In early 2018 the chief risk officer of IDB Invest, the entity created in 2015 to consolidate the IDB Group's private-sector lending, announced his departure. Rachel leaned into the opportunity and was selected for the job.

Education Parity Versus Career Parity

It comes as no surprise that a great deal of Rachel's success stems from the value of her education and the skills that she brought to the table when starting her career. But her story also shows how she was able to reach her full potential by taking chances instead of staying in her lane.

Formal education is a setting that women in most developed countries thrive in. In high school in the United States, women represent 70 percent of valedictorians. In college and graduate schools, women earn both undergraduate and graduate degrees at higher rates than men and earn higher GPAs. In the European Union in 2022, 49 percent of women between the ages of twenty-five and thirty-four had completed tertiary education, as compared with 38 percent of their male peers.[1] In the United States in 2022, women earned 59 percent of bachelor's degrees, 63 percent of master's degrees, and 57 percent of doctorate degrees.[2]

These trends have been around for a long time. Globally, the gender parity index in primary and secondary education increased from about 90 girls enrolled for every 100 boys in 1995 to an equal number of both in 2018. In the United States, gender parity in education has improved since the passage of Title IX legislation in 1972, over 50 years ago. By 1982 women began earning the majority of bachelor's degrees. Five years later they began earning the majority of master's degees and have earned the majority of doctoral degrees since 2006.[3]

The trend reverses, however, as soon as men and women enter the workforce. Women immediately lose their education degree advantage, representing less than half of entry-level positions, and they continue to lose ground at every step up the corporate ladder. In fact, Rachel is one of the very few at the top: women typically represent 29 percent of the leaders with a seat at the C-suite table to guide a company's most important decisions.

How is it possible that women are still so far from workplace parity more than five decades after reaching education parity? After all, our educations are meant to prepare us to succeed professionally. If women are beginning their careers just as qualified as men, and often even more so, there should be equal representation throughout the talent pipeline. So, what is driving these stubborn inequities?

It turns out that our educations and entry-level skills do not fully prepare us for our careers—at least, not when it comes to reaching our full earning potential. On average, globally, only half of our lifetime earning potential comes from the skills we bring to the table after completing our educations. The other 50 percent comes from our *experience capital*, the knowledge, skills, attributes, and experiences that we build on the job (see figure 2-1).[4]

There is no limit to the amount of experience capital that you can accumulate over the course of a career, and there are many ways to continue building it. For example, it can be gained through employer-provided learning and development programs, job changes that challenge you to add new skills to your repertoire, and observation, such as watching colleagues perform complex tasks or your boss handle tricky situations.

FIGURE 2-1

Experience capital accounts for nearly half of the earnings across a lifetime—much more later in a career

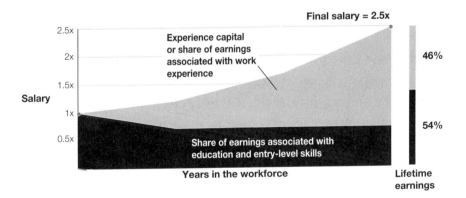

Note: Pooled results across a sample of workers in each country (US, UK, Germany, and India)

Source: McKinsey's proprietary organization data platform, which draws on licensed, de-identified public professional data, as well as 2018–2019 job posting records; UK Office for National Statistics; US Bureau of Labor Statistics; Germany's Federal Employment Agency, BA; India's National Sample Survey Organisation and Periodic Labour Force Survey; McKinsey Global Institute analysis.

Here's the rub: Men are gaining more monetary value from their work experience than women are. Invisible systemic factors are keeping women from getting the skills that they need in order to rise in the ranks in numbers equal to those of men and to be considered for senior positions. This gap in experience capital is slowing progress toward gender equality and keeping women from fully developing their skills, career opportunities, and lifetime earnings.

Women are just as capable of gaining the experience capital edge as men. They are also just as ambitious to advance and to become leaders in their organizations. They are achieving the first 50 percent of their earning potential even faster and more successfully than their male peers. But they are not fully achieving the other half—in the form of experience capital—because they are not getting the same opportunities to learn, develop new skills on the job, or make strategic career decisions in the same ways or at the same rates as men.[5]

Reaching the Doubling Point

One way to assess the curve of your experience capital is to determine when you reach your *doubling point*, which is when your current salary is twice as high as your starting salary. Your pay at any given time does not determine your lifetime earnings, but how quickly you are able to double your starting salary, relative to your peers, is an indication of the curve of your experience capital thus far.

While workers in some occupations see their salaries double more quickly than others, on average, it is useful to compare your doubling rate with that of your peers. If your salary doubles more quickly than someone in the same occupation and industry as you, it means the slope of your experience capital thus far is steeper.

For example, take two colleagues, Owen and Sydney, who are equally intelligent, educated, and ambitious. They landed similar positions at the same company fresh out of college, each with a starting salary of $40,000.

After two years in an entry-level role, Owen moved to a new company, where he was promoted twice. This helped him gain a lot of experience capital early on. Just five years into his career, he reached the doubling point with a salary of $80,000. He then jumped to a startup, where he stayed for ten years and continued to build his experience capital. Fifteen years after graduating from college, he was earning $150,000 a year as a chief marketing officer.

Meanwhile, his former colleague Sydney was earning $90,000 after fifteen years on the job. What accounts for their difference in salaries? The gap between their levels of experience capital. While Owen left their first company early, Sydney stayed for an additional four years, then rose more slowly at her next organization. She finally hit her doubling point after a full ten years in the workforce, taking twice as long as Owen to reach this milestone.

The difference between Owen's and Sydney's experiences underscores an important lesson: the more experience capital you build early in your career, the quicker you'll reach your doubling point. If you then remain on that trajectory, you will be on the path to maximizing your lifetime earnings. In other words, what you bring to your career when you enter the workforce only carries you so far. When you graduate, your skill-building journey is just beginning.

A Diagonal Path to Success

If you look back at Rachel's story with this idea in mind, you can see that she reached the C-suite so early in part because of her unconventional career path, with its diagonal and sometimes even lateral moves. That approach is an unusual but effective way of increasing experience capital, for two reasons. First, every time you shift jobs, you are gaining additional knowledge and must learn new skills. While this seems obvious, traditional career paths still involve people working their way straight up the ladder, which does not require them to gain radically new skills—often flattening the curve of their experience capital.

Second, by moving around so much within her company, Rachel built a significant network of supporters. Women and people of color tend to have a lot of mentors, who give advice, while men tend to have more sponsors, who create opportunities for them. Leaders across Rachel's company knew and trusted her. When it came to being chosen for a senior role, these relationships proved to be invaluable.

Rachel's path is not the only formula for capturing experience capital. On its face, her career appears extremely different from that of Shayna Casey, a self-described people person who loves children, crocheting, and sharing her love of learning. Growing up, Shayna imagined herself as a home economics teacher, a stable, safe job that would allow her to do many of the things she loved. At least, that was the plan until she graduated from college and faced a harsh reality. The majority of schools had stopped offering home economics classes, leaving few opportunities for teachers who wanted to specialize in the area.

Shayna also realized that teaching in general didn't allow for the upward mobility she desired. She had never been particularly motivated by money, but around this time she went through a difficult divorce and became a single mom to her four daughters. Instead of diminishing her ambitions, Shayna's circumstances motivated her to be strategic about her aspirations so that she could provide for her family.

After analyzing the job market and reflecting on her skills and passions, Shayna became convinced that the ideal occupation for her was in human resources. She loved working with people, and another major plus was geographic flexibility. Shayna's ex-husband was in the military, and before the divorce their family had been moved to the army base in Fairbanks, Alaska. Shayna wasn't certain whether she and her children would stay in Alaska, and she wanted a career that would allow her flexibility with location. Since she knew that almost every type of organization has an HR department, Shayna figured that expertise would make her marketable across industries and regions.

There was only one problem: she had absolutely no experience in HR. Shayna enrolled in a master's program in human resources management while looking for an entry-level job. Before long, she got her foot in the door as an assistant in her local school district's Employment and Educational Opportunity (EEO) office, which was responsible for making sure schools offered an environment free from all forms of discrimination.

To say that this was a busy time for Shayna would be an understatement. She worked full-time during the day, and after putting her young children to bed, she stayed up to complete her coursework. She didn't get much sleep, but she was confident the late nights would pay off in the form of a fulfilling and sustainable career that would provide greater financial stability for her family.

Although Shayna loved her job at the school district, she knew that her role was a dead end. She applied for other jobs and was thrilled when she was offered a midlevel position at an Alaska Native corporation that operated a diverse portfolio of companies in construction, tourism, and real estate.

Although it was a promising job, taking it represented a huge risk for Shayna. The salary was lower than what she was earning at the school district, which wasn't much to begin with. Shayna already was on a very tight budget, and a pay cut would mean no vacations, few luxuries, and having to stretch even further to make ends meet. Plus, the new job was seen as low in the hierarchy. It would look like, and in some ways felt like, a step down.

Shayna was only one month away from earning her master's degree and had plans to get a professional certification from the Society for Human Resource Management. She wondered if it would be better to stay put and then find a higher-level position after she'd earned the credential. But she didn't want to let the opportunity pass. Her interactions with the employees impressed her, and she sensed the company's stated commitment to developing its people was more than just lip service.

Shayna took time to learn more about the organization. After two interviews, she went to the office to meet people in person and get a better sense of the culture. From these conversations, she could tell that it was a good place to work and would offer her many opportunities to develop. She could see a career path and envisioned herself in a number of exciting roles that would help her learn and grow.

And grow she did. After accepting the job, she discovered that her cross-training experience had prepared her for dealing with the variety of relevant laws, business practices, and human resources issues. No one had to teach her how to be a good communicator since she had a natural inclination for connecting with people, but she took it upon herself to make use of courses offered by her company and outside resources to develop these skills. She honed her abilities in giving feedback, managing conflict, and presenting herself.

While risky at the onset, Shayna's decision to take a salary cut to join the corporation has certainly paid off. She was recently promoted and began earning a salary that is significantly higher than her previous job's—in fact, she has now reached her doubling point.

Key Drivers of Experience Capital

While their educations, occupations, and industries are all different, one thing that Rachel and Shayna have in common is that they both made intuitive career moves that helped maximize their experience capital. Their paths underscore our key findings about how to amass valuable skills and experiences.

The first finding is that the organizations you choose to work for early in your career have a long-lasting impact on your lifetime earnings—more so than your job title or starting salary. Picking the right employer is critical. Yes, we advocate for women to negotiate for the highest possible dollar figure, but your paycheck represents only one of a number of critical factors. When moving to a new organization, like Shayna did, opportunities for continued learning and internal advancement are just as important, if not more so, than the size of your paycheck. For Shayna, it paid off to take a temporary pay cut for a long-term boost in experience capital.

While workers in the past tended to stay put throughout their careers, today's workers tend to switch jobs and even occupations more frequently.[6] It is key to keep an open mind and focus on the big picture of your career. In addition to your annual salary, think about how to maximize your lifetime earnings and learning. They often go hand in hand.

When we assessed different work environments, we found that although employees' day-to-day tasks in a particular role may look very similar at two different organizations, their overall experiences and learning opportunities can vary widely. In other words, you may gain significantly more experience capital in one company than another, even in the exact same role or with the same title.

For this reason, it is imperative to investigate potential employers beyond their glossy websites and recruiting brochures. Don't rely on the job description and starting salary. Look at the career pathways and potential opportunities in three to five years, the female role models a few levels ahead of you who are doing what you aspire to do, what women in the organization say about the culture, and the number of women at the very top. These are just a few ideas to help you find out how a company will truly help you build experience capital.

Second, don't be afraid to start over, reinvent yourself, or make lateral moves. Today few people feel bound to one company, one occupation, or one industry throughout their careers. In fact, 80 percent of people across the countries we studied started out in one occupation and ended their careers in another.[7] This fluidity allows you to develop a valuable variety of experiences and skills. Although she stayed at the same company for many years, Rachel didn't simply climb the ladder. She broke into the C-suite because of her range of experiences.

With the world of work changing, women—who are disproportionately in the occupations that are being impacted by automation and generative AI—must be strategic about shifting industries to stay ahead of marketplace trends. Shayna had the foresight to build skills in human resources and to jump to a company that spanned multiple industries. In many ways she was starting over, which one might assume would slow down her career progression. Surprisingly, our research shows that making this type of big move to an entirely new occupation or industry early in your career is one of the best ways to maximize lifetime earnings. When the move involves shifting to a high-quality organization or a growing industry, the related boost in lifetime earnings is compounded.

Both Shayna's and Rachel's stories show that you have truly limitless opportunities. Yet with more options and far more opportunities to grow your earning potential, too many women remain stuck. When you are starting out, you have no idea where your path can and will take you—which can be exciting if you are open to it, but also stressful or even scary. If you stick to a specific trajectory that is too narrow, it's likely you will end up missing out on opportunities, learning, and lifetime earnings.

In a rapidly changing economy, it's natural to feel like your job may be at risk and to focus on protecting your role, but that kind of thinking will keep you from adapting and exploring new horizons. Opening your mind and strategically changing course will allow you to build experience capital. Although globally on average 50 percent of lifetime earnings come from experiences and skills gained on the job, we have seen the country-level variation range from 40 to 60 percent. In the United States the average is 40 percent, while it is 43 percent in the United Kingdom and Germany, and 58 percent in India. So, for some women, more than two-thirds of their lifetime earnings come from skills learned on the job.[8] The share of lifetime earnings from experience capital tends to be higher in occupations that require lower levels of education, such as fast-food workers and machine operators, but also in some professional occupations, like dancers and commercial pilots, where built-up experience over the years is very valuable to your earnings.

By applying some or all of the strategies that we'll share throughout the rest of the book, you can shape your career in the face of daunting barriers. Next, we'll take a look at the specific experiences that will make the biggest difference.

PART TWO

GAIN THE EXPERIENCES
THAT MATTER

CHAPTER 3

Seek a Company, Not Just a Job

Stephanie Carullo, the former chief operating officer of Box, says that she fell into the field of technology by accident. A native of Australia, she graduated from university with a degree in economic history, focusing on the social ramifications of economic legislation in developing nations. When she was about to graduate and it was time to look for a job, she simply interviewed with the organizations that were recruiting on campus. The one that caught her eye was IBM.

At the time, IBM's marketing was based on the fact that it solved problems for businesses, with little mention of using technology to do so. Stephanie admits that she didn't fully understand what the company did when she accepted the job offer. But she did know two things: she had always loved solving problems, and IBM had a training program that was considered one of the best in the world.

Stephanie credits that training program with a great deal of her career success. In fact, many of the lifelong friends that she made in the program hold C-suite roles today. Although their paths have varied widely and they are now spread out across multiple industries and continents, the common thread between them is the skills and network they established early in their careers.

During the program, participants learned how to advance both the soft skills that are essential when working with clients, such as communication and presentation, and the hard skills, including how to code, which taught them technical abilities as well as how to think through decision trees. But perhaps the most essential skill that Stephanie learned was negotiating.

The training that she went through was led by crisis negotiators who had experience deescalating serious situations such as bomb threats. Stephanie learned that negotiating really comes down to understanding your audience at all times and knowing the right language to use and questions to ask. This knowledge has directly and consistently helped Stephanie in her career. She explains that with the current business climate growing increasingly complex, having the ability to quickly read people and situations is essential. It regularly helps her find win-win outcomes that benefit all parties and lead to real progress.

In addition, the company brought in specialists to assess what sort of role each of the participants was likely to thrive in, which helped them develop valuable self-knowledge and took a lot of the guesswork out of their choices about future roles and career trajectories. While it is difficult to quantify, many of the women we interviewed for this book credited self-knowledge with helping them find success in their careers. The training gave Stephanie a head start in building that self-awareness.

From this launchpad, Stephanie excelled through the ranks of IBM in the Asia Pacific region, then held an executive position at Telstra, the leading telecom company in Australia. From there, she was a vice president at Cisco, a networking and software technology company in San Jose, California, before leading education sales at Apple. Her most recent role was at Box, which 67 percent of *Fortune* 500 companies use to organize file sharing and content management. As the chief operating officer she led sales, marketing, customer support, operations, and customer success—in many ways bringing all the parts of her journey together.

What grew into an incredible career in Silicon Valley started with a professional leap and a training program that laid the groundwork for her future success. Stephanie could have had the same entry-level job at any number of companies—but she chose a company, not just a job.

Effective Organizations and Experience Capital

Stephanie's story is of course unique to her, but the impact of working for an effective organization that invested deeply in her training and skill development is not. An effective organization is one that offers employees lots of opportunities to learn and grow due to a strong learning culture, has a successful competitive strategy, and has a high rate of internal promotions or cross-functional mobility. In fact, we found that early exposure to a company that supports employees' growth is the single biggest differentiator in the ability to maximize experience capital—it accounts for a full 50 percent of the variation in experience capital between workers.[1] In other words, picking the right organization to join early in your career might be one of the most important career decision you make.

Workers get the biggest boost in their experience capital from working for one of these organizations early in their careers because they simply have more time later in their careers to use the skills and experiences they gain at the start.[2] Learning and skill-building during those formative years set the foundation for future growth and your career trajectory. But even for individuals who are in their mid- to late careers and still have not found an organization that is effective and invests deeply in training, it is never too late. It's always a good time to join an organization that provides access to learning and growth opportunities.

Effective organizations provide ample chances for employees to grow, which has a lasting impact on their experience capital and therefore lifetime earnings. One way to measure this is by looking at workers' ability to move up one or more earning quintiles throughout their careers.

Earning quintiles divide the population into five groups based on their income level. Roughly one-third of US, German, and UK workers and almost one-quarter of Indian workers will move up one or more quintiles throughout their careers. While only 25 percent of workers at less effective organizations move into higher-earning quintiles, 35 percent of workers in effective organizations do. This means that working for an effective organization increases your chance of moving to a higher earning quintile by about 1.5 times—it is a big income booster.[3]

When starting out, many of us focus on landing a specific job. But the organization in which we perform that job has a more direct impact on our trajectory, as well as our feelings of satisfaction and engagement while we are in that role.

Linda Hall, who was the CEO of MinuteClinic before its $214 million sale to CVS in 2006, experienced this at her first company, where she worked for fifteen years. During this time she progressed rather rapidly from manager to vice president. Although three out of her four bosses mentored and supported her, the mostly male, one-hundred-year-old manufacturing business was a challenging environment.

Eager to connect with other women leaders, Linda formed a networking group in the 1990s called the Executive Women's Forum. The group met for three days every year—and they continue to meet over thirty years later. These meetings all share the same format: each woman takes a turn sharing what she wants and then telling the group what she needs their help with. The group then uses as much time as needed to offer support and suggestions.

At one meeting, Linda told the group that she was thinking about making a career move after fifteen years but that she wasn't sure what she should do next. One of the other women told her, "We know that you like to do hard things, but why do you have to do them in such a hard place?"

For Linda, a light bulb went off in that moment as her network helped her realize that it could be easier to grow and evolve at a different organization.

The Three Common Traits of Effective Organizations

So, what exactly does it mean to be an "effective organization" that boosts employees' experience capital?

As we mentioned earlier, our research shows that effective organizations share three traits: a strong learning culture, a proven strategy against competitors, and high rates of internal, cross-functional mobility. Said another way, effective organizations focus on learning, are clear about how they win in their industry, and promote people internally.

A strong learning culture

A learning organization is one in which people have a growth mindset and continually learn both individually and in collaboration with others. The notion of a learning organization was pioneered by Peter Senge, a senior lecturer at MIT and the founder of the Society for Organizational Learning.[4] Since the release of his book *The Fifth Discipline* in 1990, Senge's theories have been proven by research. Organizations with a strong learning culture are 92 percent more likely to develop novel products, 56 percent more likely to be first to market with their products, 52 percent more productive, and 17 percent more profitable.[5] It turns out that creating a learning culture is just as good for employees as it is for organizations.

One example of a learning environment is the global pharmaceutical company Novartis. Its chief learning officer, Simon Brown, has researched curiosity extensively and coauthored the book *The Curious Advantage* about the topic. As part of its efforts to foster a culture of curiosity, Novartis invited employees to self-nominate as "curiosity storytellers" and created physical "curiosity hives" that provided space for open dialogue and exploration.[6]

Novartis also held a Learning Month featuring over one hundred global webinars and events on different topics from internal and external speakers, including startups and academia. The company encourages its employees to devote 5 percent of their time to learning, education, and skill development and offers employees access to a range of learning platforms. It has made an organizational commitment to invest $100 million in learning over five years.

Organizations with a strong learning culture provide education and training to develop both new and long-tenured employees. They also hold post-project review sessions and forums with customers or subject-matter experts to gain new perspectives. For example, Google makes it clear from day one of someone's employment that learning is an expected part of the job and that learning and development are part of the company's core values. It puts these claims into practice by offering 360-degree feedback as part of performance management and providing feedback that is linked to individual recommendations for learning resources.

These kinds of organizations also prioritize peer development. All Google employees take responsibility for developing each other, and social learning is a big part of their learning philosophy. A full 80 percent of all training at Google is in the form of peer-to-peer development.

Another example of concrete practices comes from Stephanie's experience at IBM. She stayed with the company for fourteen years and was able to participate in additional leadership programs. At one point, the company chose twelve high-potential employees from around the globe and asked them to work together to come up with solutions to a real business problem: how IBM could transition from being a hardware business to a truly solutions-oriented business. The group met for six months while analyzing data and problem-solving, and then presented their findings and ideas to the board of directors. This initiative was the beginning of IBM's acquisition of the consulting services business of PricewaterhouseCoopers—a significant step forward for the company and a valuable learning opportunity for participants.

Leaders at organizations with a learning culture prioritize employees' growth. In addition to providing opportunities to learn, they actively listen to employees, which signals the importance of identifying problems, sharing and transferring knowledge, and exploring different points of view.

Stephanie credits one leader she encountered early in her career with nudging her toward different opportunities to learn. There were certain roles that she hesitated to go after, believing that she wasn't fully qualified, but this leader pushed her to apply anyway. As she took on these new roles, Stephanie experienced exponential growth. She was stretching herself and building her experience capital in what we call a *bold move*, which we will explore more in chapter 4.

Another good example of this type of leadership comes from Microsoft. CEO Satya Nadella famously claims that the C in his title stands for culture, and he has focused on creating a culture of learning, growth, and empathy. He's made a commitment to and role-models risk-taking and learning from "smart failure." Satya also introduced an open learning day every quarter and identifies the long-term benefits in productivity, creativity, and morale as clear business outcomes.

A proven recipe for success

The second characteristic of an effective organization is that it has management practices that strongly align with one of four proven recipes for success. No one recipe is more effective than another, as there are different ways for companies to succeed. What determines the level of effectiveness is how closely the organization aligns with the recipe, because it shows that the company is coordinated around a common strategy. Companies with very strong alignment are six times more likely than those with weak alignment to be in the top quartile of healthy organizations.[7]

Let's look at the four recipes for organizational health and success.

Leadership factory. Leadership factories drive performance by developing, supporting, and deploying strong leaders, and supporting them through coaching, formal training, and offering the right growth opportunities. Aligned with a clear purpose and direction, leaders are inspired and empowered to figure out how to deliver results, and they are held accountable for doing so. Leadership factories also set clear parameters for decision-making and dedicate significant time to developing, coaching, and motivating. Leadership factories create an environment where leaders can grow and succeed, and hold them accountable when they don't.

GE is a well-known leadership factory with a robust leadership program. Rita Kim, who is now senior vice president of retail and merchandising at LIV Golf, participated in GE's two-year rotational program after graduating from business school. Rita says that one of the most impactful things she learned there was Six Sigma, a set of techniques and tools for process improvement that is often used in manufacturing environments with low tolerance for variability or quality issues. She still regularly uses these techniques when problem-solving in her current role.[8]

At GE, Rita also learned about negotiating and about motivating and leading teams, and she had opportunities to present to the C-suite and to leaders across business units. It was an unparalleled opportunity that gave her valuable feedback and visibility within the company.

Market shaper. Market shapers find their advantage lies in coming up with products and services that the markets want (or will want) and that their competitors will struggle to respond to. Product development and strategic decisions are driven by a desire to constantly innovate and create new customer demand. Market shapers aim to delight customers by providing them with a product or service that is better than they imagined. These companies tend to test and learn, fail fast, and reward calculated risks.

Later in her career, Stephanie moved to a market shaper, Apple, as the vice president of sales for the education segment. She says that one of the most important things she learned at Apple was the importance of trusting her fellow employees. They were each a link in the value chain—an important piece of the puzzle—and Stephanie was aware that the person upstream and downstream from her was relying on her to deliver. She felt a real sense of responsibility to do her very best job and never let the team down. She never wanted to be the link that broke the chain, so to speak. This dynamic speaks to the importance of role clarity, a defining feature of a market shaper organization.

Execution edge. These are creative, entrepreneurial organizations that get ahead by involving all employees in driving continuous improvements, gathering insights, and sharing knowledge. There is a strong, self-sustaining culture of learning and improvement and of emphasizing experimentation and creative ideas, particularly from frontline employees who are closest to the work. New knowledge and best practices are rapidly communicated and adopted across the organization, supported by clear linkages between performance expectations, rewards and consequences, and healthy internal competition. Execution edge organizations work to raise quality and efficiency while eliminating waste. Their emphasis on sharing knowledge drives innovation, as well as standardization.

Toyota is a good example of an execution edge organization. In the book *The Toyota Way*, author Jeffrey Liker explains the company's 4P model: Philosophy, People, Process, and Problem-solving, which are common priorities for this archetype.[9] Toyota's operations are very rigid, and yet they are also extremely responsive to consumer demand. While this may appear to be a contradiction, it is that rigidity that makes the flexibility possible. The company uses the scientific method to set up and streamline all of its operations, which drives innovation and allows problems to be identified and corrected quickly. Execution edge organizations continuously improve—even if just a little bit every week or month—to get more effective over time.

Talent/knowledge core. These organizations create value by continuously searching for and attracting top talent and then developing and inspiring them. Their goal is to assemble and manage high-quality workforces and knowledge bases, and they succeed, thanks to highly skilled individual performers. As such, they often invest in skill training and sponsor continuing education or graduate school studies for employees. Talent/knowledge core organizations also provide structured and accelerated career development plans. They encourage employees to follow their passions, chart their own courses, and blaze new trails when necessary.

JPMorgan Chase is a good example of a talent/knowledge core organization. The company made a $300 million investment in employee training and development, and it provides additional skills retraining for employees who are transitioning into new roles at the firm. It also has a structured career development plan with specific hierarchies that employees work their way up as they accelerate.

Internal mobility

Effective organizations have a higher rate of internal moves than less effective organizations. These can be upward or lateral moves; both go a long way toward helping employees build experience capital. Many effective organizations also go a step further and create internal mobility strategies to gain a competitive advantage.

Less effective organizations tend to overlook internal talent and untapped potential. They opt to keep employees in their current roles, perhaps to avoid the costs of transition periods and ramp-up time. Effective organizations, meanwhile, help employees find roles that are the right fit and allow them to reach their potential, which of course increases retention. One study showed that employees in the United States stay 41 percent longer at organizations with high internal mobility than those without.[10]

High internal mobility also helps create an agile culture of workers who are invested in their organization because they feel that the organization is investing in and values them. This drives engagement and feelings of job satisfaction. For example, Ingersoll Rand, an American multinational company that provides flow creation and industrial products, introduced an internal career program that helped people seek new opportunities within the organization. Employee engagement increased by 30 percent.[11]

The importance of diversity in organizations

Beyond the three traits that identify effective organizations, it is worth noting the relevance of diversity in the performance of those organizations. Diversity on senior executive teams (direct reports to the CEO) is correlated with better organizational and economic performance, as organizations with leadership teams that have more gender diversity show higher levels of innovation and improved decision-making.[12] We also know that among younger generations of managers and leaders (Millennials, Gen Z, and others), diversity and inclusion is considered table stakes for the type of culture they want to be a part of.

Companies in the top quartile for gender diversity on executive teams are 39 percent more likely to outperform their peers economically (as measured by total returns to shareholders) than companies in the fourth quartile.[13] This is correlation, not causation, as you cannot put a company through a double-blind scientific test. However, the correlation suggests the value of diversity.

Here's what can drive that value: businesses run by culturally diverse leadership teams are more likely to develop new products and make better decisions.[14] Within diverse teams, employees can become more aware of their own potential biases and may be more open to the idea that their team did not come up with the best solution the first time around. They can be more open to the notion of continuous improvement, which leads them to consistently reexamine facts and remain more objective, making them less prone to errors.

These patterns repeatedly play out in research. In one study published in the *Journal of Personality and Social Psychology*, scientists assigned two hundred people to mock jury panels.[15] These juries were either all white or included four white and two Black participants. The groups were then shown a video of a trial with a Black defendant and white plaintiffs and had to decide whether the defendant was guilty. The diverse juries stuck to the facts related to the case more than the homogenous juries did. They also used a more logical decision-making process and made fewer factual errors when discussing available evidence.

In another experiment, scientists gathered groups of financially literate people in either ethnically diverse or homogenous teams.[16] In simulated markets, the participants had to price different stocks. The individuals on the diverse teams were 58 percent more likely to price stocks correctly, while those in homogenous groups were more prone to pricing errors.

Levels of diversity and inclusion also have an impact on employee experience, performance, and ultimately experience capital. Those are dramatic differences in how employees feel in the workplace.

Organizations that provide an inclusive workplace are better able to attract and retain diverse talent, which is becoming increasingly important to employees. Today 60 percent of women say that they look at the gender diversity of an organization's leadership team when deciding where to work, and 40 percent claim that a company's commitment to diversity, equity, and inclusion (DEI) is becoming more relevant when switching jobs.[17]

Nikki Sorum, a financial services executive and the former head of sales and distribution at financial services provider Thrivent, points out a more direct connection between an organization's diversity and employees' experience capital. As she navigated through a career in financial services, she found that not only did the diverse teams she led perform better than homogenous teams, but they also provided her and other team members with better opportunities to learn. We are more likely to learn new things when we work with people who are different from us—a simple but important way of boosting our experience capital.

What Is More Important: Your Boss or Your Organization?

Many of the women leaders whom we spoke to cited their experiences with good bosses as a primary driver of their experience capital, but the research clearly shows that exposure to an effective organization actually plays a bigger role than an individual manager. So, which is really more important—your boss or your organization? Ideally, you would have both a great organization and a great boss. If forced to choose between the two, though, the data says that opting for an organization that invests in its people has a greater impact on your career and experience capital.

That may be because effective organizations that nurture and develop great leaders are likely to provide a longer-lasting advantage in your career than a good boss will. Individual bosses may shift as they take on a new role, you change jobs, or there is a broader company reorganization. If you choose to stay at your company, though, that advantage and the investments in your learning are likely to persist longer in your career.

We know that your boss plays a large role in shaping your day-to-day experience and determining the level of your job satisfaction. A study of thirty-five thousand employees showed that the single largest influence on their job satisfaction was whether they had a highly competent boss; often it was even more important to them than their salaries.[18] Yet the majority of employees are not happy with their bosses. In fact, 75 percent of respondents said that their boss was the most stressful aspect of their jobs.

Clearly, it's important to spend time getting to know your prospective boss before accepting a job offer, since it is a good way of assessing a company's culture and finding out what your day-to-day experience might be like. But no matter how much you like your boss, know that if a company does not support your growth, gaining experience capital will simply be more difficult. Often your boss will only be your boss while you are in one role, so your likelihood of advancing is more dependent on the overall organizational culture than your individual manager.

As a Black woman executive who started her career in the 1970s, Pam Scott has faced her share of both supportive and difficult bosses and workplaces. Early on, as an analyst at Citibank, she felt supported by the company. She was able to move up to become the manager of a small team focused on high-net-worth individuals. At that time, Pam says, her power base was still relatively low, so she wasn't seen as a threat to others' position or power. The greater challenges came as she advanced in the organization. The more responsibilities she had, the more pushback and resistance she faced.

Pam moved between a few companies and roles throughout her career, transitioning to a client-facing job and eventually to managing multiple teams. She also spent a lot of time presenting and hosting functions at conferences, not only giving her opportunities to travel, which she loved, but also helping her become highly visible in the marketplace. Then, when she was passed over for a promotion that she believed she deserved, she knew that she had a high-enough profile to easily bring her skills to another organization that would value her more.

Pam switched to a new company specifically to work for a boss she knew from earlier in her career and greatly respected. Unfortunately, he was soon replaced by someone who wasn't as enthusiastic about Pam or building her team. She was left without the resources she needed to do her job effectively, and when she appealed to the higher-ups, they said that there was nothing they could do; her new boss was free to spend his budget as he wished.

Pam's situation highlights the importance of both having a good manager *and* working at an effective organization. Especially as a woman of color, it was important to her to feel that her boss respected her. Plus, this person was her spokesperson and advocate during conversations about budget. But choosing to work for a certain organization is a bigger investment—a bigger bet from a career perspective. It's important to weigh these two factors when making decisions.

Pam learned from her experience and began talking to another leader she knew about switching companies again to work for him. But this time, she made sure to do two things: First, she asked around about what it was like to work for him, since he had never been her direct manager. Second, she did her research on the company to make sure it was an effective organization. This way, she made sure that she would have both the day-to-day and the long-term support she needed to maximize her experience capital.

Identifying Effective Organizations from the Outside In

We know which traits define an effective organization, but many early job seekers, particularly women and members of Generation Z, focus on other factors instead. They often prioritize flexibility in terms of their lifestyles and where, when, and how they get work done. In addition, women tend to look for organizations that offer transparency in their pay and benefits, while members of Gen Z are looking to be recognized and rewarded for their work. They are less financially secure than other generations and also prioritize salary and stability when choosing an employer.[19]

While many factors can make a company attractive to work for, none of them will boost your experience capital as much as working at an effective organization. Luckily, factors like work flexibility and the qualities of an effective organization are not mutually exclusive. Such a company is more likely to offer transparency, recognize and reward employees, and offer competitive salaries and/or flexibility. So, by focusing your search on effective organizations, you will hopefully end up getting the best of both worlds.

The question, then, is how to identify an effective organization from the outside looking in. Kera Yang's early career experience shows how crucial it is to do this research before accepting an offer. Kera, who identifies as a person of color and a member of the LGBTQ+ community, graduated from the University of Michigan's Ross School of Business and then joined a rotational program at a large telecommunications company. The program cycled participants through three different positions in two years. To Kera, this sounded like a good opportunity to build the foundational skills that she could draw on throughout her career.

Kera did gain some skills throughout the program, particularly during her first rotation, which was in the planning and analysis group. There she learned how to present data in a format that is readable and consistent and how to communicate effectively with everyone from team members to senior leaders. But Kera found the other rotations to be less well organized, and her managers were young and new to the company, so they were unable to provide Kera and the other trainees with much coaching or guidance.

Worse, Kera learned after she was already in the program that her salary was much lower than those of her peers at other companies. She felt undervalued and knew that starting her career at such a low salary would make it difficult to negotiate fair pay in her next role, particularly if she stayed at the company. But there was a catch—trainees who did not stay at the company after the two-year program had to repay its expenses, which were significant and, with her low salary, would put Kera in debt. So early in her career, she felt stuck, like she wasn't reaching her potential.

How could Kera have known that her company would not support her development as well as she had expected? From the outside, the training program seemed to be an ideal opportunity for growth.

There are both formal and informal sources that you can use to assess whether an organization will be effective in supporting your growth and development. The most obvious places are company websites and information from the human resources department, but there are a few things to look out for.

Ignore vague buzzwords about training and focus instead on specifics and quantifiable metrics. For example, look for answers to these questions: How many hours a year (or what percentage of time) do employees have to invest in their personal learning? How does that learning actually happen, and what company support and resources are there to ensure that it happens? What is the promotion structure? How high is employee turnover? What percentage of employees make cross-functional moves within the organization? Does the company offer access to on-demand education programs or sponsor graduate studies? What kinds of formal sponsorship and mentorship programs exist?

It's also a good idea to spend some time researching the organization via high-quality external sources such as *Harvard Business Review*, *Forbes*, the *Wall Street Journal*, and the *Economist*. What do they say (if anything) about the organization's culture?

Sometimes, formal sources of information on an organization are scarce. Whether or not you can find plentiful information, try to supplement that with informal sources. These can include current or former employees whom you speak to directly or who have written or spoken publicly about their experiences. Look at online sources such as Glassdoor, Indeed, and Fishbowl. And when interviewing for a job, never forget that you are interviewing the organization, too. Take every possible opportunity to speak to current employees, and not just the ones who interview you. Ask about the culture. Research the CEO and executive team, and learn as much as you can about their values, leadership styles, and how they interact with others.

Nikki Sorum, the financial services executive mentioned earlier, also suggests looking at the makeup of an organization's board of directors. As she was nearing the end of her tenure at Thrivent, she attended an executive education course about women's participation on boards. She found it fascinating to hear some of the other women talking about why they were so passionate about serving on boards. They shared how the board plays a large role in shaping an organization by overseeing its ethics, strategy, and CEO; therefore, women can play a direct role in creating equality in an organization from their seat on the board. Directors are the people shaping the organization from the very top.

. . .

The earlier in your career that you work at an effective organization, the better, since it will give the skills you gain there more time to compound, maximizing your experience capital. However, no matter what stage you're in, it's not too late. If you are more than five years into your career and have not had a chance to work at an effective organization yet, it's worth carefully selecting your next employer using the strategies in this chapter. By combining them with the other tactics in the book, you can compensate for time spent at a less effective organization and boost your lifetime experience and earnings. Next, we'll explore how to make the right job moves to maximize your experience capital and progress in your career.

CHAPTER 4

Making Big, Bold Moves

Growing up in Grand Rapids, Michigan, Noorain Khan was always passionate about human rights. As a practicing Muslim, she started getting involved in youth organizing at her mosque when she was in middle school. And throughout her education—which took her from Rice University as an undergrad, to the University of Oxford, where she was a Rhodes scholar, and finally to Yale Law School—she pursued multiple internships in the world of public interest.

At Rice, Noorain triple majored in women's studies, political science, and religious studies, and at Oxford she focused on migration studies—seemingly disparate subjects that all tied to her passion for human rights. Noorain's goal was to find a way to bring these subjects together in her career to make an impact.

She always assumed that she would enjoy a career in the public sector, and her education positioned her to do so. But when Noorain was graduating from law school, her advisers and mentors encouraged her to instead begin her career at a corporate law firm. To Noorain, this seemed like a bit of a left turn; she knew that corporate law was not her passion. But they explained that since nonprofit law is based on corporate law, gaining expertise in the area would serve as a valuable foundation no matter what Noorain ultimately decided to pursue.

She took the advice and spent about two and a half years as a corporate associate at a small and prestigious firm in New York City. Her time there was indeed educational, as well as high pressure. There were nights when she stayed up working on a deal that her team managed to close just before sunrise. Still in her pajamas, she would rush down from her apartment in the morning to grab a newspaper from the corner stand and see the deal announced on the front page. That feeling, she says, was unparalleled. It was exhilarating.

Yet the pace was exhausting, which was compounded by the fact that Noorain never gave up her public interest work. She just did it on the side—on every weekend and the rare day off. During her first year at the law firm, Noorain billed 3,100 hours. That's roughly the equivalent of working five twelve-hour days a week. And it doesn't include any of the time she spent volunteering. She had gotten good at allocating her time in fifteen-minute increments, but she was quickly becoming burned out and knew that this pace wasn't sustainable for the long term.

The organization that Noorain felt the most passionate about volunteering with was the Girl Scouts of the United States of America. She had joined the Girl Scouts as a Brownie when she was only seven years old, and for her it was a source of sisterhood, growth, adventure, and fun. She has been affiliated with the organization ever since and says that it has been the single most important influence in her life outside of her family and her faith.

During her second year at the law firm, Noorain took an entire week off of work—a first for her—to travel to Chicago for the Girl Scouts' one-hundredth-anniversary celebration. Just as she was ushering girls from eighty countries into their seats for the main event, Noorain received a text from one of her colleagues that read, "I know you're on vacation, but we need you to look at some documents within the next two hours."

This was the pivotal moment when Noorain realized that her current situation no longer made sense. She had indeed learned a lot at the law firm that would provide a solid foundation for a future in public service, but now it was time to take what she'd learned and move on, hopefully finding a way to combine her passions with her profession.

Trends in Job Moves

The moves you make throughout your career, between roles, organizations, occupations, and industries, will all play an enormous role in shaping your career trajectory and the growth of your experience capital. There are many factors to consider when deciding when and where to leap. Today's workers must weigh these factors and make these decisions more frequently than in the past, but doing so strategically and effectively does pay off.

It used to be that employees worked their way up the ladder at one organization throughout their careers. This type of trajectory does provide stable employment and perhaps greater predictability, but it also may keep the curve of your experience capital relatively flat. When you stay in the same occupation, organization, or industry, you are likely to deepen your skills and make them more specific and potentially valuable within one particular context. You improve your existing skills over time by becoming more senior and taking on more responsibilities. But these skills may not necessarily be broadly applicable across organizations or roles. Sometimes you can grow well within an organization by progressing and taking on broader responsibilities—particularly if you are in an effective organization as described in chapter 3—and sometimes you can grow well by stretching yourself in a new group, organization, or industry (if you choose well, of course).

There are some professions that do require personal mastery, and in these roles honing the same skills instead of gaining new ones does pay off. For example, surgeons, writers, and chefs may benefit more from continuing in the same occupation and simply getting better and better at their craft. These roles tend to be clustered at either end of the education spectrum: either they require advanced degrees (in the case of a surgeon) or are not associated with a specific degree at all (in the case of a writer). But the majority of workers in the middle of this spectrum benefit from taking on new roles that require them to gain unique skills instead of just improving those they already possess.

Further, the nature of work is evolving as the world around us changes faster than ever, which has led to rapid shifts in the types of skills that are the most valuable and in demand. Workers today must be nimble and continue adapting their skills to meet the market's needs. One way to do this is to make the right job moves at the right time to gain opportunities to build new skills.

Some of today's workers seem to understand this intuitively. While more than 40 percent of Baby Boomers stayed at the same organization for more than twenty years, 91 percent of Millennials say that they expect to switch jobs every three to four years.[1] Indeed, the average worker both in the United States and around the world now changes roles (though not necessarily employers) every two to four years. This number includes moves that are voluntary and involuntary.

Interestingly, these data points are connected. With Baby Boomers staying in the workforce longer than previous generations, there isn't always room at the top for young, upwardly mobile workers. Accordingly, sometimes younger workers look to other organizations for opportunities, even if they're otherwise happy where they are.[2]

Historically, and especially during economic downturns, most job changes have simply been due to workers being laid off. But today, voluntary moves are far more common than layoffs and firings. From 2010 to 2020, in the decade before the Covid-19 pandemic, for every 1 worker who was fired or laid off, there were 1.4 workers who quit voluntarily.[3] There are many reasons for this shift. Among them are reduced unionization, fewer defined-benefit retirement plans, and a growing share of independent workers.

In the United States, unionization began decreasing in the 1960s, breaking down some of the direct connections tying employers to employees. Defined-benefit retirement programs that are associated with a specific organization are another structural element of this employee-employer relationship. In the United States, these benefits (often known as pensions) have been disappearing for decades in favor of 401(k)s, which are more portable from employer to employer.[4]

It's important to note that as these connections between employers and employees deteriorate, there is less of an incentive on each side to invest in human capital. As worker tenure decreases, organizations see a lower return on investments in their people, from capability building to benefits. The resources they put into helping their employees learn and grow will benefit another organization when that worker moves on.

Besides making more frequent job moves, today's workers are also moving into new industries more frequently than ever before. These employees are seeking the traditional perks of moves, such as better compensation, benefits, and advancement opportunities, but in many cases those are table stakes. They are willing to make big moves for other reasons too.

Millennials and members of Gen Z value flexibility more than previous generations, and value having control over their careers. Flexibility includes the ability to work remotely, have customized schedules, and create better work-life balance. These generations are also more likely to have and recognize mental health concerns. During the pandemic, for example, one-third of US Millennials received treatment from a mental health professional.[5]

In addition, Millennials and Gen Zers are more likely than previous generations to "vote with their feet" by choosing to work for organizations that align with their values.[6] Many of these factors lead them to seek out new organizations and industries if they are not happy with their current employer.

While the reasons behind increased job moves are complex, it's clear that they do pay off in the form of experience capital and therefore lifetime earnings. However, not all job moves are created equal. Our data shows that there are two types that have the greatest impact in helping you build experience capital: big, early moves that involve starting over in a new occupation or industry within the first five years of your career, and bold moves, which involve switching to a job that requires a significant share of new skills.

Big, Early Moves Matter

Once she realized that her career in corporate law was no longer serving her, Noorain Khan knew that she needed to make a big move. She had only been at the law firm for a little over two years, and while some workers may have worried that it would reflect poorly on them to start over so soon, Noorain had learned a lot and believed that many of the skills she gained would be transferrable to whatever she decided to do next.

She knew that she would have to take a significant pay cut in order to move into the public sector, but she felt strongly that she could no longer sustain her life at the law firm and wanted to follow her passions. It didn't make sense to stay in a role that she already knew was not the right fit; compared with doing something new, staying in an unsustainable position felt like the bigger risk.

Once she returned from the Girl Scouts' anniversary celebration, Noorain began looking for a chief of staff role at nonprofit and government organizations. She believed that these positions would have the fast pace that she had enjoyed at the law firm and allow her to use the skills she had gained as a corporate lawyer.

Noorain soon landed a job as the chief of staff to the CEO and cofounder of Teach for All, a global network of organizations with the mission of expanding access to education. As she expected, the role required her to take a 70 percent pay cut, but Noorain felt that it was worth it and hoped she would move up quickly once she gained additional experience in the nonprofit world.

Ten years later, this both has and hasn't happened. A full decade after making the jump, Noorain is just now getting close to earning the same salary that she was making in corporate law. She is hoping that with her next job move, she will finally reach this milestone. However, she says that the move has more than paid off in terms of her personal fulfillment and impact. Every day, she has a chance to do the type of work that she previously squeezed in on nights and weekends, and devoting herself to this work full-time has allowed her to make a real difference.

Starting Over Doesn't Mean Losing Ground

There are many reasons you might choose to start over early in your career. Like Noorain, perhaps you took a job that you knew would be more of a training ground than a lasting career choice. Or perhaps you entered a field you were excited about or that your family expected you to join, only to learn that it wasn't actually right for you. Maybe you read the previous chapters and realized that your company is not an effective organization that will help you maximize your experience capital or that you have fallen through the broken rung.

Whatever the reason, instead of holding you back, making a big move early on can actually thrust you ahead in your career. In fact, doing so within the first five years of your career is one of the best ways to maximize your experience capital—second only to being exposed to an effective organization early on. The beginning of your career is a critical time for building experience capital, and making big moves during this period is a productive way of learning new skills. People who do, have experience capital that, on average, accounts for 60 percent to 80 percent of their lifetime earnings. This number is much higher than the average of 50 percent, and this strong experience effect can translate into higher lifetime earnings.[7]

So, what exactly does it mean to make a big move? It's not just any job change. Rather, it means starting over in an entirely different occupation or industry, like Noorain's shift from corporate law to the public sector. It makes sense that people who strategically make these types of moves amass higher-than-average experience capital. The earlier in your career that you gain skills and experiences, the more time you have to use those skills across your career. And, of course, it would be hard *not* to gain new skills when starting over in a new occupation or industry.

This is exactly what happened to Noorain. The learning curve she faced ten years ago was nearly as steep as the pay cut she took in order to make the leap. Noorain had jumped into the world of nonprofits without fully understanding the organizational structure and found that it was far less hierarchical than in corporate law. In her new world, it took work to convince others to collaborate on projects, and Noorain found herself spending a lot of time educating others and building consensus before she could take any action—which led her to enhance the relational skills that had always come naturally to her.

Because the market for chief of staff roles was so small, Noorain had also accepted her job without taking much time to get to know her boss, who was the CEO of the organization. They turned out not to be a great fit for each other, and after just about a year in her role, Noorain started looking elsewhere. When she heard that the Ford Foundation had hired Darren Walker to be its new president, she was determined to work for him. She had heard him speak in the past and knew that he was a dynamic leader with grand ambitions that aligned perfectly with her own.

After Noorain interviewed to be Darren's chief of staff and met with the leadership team, she was more excited than ever about the possibility of working at the foundation. She couldn't believe how many impressive people it had, and she floated home from her interview already brainstorming about all of the exciting things that she and her new colleagues could accomplish together . . . and so she was incredibly disappointed to learn that she didn't get the job.

There was a silver lining, though. Darren called Noorain personally to say that he had been impressed with her, and he promised that he would find another job for her at the foundation. Noorain took him at his word and quit her current job even without a solid offer from Ford. It was a big risk, and got even bigger when he came back and offered her two jobs to choose between—and she decided to turn them both down.

From the outside looking in, the decision was perplexing. Noorain had already quit her previous job and desperately wanted to work at Ford. Why would she reject two job offers? The answer is that neither of those jobs reported to Darren. In her previous role, Noorain had learned about the nonprofit organizational structure and how important it was to have a strong relationship with her boss. She was willing to wait in order to work with someone she knew she would have that sort of connection with. Noorain felt that the Ford Foundation was an effective organization, and by prioritizing having that kind of employer as well as having a good boss, Noorain stood to dramatically increase her experience capital.

It took another three months, but Darren finally called Noorain with a job that was exactly what she'd been waiting for. She became the program officer for the office of the president, working directly for him to create a strategy for the Ford Foundation's philanthropic budget of $60 million to $80 million per year. Since then, she has moved up to a leadership role as director and has been able to make grants that support economic, racial, and gender justice, bringing together her disparate college majors and, more important, her passions.

Though she admits that it might sound over the top, Noorain says that she genuinely can't believe she gets to do her job every day. She feels incredibly grateful to have a chance to work with people she deeply respects, each doing their part to make the world a better place. With the Ford Foundation's mandate to fight inequality, a supportive boss like Darren, and plentiful resources, Noorain has been able to make a real impact. Plus, she feels truly supported and celebrated as a leader who is a woman of color.

Although Noorain is still catching up on her salary in corporate law, the skills and experiences she has gained over the past decade have put her in a position to create enormous impact, live a fulfilling life, and continue investing in herself. While we are using financial earnings as a proxy, there is real value and gratification in knowing that you're doing work you are passionate about and that you are making a positive difference in the world. Our goal is to ensure that you have all the knowledge of how to maximize your experience capital so you can make the decisions and trade-offs that are best for you.

Bold Moves Build Skills

Unlike Noorain, Holland Morris started her career in a field she was passionate about and had always planned to spend her life pursuing—teaching. When she was in high school, Holland had been deeply unhappy, but she'd had a strong connection with her English teacher, who inspired her love of reading and writing. In some ways this saved her, and she dreamed about having the same type of impact on teenagers through a teaching career of her own.

After graduating with a master's degree in education and curriculum development, Holland began her first year of teaching, as she describes it, bright-eyed and bushy-tailed. She had lots of creative ideas that she was eager to implement, but all of that enthusiasm quickly dwindled. The kids simply did not respond to her the way she had expected, her day-to-day was exhausting, and Holland started to doubt herself and her methods.

To add to a difficult first year of teaching, Holland was working thirty hours a week as a bartender to make ends meet. She had always known that teaching wouldn't be particularly lucrative, and she'd been working in hospitality since she was fifteen, so she didn't mind continuing to bartend. But she underestimated how exhausted she would be every day after teaching all day and bartending at night.

By year two, Holland was already somewhat disillusioned, but she was far from ready to give up on her goals. Over the next few years, she taught many different classes across grade levels and learned a lot about which subjects she enjoyed teaching the most. Though she didn't always get her first choice of class assignments, she was able to spend enough time doing what she loved to make her job feel more sustainable. During this time, Holland was able to achieve some of her ambitions outside of the classroom. She became the English department chair in charge of curriculum, led school-wide conversations about state testing, mentored new teachers, and served as a class adviser.

After seven years on the job, Holland was proud of everything she had accomplished, yet she was still bartending to make ends meet. She felt that she was at a turning point, and she was torn. She loved the time that she spent at school working on curriculum and in the classroom. But she was beginning to resent bringing work home at night and on weekends, especially since she still had a second job.

Most of all, she was tired, and this all came to a head when she had to take time off from work to care for her father, who had been diagnosed with cancer. It was as if Holland hadn't realized how exhausted and demoralized she really was until she was forced to take a break. After her father passed away, she told her school that she was leaving at the end of the year, despite the fact that she hadn't yet lined up another job. She still had her bartending gig and knew that she could always pick up extra hours until she found a new full-time role.

At first, Holland assumed that she would take a job at another school. But after she received a few offers, she found that she wasn't excited about any of them. She finally realized that it was time to move on from teaching. But how? Outside of hospitality, teaching was the only job she'd ever had, and other career paths were not so obvious to her.

Holland had a sense that she might like working in a corporate environment and rewrote her résumé with that in mind, expressing how all of the skills she'd used as a teacher would translate to the corporate world. For example, lesson planning turned into project planning, communicating with parents and administrators became communicating with stakeholders, classroom management became team management, and creating and implementing curriculum turned into overseeing projects. Not everything that Holland had done as a teacher translated—she wasn't sure if she would ever find a role that valued her knowledge of eighteenth-century literature—but when she was done, her résumé showcased a lot of transferrable skills.

Holland applied and interviewed for a few corporate jobs and ended up landing one as a learning and content specialist at Tripleseat, an event management software company for the hospitality industry. The role involved educating both internal teams and customers about new features and product updates. With her background in hospitality, Holland felt this was a good fit, and she told herself that she would still be teaching; it was only the content and the age of the students that had changed.

Indeed, the foundational skills Holland gained as a teacher have served her well. After a year, her boss started giving her opportunities to take the lead on more complicated, multistep projects. For example, she led the creation of a sixteen-piece learning guide to onboard new clients, and she is now leading a revamp of the learning management system. The company is also paying for her to take a project management class to further hone these skills.

The longer she stays at her current job, the more Holland realizes how many of her teaching skills actually serve her today. For example, she learned in the classroom how to quickly pivot when something doesn't go according to plan. When she's conducting customer trainings, she's good at reading the room to assess if something isn't landing and finding a way to communicate information more clearly.

Yet her new job also required Holland to build many new skills, and that is what has given her the biggest boost in experience capital.

Going the Skill Distance

We use a metric that we call *skill distance* to evaluate how big of a stretch someone's new role is compared with their previous job. Skill distance measures the percentage of new or nonoverlapping skills required for the new role. In general, the median skill distance per move is roughly 25 percent, meaning that 25 percent of the skills required for the new job were not used in the person's previous role. When a move has a skill distance that is higher than this average, we consider it a *bold move.*

The data clearly shows that one of the best ways to gain experience capital is to make several bold moves throughout your career. Your pay goes up the most when you take a new job that requires novel skills and your learning curve is the steepest. When you make multiple bold moves throughout your career, the impact on your experience capital is compounded.

Of course, career jumps with high skill distance do not come without risks. The chances of succeeding in the new role, given that it requires a deeper set of new skills, are not guaranteed. In fact, 20 percent of people in our sample who undertook bold moves early in their careers moved down income quintiles. But the long-term potential upside and growth are greater: higher-risk career jumps, and higher financial rewards when it works out. Meanwhile, 80 percent of people moved into higher earning quintiles or at least stayed in the same quintile while growing their incomes.

Interestingly, our analysis shows that when women make moves, those moves are just as bold and just as frequent as men's moves. However, men are more likely to move to growing occupations from declining ones. Men's moves are also likely to increase their pay compared to women's, who often see a decrease in pay. These are two of the primary drivers of men's greater experience capital.

In the United States, the most upwardly mobile workers averaged 4.6 moves with an average skill distance of 40 percent per move. Compare this with workers staying in the same earning quintile, who averaged 3.7 moves with an average skill distance of 30 percent per move. In Germany and the United Kingdom, upwardly mobile workers move even more frequently, on average 5.2 and 5.3 times, respectively. They also stretch themselves even further, with an average skill distance of 45 percent per move. In India, on the other hand, growth tends to be more incremental: the average skill distance per job move in upwardly mobile workers is 30 percent, compared with 20 percent for those who stayed in the same earning quintile.[8]

Holland's move from teaching can certainly be considered a bold move. When taking her new job, she received a pay increase of 50 percent. Finally, she no longer had to bartend in the evening to make ends meet! In order to get this increase, however, she had to stretch outside her comfort zone and gain many new skills that she did not need as a teacher. These were primarily technology skills and the soft skills of working on a team and developing goals in collaboration with her peers.

Notably, as we'll discuss later, these are the same skills that will be in demand more and more in the future. So, Holland not only boosted her experience capital by making this bold move but also set herself up well for future roles through the specific skills she gained in the process.

Gaining Opportunities to Make Big Moves

Whether you are looking to make a big move early in your career or are considering making a bold move later on, it can take some work

Gateway Jobs

One way to become better qualified for a higher-paying job is to take advantage of gateway jobs. These roles give workers opportunities to build skills and experience before jumping to their target occupation. Taking one is a common way for frontline workers to gain the necessary capabilities for corporate jobs.

For example, a medical assistant may wish to become a radiation therapist but lack some of the necessary skills and experiences. A gateway job as a radiological technologist would provide those capabilities and act as a launching pad toward the target occupation. Another common example is a worker who starts as a customer service representative. They may take a gateway job as a frontline supervisor of production before landing in their target role as a quality control system manager.

Whether or not you are starting on the front lines, it may be helpful to think of your career progression as a series of gateway and target roles. Think a few moves ahead, and then look at the skills and experiences you need to get there. What roles will help you build those skills, and how can you signal them on a résumé and in interviews?

The good news is that there are not many educational hurdles to accessing gateway jobs, since 70 percent of job progressions to gateway roles hinge on interpersonal skills.[a] However, since these skills are hard to quantify, it is easy for biases to interfere with women's ability to gain these opportunities. Skill signaling—how you communicate your abilities to others—therefore becomes a critical factor when applying for gateway jobs.

Note

a. Lareina Yee et al., "Race in the Workplace: The Frontline Experience," McKinsey & Company, July 2022.

to get that opportunity. It's a simple truth that you won't be able to build your experience capital by making a bold move if no one gives you the chance to stretch and challenge yourself in new roles. Treat this process as your own personal workstream. Nobody can look out for you as well as you can, and nobody can proactively steer your career as well as you can. You are in control of your trajectory to maximize your experience capital. Here are a few steps you can take.

Bet on yourself

The first step is to make sure you are reaching for roles with a high skill distance. In 2014 an internal report from Hewlett-Packard revealed that men tended to apply for jobs when they were 60 percent qualified, while women did not apply unless they were 100 percent qualified.[9] This finding has been widely reported, sometimes with the related assumption that women lack the confidence to go after bold moves.

However, a survey of men and women revealed that women's reasoning is typically a little different. In fact, when they did not apply for jobs that they weren't fully qualified for, it was primarily because they simply didn't think they would be hired. They didn't want to waste their time or risk the failure of applying.

There were also other reasons that women cited far more frequently than a lack of confidence. These included wanting to respect the time and energy of the employer, who had made the qualifications clear, and the fact that they were simply following the guidelines. In fact, only 9.7 percent of women said they didn't apply because they didn't think they could do the job well, as compared with 12.4 percent of men.[10] So, for women it was risk aversion and concern for others as opposed to a lack of confidence.

It appears that some women are misunderstanding the hiring process, and this may be holding them back from applying for stretch roles. Let this be your wake-up call: You do not need to wait to apply until you meet all of the qualifications. If you only go after jobs that require the skills you already possess, you are not maximizing your experience capital. Period. In fact, you are undershooting your potential, and instead of maximizing your learning curve, you are flattening it.

Going to another company to perform largely the same role and activities may yield a pay bump in the short term but won't lead to real growth over the longer term. When you feel you have learned all you can from one employer, you should not only go—you should boldly go in search of learning opportunities elsewhere.

Of course, there are some women (and men) who do struggle with self-doubt, including many amazing women senior leaders whom we know. If doubt is holding you back, you need to find a way to believe in your potential to gain new skills on the job. After all, if you don't think that you are the best candidate for a role, you won't be able to convince anyone else.

To build confidence, it may help to think about challenges you've met in the past and what you've learned from them. Ask friends or colleagues how they see you and which of your qualities they value. Doing so may help you recognize and appreciate new things about yourself and gain the confidence you need to stretch.

Even if self-doubt lingers, try to separate those feelings from the process of pursuing new opportunities. Get the opportunity first, and then figure out if you want to take it or if you are the right fit for the job. Once you are offered a role, you can go through a thoughtful decision-making process about whether this is the right role at the right time. But if you let insecurities keep you from going after opportunities in the first place, you're likely to remain stuck.

Even if a particular role isn't right for you or you don't end up getting it, you've still positioned yourself to gain another opportunity in the future. Just think of Noorain and the first job she applied for at the Ford Foundation. Although she was not offered the role, she made an impression that led to an offer later on. If she hadn't gone after that initial opportunity, it's highly unlikely she would have had ten successful and fulfilling years at the organization.

Build your narrative

After you've aimed for roles with a high skill distance, the next question to ask yourself is how you can convince leaders to bet on your potential. This is especially important if you've landed in a first or second job that turns out to be the wrong fit. Many women fear that being in this situation will come across as a misstep or even failure, but there are ways to reframe early moves so they are seen as triumphs instead.

Before beginning a job search, create a narrative around your early role(s). How you talk about your prior experiences will determine whether they are perceived as missteps or learning opportunities that have provided you with valuable skills. It is key to keep these narratives focused on the positive and the learning aspects, rather than what made you unhappy or frustrated.

For example, our colleague Kyla, who identifies as Asian American, left McKinsey early in her career to work at a nonprofit organization. Like Noorain, she thought she would be more fulfilled and make a greater impact if she devoted her career to the public sector, and she took a significant pay cut in order to do so.

At McKinsey, Kyla had gotten a lot of feedback about not speaking up enough. She knew it was something she had to work on, and her new role gave her plenty of opportunities since part of her job was fundraising for the organization. Having to ask strangers for money made her uncomfortable initially, but as she got better at it, she felt a lot more comfortable speaking to just about anyone.

At the same time, Kyla felt that she wasn't making as much of an impact as she wanted in her new role. She felt there was too much time spent writing grant applications and reporting on work done instead of actually doing the work to make a difference. After she had been there for about two years, she started to regret making this move and especially taking such a big pay cut in order to do so. How would she ever get back to the salary she was earning previously and avoid flattening the curve of her experience capital?

One way is to pursue graduate school. Business school, law school, or a master's degree can serve as a helpful reset point in your career and give you the chance to make bold moves to build your experience capital. But attending graduate school to build experience capital is certainly not required. After the two years, Kyla highlighted the new skills she had gained at the nonprofit, such as fundraising and strategic planning, and she thrived upon her return to the corporate world.

Activate your network

Especially when you're not the most obvious candidate on paper, it's unlikely that you'll be given a chance at a stretch role by just submitting your résumé. Personal connections are the key to new opportunities. Begin to systematically free up time on your calendar for coffee chats, lunches, and so on, and use them to talk to people in areas you are interested in. Ask them about their roles, and test whether their industry or field is truly an area of interest. Ask each person you meet whom else they think you should talk to—and if possible, ask them to introduce you to those connections with an email, text, or message through LinkedIn or other professional networking app. Continue doing this until you know exactly what kind of opportunity you are looking for.

Next, work to gain clarity on the path to get there. Be straightforward and clear with people: "I'm really interested in this area and want to find an exciting role in this space. How can I best prepare myself and build the right skills?"

Once you've completed any recommended action items, update your connections on your progress if doing so feels natural. In the meantime, keep putting out feelers and telling other people in your network about your objectives. This is especially helpful in the case of sponsors or mentors who are likely to be in the room when hiring and promotion decisions are being made.

Signal the right skills

To get opportunities, skill-signaling can be just as important as skill-building. Often, job seekers have the skills that are required for a role but fail to signal this on their résumés, LinkedIn profiles, or in other ways. This is what we call a *skill-signaling gap*.

A review of 6.4 million LinkedIn profiles of young people in Brazil, India, Indonesia, and South Africa, and of hundreds of thousands of job postings, revealed that the skill-signaling gap is widest when it comes to soft skills like teamwork, conflict resolution, and communication. Soft skills made up 25 percent of the top twenty skills listed in job postings but did not appear in the top ten skills listed on these LinkedIn profiles, which focused on job-specific technical abilities instead.[11] What that means for you is to make sure you signal all of your skills, including softer ones.

Similar to when Holland wanted to transition out of teaching, you can create a skill-based résumé that will make it easy for potential employers to see the expertise you already have that is valuable to their company. Look at the requirements in job listings, and make sure you do not leave a skill-signaling gap. Then highlight your qualifications with specific examples that are relevant for your ideal role. Mention projects you were a part of or led, and try to quantify their impact or scale, which can make your experiences clearer and more objective for those reading your résumé. It will also make it much easier for employers to envision you in the new role. Don't depend on them to translate the skills you have into what they are looking for. Help them understand how you have built the abilities they need, even if it was in another context or industry.

You can even use signaling phrases when you are describing experiences and stories, such as, "What I learned from that experience that is most relevant to this role is . . ." Or, "The skills I learned were how to build a strong team even with significant differences, and I think that would apply in this role because . . ."

Here are some examples of how to signal the right skills on your résumé:

- Instead of "Captain of sports team," try "Able to lead teams and influence others to achieve results."

- Instead of "Wrote master's thesis," try "Able to manage long-term projects including complex data analytics and synthesis of key information" or "Demonstrated excellent written communication skills."

- Instead of "Ran meetings," try "Able to communicate clearly to both large and small audiences."

- Instead of "Quarterly planning," try "Able to think strategically to develop short-, medium-, and long-term business plans."

It is even better if you can add metrics to your descriptions to quantify and show clearly what you have done and how it might translate. For example, if you ran a project that had a $1 million budget, or that included one hundred people or served five thousand customers, note that in your skills description.

When you land an interview, you have another opportunity to signal your skills by sharing stories and experiences that apply to the new role. Prepare well beforehand and do practice interviews with a friend to make sure you seize the opportunity. When she was preparing to go back into the private sector, Kyla wrote down all the potential questions she thought she might get in an interview and practiced answering them out loud—even in front of a mirror sometimes—to get comfortable with how she sounded and what she wanted to emphasize.

Most of the time, interviewers will open with a general question such as, "Tell me about yourself." This is a pivotal moment to make a good impression and reveal something that's not on your résumé, drawing them into your "why." Ideally, after you take a few minutes to answer the question, your interviewer will feel that they know you a bit more personally and start rooting for you to get the job, though that requires you to reveal something personal and professional about yourself. Talk about your passions and how they connect to the job, as well as how the experiences you have gained so far have prepared you to succeed in it.

If there is an elephant in the room, it's a good idea to address it head-on; for example, if the position would be a stretch role, and you and the interviewer both know it. Instead of allowing that fact to linger in the background, make a clear statement, such as, "I may not be the most obvious candidate, but here's why I think I would do an excellent job . . ." Then reiterate why you are so enthusiastic and all of your existing skills that do apply.

Finally, end strong by restating why you believe you are the right person for the job. Again, if you don't believe it, you won't be able to convince others. So, really own the fact that you believe in yourself, the skills you have built, and your potential to apply them to have an impact—and hopefully your potential employer will believe in you, too.

Next, we will explore the different types of roles you might consider moving into and which ones can best help you build experience capital.

CHAPTER 5

The Power Alley

Amy Weaver grew up in Seattle in an extended family full of lawyers—she says she stopped counting at twenty. From a young age, she had no doubt that she would follow the same route, and she did. Amy had always loved to travel, and two years after graduating from Harvard Law School, she joined a renowned Wall Street law firm based in Hong Kong. She enjoyed the work, but a few years later she longed to return to her roots and moved back to Seattle for a job at a midsize law firm.

Several years on, Amy began to feel conflicted about her career. She was on the verge of making partner, which had always been her goal. But she felt that she was missing something at work and longed to make a greater impact. When an opportunity came up to become the deputy general counsel at travel website Expedia, Amy found herself at a crossroads.

Though Amy had grown up around lawyers, none of them had ever gone in-house at a corporation. At the same time, this was an opportunity to break away from expectations, take on new responsibilities, and open up new doors in her career. Expedia was a world-class company in an industry Amy was passionate about. Going in-house would also expand her ability to work in the tech field, setting her on a bigger and bolder path. So, she took the chance and accepted the offer.

After five years at Expedia, Amy was ready for another leap. She wanted to take on a new challenge and find an opportunity to help shape a company more directly, and she moved on to become the general counsel for Univar Solutions, a global chemical distribution company. Amy was the first female executive in the company's one-hundred-year history. Although she had less of a personal passion for the chemical industry than for travel, she was excited for a more senior role at a huge and well-established company that was conveniently based in Seattle. The company was also planning to go public, which was exciting to Amy.

A year later, the company went through some major changes. The CEO left, and Univar decided not to go public after all. Even worse (at least for Amy), the company was moving to Illinois—two thousand miles away from her family and her roots.

At the time, Amy and her husband were raising three young boys, and she was juggling the ambition to have a remarkable family and career. For weeks she woke up every night at 2 a.m. thinking, *What did I do wrong?* She felt that she had made all the right choices in her career, and yet it had gone sideways, and she was deeply afraid that her career would never recover. She knew that she needed to make another pivot.

Without having another job lined up, Amy made the tough decision to leave Univar. She couldn't justify uprooting her family in order to stay, especially when the company was going in a different direction. After a few more sleepless months, Amy received a call about a role as senior vice president and general counsel at Salesforce, a cloud-based software company. There were only two problems: the role was two levels down from her previous job at Univar, and the company was based in San Francisco.

Amy flew out to interview at Salesforce anyway and was almost disappointed by how much she loved the company, the executive team, and their values. They were also growing rapidly, with revenues at $3 billion and increasing 30 percent a year. Amy was excited by the work they were doing. She knew in her gut that she was going to have to move her family to California to take a lower role in a bigger company.

A few years on, the company's chief operating officer left and his responsibilities were split up, with corporate security now falling under Amy's purview. This was an entirely new world that she had no experience in. The logic was that legal and security were both ways of protecting the company and minimizing risk. Despite her inexperience, Amy made some tough decisions that proved to her that she could succeed as a leader without subject area expertise.

This confidence became even more important three years later when Amy took over the role of chief legal officer. She was now leading audits and government affairs in addition to security. It was challenging, but as a member of the C-suite, Amy now had a seat at the table and was able to have a real impact. For example, she helped lead the company's vocal public stance against laws that discriminate against the LGBTQ+ community and its strong stance when it comes to diversity and equal pay for women.

Then Covid-19 hit. In her role, Amy was responsible for making decisions about employees' health and well-being. Suddenly, she had to learn how to lead a company through a global pandemic. She thought back to other times she had done things without training, such as taking on corporate security, which gave her the confidence to step up and lead.

What Is the Power Alley?

In the previous chapters, we discussed many of the factors outside of your specific job function that affect your career trajectory and lifetime earnings. But, of course, your role itself is also quite important, and not all types of roles are created equal when it comes to building experience capital. In particular, there are two types of roles that are career accelerators: leadership roles and those with profit and loss (P&L) responsibilities. Together, we call these jobs the *power alley*.

We have all heard that women should have a seat at the table. These positions are seats of power, where decisions are made and women's voices can be heard. It is important for women—and for the organizations they work for—that they are equally represented in these rooms. To shape organizations and have an impact, they need to be in "the room where it happens," to borrow a line from the musical *Hamilton*. These rooms line the power alley.

Yet many women have been conditioned to shy away from the idea of power and are still perceived negatively for being ambitious and seeking power.[1] But there is nothing wrong with having positive ambition or wanting to be in a position to make decisions and an impact. It is important for women to own their ambition, including their ambition to hold powerful jobs.

Further, as Amy says, power is often misunderstood. It's not about pounding the table, yelling, or making demands. And it's not about control or domination. Nor is it about forcing others to do things your way. Real power, Amy says, is about getting things done. It is about exerting your influence to make a difference. And there is a way to do that while leading with kindness.

The best way to gain this type of influence is to create a career path that lands you squarely in the power alley. These roles open up opportunities, accelerate the growth of your experience capital, and help you navigate your career in an upward trajectory—even if it takes some side steps to get there.

While P&L and leadership roles both lie in the power alley, there is no one path to get there. It is possible to shift from leadership roles to P&L roles and vice versa. Amy's story is a good example of someone who earned at a seat at the table by making smart moves throughout her career. The wider the variety of power alley roles you can fill, the better. Yet it comes as no surprise that women are underrepresented in these influential jobs.

Leadership Roles

Six months into the pandemic, the chief financial officer of Salesforce was preparing to leave, and the company was running a search. During an online meeting with the CEO, Marc Benioff, Amy told him, "I've thought of a couple more names for the CFO role." Marc responded, "I thought of one, too—Amy Weaver." In Amy's mind, this did not compute. "Oh," she said, feeling baffled, "she's not on my list."

Marc asked Amy to think about it, but she was skeptical that it was a good idea. The potential move to CFO was unprecedented; as far as Amy knew, no one had ever gone from head of legal to head of finance in a *Fortune* 500 company. Shortly after the discussion, she talked to a member of the executive team. "I'm not qualified for this role," she told him. "It's true that you're not qualified to do the role that your predecessor did," he said, "but that's not what we want. We want you to take the role and really make it your own."

This conversation is ultimately what influenced Amy to accept the job. She greatly appreciated the freedom she would have to recreate it in a way that matched her skills and style of leadership, and she was excited by what she could do. And she succeeded: During the time she was at Salesforce prior to becoming CFO, its sales went from $3 billion to $21 billion. While she was CFO, the number increased to $35 billion.

Amy had always been passionate about embracing kindness as a critical strength as a leader, rather than a weakness. When she treated her teams with kindness and respect, they were happier, less likely to leave or burn out, and more productive and innovative. Becoming CFO was a chance to not only redefine a role but help redefine leadership from a bigger platform. She was deeply qualified for a C-suite role—she just did not have the obvious résumé of someone who came up in finance. Luckily, Marc saw a broader set of criteria and capabilities for the CFO role.

While she already had influence as CLO, Amy's influence was now even bigger. The CFO operates some of the most powerful levers in the company, such as where to invest and where to pull back. And although she's led major transactions and improved the company's overall financial operating model, Amy says that one of the greatest impacts she's made has been showing other people that they can get ahead. So many, including one woman who was hesitant about moving into a CEO role, have reached out to say they took a career risk because they were inspired by what she'd done. This is what you gain when you have a seat at the table: the power to inspire and empower others.

Leadership and Experience Capital

In a leadership role like Amy's, you have a close-up view of the company's decision-making process and are able to influence those outcomes. Doing so is one way to make a difference and build experience capital by gaining knowledge about the company without working in the P&L roles that represent the core of the business. When you have a leadership role, you and your work also become far more visible. You have an opportunity to build more senior networks that can open doors for you, and your leadership position allows you to open doors for others.

As a leader at any altitude, you can simply have a greater impact than you can as an individual worker. Senior leaders, of course, shape entire organizations, and managers influence their teams. In fact, employees are more likely to quit their jobs due to their immediate boss than due to their CEO because of the outsize impact that managers can have.[2]

Becoming a leader is also one way of rapidly building new skills by stretching your skill distance. Individual contributors only have to focus on their own performance, while leaders must learn to delegate, provide feedback, and motivate others (and much more). All of this requires excellent communication skills that are transferrable across organizations and industries.

Further, there is a ceiling for how high most individual contributors can rise in an organization, while nearly all senior roles involve leadership and require leadership skills. Therefore, holding leadership positions in your career provides a foundation for you to continue advancing.

Yet, as we have already discussed, women are vastly underrepresented in leadership roles, starting from early-career managers and continuing all the way through the pipeline, dropping in numbers more and more at every step along the way. The result is that very few women actually have decision-making authority, whether they are in senior staff roles or line roles.

While it is important for women to move into more powerful jobs, it is equally essential that we empower women in every role they fill. It is worth considering why some positions are considered more powerful than others. Is it simply because of who has historically filled those roles?

The Historic Devaluing of Women's Work

Women have historically been paid less than men for the same work. And when women enter fields that have traditionally been dominated by men, pay for the exact same jobs tends to decline for both men and women. This is true even after controlling for education, work experience, skills, race, and geography. For instance, when women's representation dramatically increased in design, average wages for identical jobs fell by 34 percent. When large numbers of women became biologists, wages dropped by 18 percent.[3] The same phenomenon has been observed in the field of recreation for jobs working in parks and running camps as well as in nursing.

While there is still a pay gap between women and men in the same occupations, the biggest driver of the gap is now the differences in the occupations and industries in which men and women typically work. The workforce is significantly segregated by gender, and jobs in industries that are disproportionately held by women—such as health care and teaching—tend to pay less than those traditionally held by men. This is true even in jobs with similar education and experience requirements.

The dynamic also applies to the office work women often do that doesn't directly boost their careers yet is beneficial for their employers. For example, women perform a disproportionate amount of emotional labor, such as regulating others' emotions during conflict and listening to people vent. Women leaders are also two times as likely as men to spend a significant amount of time on diversity, equity, and inclusion (DEI) work, which dramatically improves retention and employee satisfaction but isn't often formally recognized. Forty percent of women leaders say that DEI work isn't acknowledged at all in performance reviews.[4] That's another example of women's work being devalued, even when it is of benefit to others.

The power imbalance may also be a self-perpetuating phenomenon. Historically, women have been steered away—either overtly or not—from pursuing high-paying, traditionally male roles. And when young women are deciding what to study and which careers to pursue, they tend to choose areas with women they can look up to. As civil rights activist Marian Wright Edelman said, "You can't be what you can't see." Combine this with stereotypes about women's strengths—such as their being better at soft skills than at quantitative disciplines such as engineering, computer science, physics, math, and science—and it becomes difficult for women to imagine themselves in certain powerful roles.

Further, some women choose not to obtain certain jobs for a better lifestyle and greater flexibility. Many senior positions originated at a time when women rarely worked outside the home. There was an assumption that the men in these jobs had wives at home to handle caregiving for the children and all the work related to the home. This means that these jobs were not designed to balance work and family life.

To a great extent, this remains the case today, despite the increasing numbers of women breadwinners. Globally, about 31% of women contribute significantly to the household income. In the United States, women are on equal or even greater financial parity in 45% of households. Spouses earn roughly the same amount of money in 29 percent of couples, and the woman earns more than the man in 16 percent of couples.[5]

However, women spend more time on caretaking and household chores than their male partners even when they are the primary breadwinner. The only type of male-female marriage in which men spend more time on caretaking is when the woman is the sole earner. And in these marriages, women on average still spend the same amount of time as their partner on household chores.[6]

Further, as men advance in their careers, they do less household work, but the opposite is true for women. Fifty-two percent of women at the senior manager level and up say that they are responsible for most or all of their family's housework and childcare, compared with only 13 percent of men at the same level. For many women, this makes senior roles with little flexibility very difficult to attain and keep.[7]

Identifying as a Leader

Of course, bias is a huge factor in the power imbalance, especially when it comes to leadership roles. Becoming a leader is not just about applying for a job or a promotion. It requires being seen—both internally and externally—as someone people will follow. This is often a struggle for women, as gender bias creates a mismatch between how they are perceived and the expectations of a leader. Women are just as ambitious as their male counterparts, but they often face microaggressions that undermine their authority and send the message that they are not welcome.

For example, women leaders are twice as likely as men to be mistaken for someone more junior, and far more likely than male leaders to have colleagues question their judgment or imply that they aren't qualified for their jobs. They are more likely to experience having others take credit for their ideas too—37 percent say it has happened to them, compared with 27 percent of men. Women leaders are also more likely to report that personal characteristics, such as their gender or being a parent, have contributed to their being denied or passed over for a raise, promotion, or chance to get ahead.[8]

Black women leaders are even more ambitious than other women at their level. Fifty-nine percent want to be top executives, compared with 49 percent of women overall. But Black women are also more likely than other women of color to receive signals that it will be harder for them to advance. Compared with other women at their level, Black women are more likely to have colleagues question their competence and to experience demeaning behavior. And 61 percent of Black women leaders say they've been denied or passed over for opportunities because of personal characteristics, including their race and gender.[9]

These experiences disrupt the learning cycle at the heart of becoming a leader in the power alley. According to research published by *Harvard Business Review*, the process of internalizing a leadership identity—truly believing it about yourself—starts with taking purposeful action. For example, if you lead in a meeting or on a project and others affirm your actions, leadership becomes a stronger part of your identity and something that you believe is part of who you are. Over time, this encourages you to take additional actions that are further and further outside of your comfort zone and can lead to personal and professional growth. But if others reject your action, signal their distrust, or disrespect your leadership, it can prevent you from seeing yourself as a leader. It can become a vicious cycle, or a virtuous one.[10]

Yet we know that women do make effective leaders. Employees with women managers are more likely to say their manager checks in on their well-being, helps them manage their workload, and promotes inclusive behavior on their team—all things that are becoming more and more important to workers.[11]

Amy Weaver argues that rather than forcing women to contort themselves to fit into the mold of the leaders of the past, we should change how we define leadership and what an executive looks, sounds, and acts like. Doing so will be helpful to women, to people of color, and to many men who feel constrained by narrow definitions of leadership. Further, we should rethink whether certain roles should hold the most power just because they have in the past—and likely because they were held by men. In other words, instead of just encouraging women to take on powerful roles, we should empower the roles held by women.

Profit and Loss Responsibilities

After business school, Fuencisla Clemares (who goes by Fuen) went into consulting. She enjoyed it and learned a lot, but after six years she was ready to make a move. Her bosses had always told Fuen that she was a strong thinker as well as a very good executor, and she felt that she was missing out on the second half of that equation—acting on the advice she gave to her clients and owning the results of her decisions.

In consulting firms, consulting jobs are considered line roles, as working with clients is how the firms make money. However, strategy or advisory jobs are considered staff roles, since they support the business rather than directly driving revenue. A typical move for someone like Fuen would have been to go in-house in a strategy role for a company, but that would put her in the same position she was already in, advising others instead of implementing her ideas.

Luckily, Fuen had a strong relationship with the French multinational retail corporation Carrefour, and when a line role opened up in sales as the homeware director, she was able to position herself to get the job. She was thrilled, and thrived in the role despite the steep learning curve she faced. Finally, she was in the center of the action, driving execution. She had P&L responsibility, could see the impact of her decisions in daily results, and got feedback in real time.

For example, Fuen made calls about product promotions and soon saw the promotions being implemented in stores. The customer response and the impact on sales were immediately clear. If she made a big bet on a promotion and it didn't work, she had to change course quickly. Her team checked their sales numbers three times a day to make sure they were hitting their targets. It was intense and pressure was high, but Fuen found it energizing to work at such a fast pace.

Soon, she was able to transition into a role that gave her a chance to have an even bigger impact, as sales director at Google. Fuen was not a technology expert, so she knew that she would have to approach the opportunity carefully. In her interviews, she focused on her retail expertise, learning potential, and ability to translate between business and technology. While she had no background in technology, she knew that she could understand it well enough to support its impact on the business, which was exactly what Google needed.

As soon as she began her new job, Fuen felt confident that she had the potential to grow and thrive within the company, and she was extremely proactive about her next move. Her boss was the CEO of Google in Spain. She knew that he would likely leave the company within three to five years, and she told him very clearly that she wanted his help to put her in the right position to fill his role when he left. She already had a solid case for it with her extensive P&L experience.

Fuen asked her boss two main questions: "What are the gaps you see in my skill set and performance that I need to address? And how can I make sure that when the time comes, the decision-makers know me and feel comfortable putting me in the role?"

Together, they came up with a plan. Fuen's boss pinpointed the leaders who would likely choose his replacement and made sure that she had the opportunity to work with them on high-profile projects. He also gave her feedback around thinking big and becoming an inspirational leader. Fuen recognized that she took a cautious, rational approach to leadership. That had served her well in her career thus far, but in order to step into a more senior leadership role, she had to let herself take more risks and dream a little bigger.

It didn't happen overnight. But between the new opportunities that her boss opened up and the work she did to fill in her leadership gaps, Fuen was more than ready when her boss ended up leaving a few years later. She has been in his former role ever since.

P&L Roles and Experience Capital

As a senior leader with P&L responsibilities, Fuen has had a chance to reflect on her various roles. She says that whenever you're managing people, you have a chance to support them and the company, but when you run teams with P&L oversight, you have an opportunity to have a broader external impact. In her current role, she feels a deep sense of purpose knowing that she is aiding the digital transformation of her country.

Yet Fuen has observed that there are few women sales executives, and she has seen women hold themselves back from going after such roles, making the mistake of thinking they won't be able to do it. But she has also seen that when they try, they do an incredible job. These women bring important things to the table—their unique approaches, perspectives, and ways of building relationships.

Fuen encourages young women to try different types of roles before deciding what they want to do, but she considers it critical to hold a line role at some point during a career. She says it is the best way to deeply understand the business, make an impact, and rise to a more senior, powerful position.

As Fuen describes, line roles that manage P&L accelerate the growth of experience capital and can open up lanes to the C-suite. The people in these jobs directly generate revenue for an organization, while staff roles support the business in other ways.

Most women starting their careers don't fully appreciate the key differences in choosing a line role versus a staff role, but the decision can greatly affect their trajectories. First of all, holding line roles, particularly early in your career, directly impacts lifetime earnings. Workers who start out in P&L jobs have 20 percent higher lifetime earnings on average than those starting out in staff roles. We estimate that across sectors, workers in line roles earn salaries that are 14 percent to 31 percent higher than those of their peers in support roles.[12]

Further, *Fortune* 500 CEOs who are promoted from within a company typically come from a line role (usually running the biggest or second largest business unit) rather than a staff one. And P&L management experience is often a requirement for the C-suite.

While support roles are important and certainly contribute to a company's success, line jobs represent the core of the business. There is no way around this. As such, the people in them hold a great deal of the power in the organization and are more likely to progress to senior positions.

The P&L Gap

Unfortunately, women's representation in line roles suffers from what we call the *P&L gap*. Men gain ground in both staff and line jobs as they move through the pipeline. There are 1.5 times as many men in executive staff roles as women, but four times as many men in executive line roles as women.[13]

Yet men who start out in line jobs later shift into executive staff jobs at a disproportionately high rate. For example, men's representation in staff roles doubles as they advance through the pipeline toward senior-level positions, while their representation in line roles increases by approximately 10 percent.[14] This is a well-understood trend that extends beyond the corporate context. For example, cooking, teaching, and fashion are typically considered "women's areas," yet an unequal number of head chefs, school principals, and lead designers are men. With women losing so much ground in line roles, there are simply more men available to become CEO or to be considered for the C-suite—which helps explain why only 10 percent of S&P 500 companies have women CEOs.

In the United States, women of color (including Asian Americans, Black, Latina, and Native American women) hold an extremely small share of line roles on executive teams: 7 percent, or one out of every fifteen senior leaders reporting to a CEO. For example, Black female executives are more than twice as likely to be in staff roles as in line roles.[15] Of course, that contributes to the infinitesimally small number of CEOs who are women of color: currently three in the *Fortune* 500.

The P&L gap occurs at every stage in the pipeline, but the career stage that sees the highest percentage of women shifting away from P&L responsibility is the early executive level—typically around vice president. Approximately 80 percent of executive men have P&L responsibilities, compared with only 63 percent of women.[16] Executives without P&L responsibilities tend to have less influence, and with men already disproportionately represented at the executive level, this is a double hit to women's potential advancement.

P&L Roles and Understanding Revenue

It may be especially strategic to seek a line job early in your career. Many organizations offer programs that help workers in line roles shift into staff roles and back, but fewer offer opportunities for staff employees to explore line opportunities. Of course, when you understand the core of the business, it is easier to make internal moves and lead the organization effectively; more importantly, you are seeing how the business makes money. If there is no obvious path from staff to line roles, workers are left on the outside, without knowledge of the core business.

Jenny Abramson didn't intentionally seek out a line role. When she was graduating from business school, she was torn about what to do next. She had worked in consulting and had experience in the public sector, and she wanted to work for a company with a mission that she was passionate about. As a strong believer in the importance of a free press, Jenny took a job as a sales representative for the *Washington Post.*

At the time, this felt to Jenny like a somewhat odd career choice for someone with her background and education. She thought she would be a better fit for a different role in the organization. But the president told her, "If you want to do well here, you have to understand how the company makes money." This perspective has changed the course of Jenny's career.

In her first year, Jenny was promoted to a line role as the jobs manager, which oversaw the team selling advertising space for job openings. Holding a P&L role helped Jenny get more comfortable with and far more knowledgeable about money. The insights she gained served her throughout a long career at the *Post*, ultimately running two large organizations and helping to create and launch *Washington Post* Live along with other startup businesses. She later built on and used these skills as the founder and managing partner of Rethink Impact, a venture capital firm that invests in female leaders who are using technology to solve the world's problems.

Jenny's advice for women is to get comfortable with money, to manage money, to set goals against money, and to practice negotiating for money—and not just when it comes to your salary. The more you negotiate for your business or team, the better you'll be at talking about money in terms of incentive alignment, which will help you when it's time to address your own pay. She says that although entry-level staff roles might initially seem more appealing than line roles such as the one she took in sales, the opposite becomes true as you move through the pipeline, and the more senior line roles hold significantly more power and influence.

Gaining a Seat at the Table

As you look ahead to your career trajectory, think about how you can position yourself to hold leadership and/or P&L roles in the power alley. Doing so will help you maximize your experience capital, as you'll gain opportunities to learn about every aspect of the business and how money and decisions are made.

First of all, ask yourself whether the roles you've held so far, including your current job, have been line, staff, and/or leadership roles. If you're not sure, look at whether your role is core to the business. Do you directly drive income and manage P&L, or do you support other teams that create revenue? Remember, this varies from industry to industry. For example, a publicist working at a PR firm is core to the business because the firm makes money by doing public relations. However, a PR executive for a technology firm is a staff position, because that company does not make money by doing public relations.

There are also different types of leadership roles, all of which boost experience capital. Of course, being a manager, at any level, is this kind of position. But there are other types of leadership that are often overlooked. For example, sitting on a functional council or board, overseeing a high-profile project, or heading a location or affinity group at your organization are all forms of leadership. Through any of these positions, you can become more visible to higher-ups, gain a more senior network, and build the power to make decisions that affect the overall organization.

Once you identify the type of power alley role that you want, make a plan to reach for it. That can mean directly asking your manager or others what you need to do in order to be qualified for that job—Fuen's approach when preparing to step into her boss's position. But also, don't be afraid to make a lateral move to better position yourself to enter the power alley.

Next, we will take a close look at which industries and occupations offer the greatest opportunities and how you can make a move from one to another.

CHAPTER 6

Go Where the Jobs Are

When Kristie Lazenberry was a student at the University of Minnesota, she had a job working part-time at the local chapter of the Young Women's Christian Association (YWCA). Its mission is to eliminate racism, empower women, and promote peace, justice, freedom, and dignity for all. Being half Black, Kristie had a lifetime of thinking about racism and what made good allies, and her experience at the YWCA inspired her lifelong passion for work in DEI. In her words, it planted the seeds that she would pursue later in her career.

At the time, however—this was over twenty-five years ago—there was no such thing as a job in DEI. Careers in the area did not exist. Kristie never expected her passion to become anything more than something she pursued on the side.

She was no stranger to side projects. Kristie was also a musician with her own band and independent record label, and she spent most of her time writing, performing, and recording music. Her band, 94 East, even recorded with the Minnesota native Prince. But, like many aspiring artists, Kristie needed a day job.

Over the next two decades, that day job went from receptionist to graphic designer to knowledge manager. In this last role, Kristie managed data and the digital records of confidential documents for a large global company. As part of her job, she worked with multiple teams to develop a tool to make the document and knowledge storage system more technologically advanced. The first iteration of the tool required a person to work with the technology. The second iteration, however, performed the necessary tasks completely. Before long, the very tool that Kristie had helped develop ended up replacing her.

Kristie needed a new job, and she ended up making a lateral move to a position as an administrative assistant for the Itasca Project. It was an initiative started by senior business leaders from Minneapolis and St. Paul to focus on issues to improve economic development in the area. One of its goals was to create greater racial equity and higher standards of living, so Kristie was excited for her new job, despite the fact that it didn't pay as much.

Since college, Kristie had continued working with the Minneapolis YWCA during her free time. She trained to become a DEI facilitator and ran workshops there at night and on weekends. Then in 2015, Itasca faced criticism for the lack of diversity on its leadership team. Knowing about Kristie's work with the YWCA, they asked for her help.

She was thrilled, and started holding weekly sessions focusing on DEI at Itasca, first with the leadership team and then more broadly. Kristie describes these early sessions as basic: she simply facilitated conversations with the team about where they were in their life's journey of understanding racism and bias. Yet these discussions were extremely impactful for the business leaders and ultimately for the Itasca Project itself.

After a few years, Kristie wanted to expand her DEI work. The St. Paul Area Chamber, a local business network, had acquired a program called the DEI Collaborative, and it hired Kristie to become the program director. In this role, which she still holds today, she gathers ten to fifteen C-suite leaders from Minneapolis and St. Paul once a month for a two-hour session. They don't use presentations, a whiteboard, or a screen. Instead, they sit in a circle with nothing in between them and share their personal narratives and discuss the social systems around them.

Kristie says that she has seen countless tears as people dig into their histories and unearth the foundation of why they think the way they do. It's incredibly meaningful work that she loves, and after a long and winding career, the seeds that were planted in her in college can finally bloom.

Occupational Changes Are Happening Faster and Faster

Although Kristie's career path is certainly unique, it speaks directly to the types of occupational shifts that have been going on for centuries. As new tools and technologies develop, some job categories shrink or disappear altogether. Yet those same advances open up space for entirely new occupations. Ideally, more new jobs emerge than disappear.

With projections of economic growth and demographic shifts, we are expecting to have more jobs in the future than we do today—both globally and in the United States. And the good news is that those jobs will be higher-wage jobs on average; the catch, though, is that they will require higher skills. So, the critical question for society and for individuals is, How do we build the skills that we need for tomorrow's jobs in the workforce that we have today? For those who can make that shift, the future is promising. But at an overall country level, the degree of reskilling and upskilling that is required is greater than what we have done before and will require innovation.

For some time now, occupational changes have been occurring faster and faster. With the long-term impact of Covid-19 on top of long-term trends in automation and, more recently, generative AI, these changes are happening on a bigger scale than ever. During the first three years of Covid in the United States, nine million occupational shifts happened— 50 percent higher than the pre-Covid rate. Many of the shifts were workers taking higher-paid and higher-skilled jobs. All told, in the United States, twelve million occupational changes will need to happen between now and 2030 to fill the jobs we will need in the future. Most of the jobs in shrinking occupations from which people will need to switch are held more often by women. That number represents 7 percent to 8 percent of the workers in the United States today. Across the United States, Japan,

Germany, France, Spain, the United Kingdom, China, and India, an estimated 107 million additional occupational switches may need to happen by 2030—an estimated 7 percent of the workforce.[1] As mentioned previously, generative AI and automation technologies have the potential to automate 30 percent of today's work activities by 2030 and could automate between 60 and 70 percent of work activities beyond 2030. While it can take years—perhaps even decades—for our economy to fully absorb these changes, this represents a dramatic change to how we work.[2]

In the European Union, about 12 million cumulative occupational changes will be required (around the same number as in the United States) between now and 2030 to fill the jobs needed in the future. Making it happen will be more challenging in the EU than in other places, however, since that number is roughly twice the annual rate of occupational change that has happened historically, and they will be happening in the context of a more rigid job market, given employment rules.[3]

If the past few decades are an indicator, many workers will be caught off guard by what may seem like the sudden fall of entire occupations and even industries, leaving them with few options. But these changes rarely happen all at once. Although Kristie helped develop the very tool that ended up replacing her, she looks back now and wonders why she never worried about her next job as an assistant becoming automated too. Fortunately, she had already moved on to DEI work; administrative assistant jobs are now shrinking rapidly, as technology can indeed handle many of the related tasks.

Whether you are just starting out in your career or are more established, it is important to understand the shifts that are happening and those that are coming in the future. When choosing an occupation, it pays to be strategic and pick an area that is growing, where the wind is at your back instead of in your face, so to speak. Meanwhile, if you are currently in an occupation that is shrinking, you will need to think more urgently about reskilling and upskilling to find your next job.

Of course, working in a growing or stable occupation is helpful to protect your livelihood, but it is also an important way of continuing to boost your experience capital. In a shrinking field, you are less likely to gain skills that will continue to be marketable going forward. For instance, if Kristie hadn't helped develop the technology to automate the storage system, she would have been working with antiquated tools, flattening the curve of her experience capital.

It therefore pays in the form of experience capital and lifetime earnings to be strategic about your career path. When you are able to find work in growth areas that require more cutting-edge skills, you are positioning yourself to be in demand with greater choice and control over your career. In the next few chapters, we will discuss the specific skills that will be the most valuable.

Growing Occupations

So which occupations are growing and which ones are shrinking? In the United States, the largest future job gains by 2030 are expected to be in science, technology, engineering, and mathematics (STEM), which is set to grow by 23 percent; transportation, which will grow by 9 percent; and 30 percent for health care, which could see demand for 3.5 million more jobs for aides, technicians, and wellness workers, plus an additional 2 million jobs for health-care professionals. In particular, nurses and home health-care aides are two of the fastest-growing occupations.[4]

This should come as no surprise if you look at demographic trends. The global population continues to age—which is good news in some ways as people live longer, but birth rates in some developed countries are below the population replacement rate. The old-age dependency ratio (the number of citizens over age sixty-five per one hundred working-age people) is highest in China, Japan, and South Korea. In 2023 it was fifty in Japan and twenty-six in Korea, but in both countries it's expected to be closer to seventy by 2050. Among emerging economies, China is aging the fastest, and by 2050 Asia will have 400 million additional people who are 65 and older, on top of the 384 million today.[5]

To put this in perspective, South Korea has a fertility rate of 0.7 children per woman, which is far below the replacement rate of 2.1 that keeps a population level steady. This means that, on average, for every 100 grandparents in Korea there will be 12.25 grandchildren and 4.3 great-grandchildren—a generation size decline of about 88 percent to 95 percent across four generations. In contrast, Uganda has the highest fertility rate, of 6.8. There, 100 grandparents will have 1,156 grandchildren and 3,930 great-grandchildren. This means 4.3 great-grandchildren in Korea versus 3,930 in Uganda—the difference in just four generations is staggering. And these trends are not even counting the effect of when women give birth. In high-fertility countries, women tend to give birth at earlier ages, further compounding the effect on the population.

The aging phenomenon in South Korea is also happening in the United States and Europe, just to a lesser effect. In fact, the workforce of the next decade (given birth rates globally and the number of children already born) will be primarily in India and across Africa. Most other areas are either stagnant (with fertility rates roughly at the replacement rate) or dropping. One reason is that fewer young people want to have children, given the state of the environment and other pressures. For example, the United Kingdom has seen the rise of BirthStrike, a movement to avoid having children because of global warming.[6]

The other reason, however, is great news for humans: we are living longer. Plus, the retirement age has been pretty steady globally, meaning that we have more years of people not working post-retirement.

These demographic shifts will affect the job market across all industries, not just health care. People who are retired have very different priorities and spending patterns compared with those who are still working, which impacts consumer products and what people buy, how they invest and spend, pharmaceutical sales, and broader consumption across industries.

The second biggest growing job category is in STEM as the economy continues to digitize. Employers in banking, insurance, pharmaceuticals, health care, and most other industries are undertaking major digital transformations and will continue to need workers with STEM skills.

In addition, the US transportation services category, which includes order fulfilment, delivery workers, and ride-hailing drivers, is expected to see job growth of 9 percent overall between now and 2030. To a slightly lesser degree, occupations in business and legal professions and management, as well as in education and education training, are also expected to see continued growth.

Shrinking Occupations

Meanwhile, the job categories that are shrinking the most fall into four main categories. The first is customer service and sales roles, which are affected by the shift to e-commerce. These jobs also involve a high share of data collection and elementary data processing, all tasks that automated systems can handle efficiently and effectively. For example, as consumer product purchases move online and some stores close, logistic centers will grow, tech jobs to code the apps and websites will grow, and jobs in transportation to deliver the goods will grow, even if the exact mode of transportation looks different and is more efficient in the future.

Second is food services roles that can be automated and that are impacted by a shift toward remote work. Think of using an iPad or your phone to order at restaurants. While waiters and bartenders and cooks are still needed, fewer are needed than before and they focus their time more on delivering food, greeting and seating customers, and fixing issues when they arise.

Third is production jobs, which are shrinking despite an upswing in the overall US manufacturing sector. In manufacturing, there is now greater demand for skilled technical and digital roles and fewer traditional production jobs as automation increases.

Finally, office support and administrative assistant roles will continue to shrink due to both automation and more remote work, with fewer people coming into physical offices.

Together, these four categories of shrinking occupations account for almost ten million (roughly 85 percent) of the twelve million occupational shifts expected by 2030 in the United States.[7]

Women are disproportionately represented across three of the four categories, in particular office support, customer service and sales, and food service roles. As a result, US women are projected to be 1.5 times more likely to have to switch occupations by 2030 than US men. And globally, 40 to 160 million women may need to transition in this time frame. The wide range represents the differing pace of automation around the world, taking into account technology capabilities to automate work as well as the wages of the people doing the work that is being automated.[8]

In addition to women, workers of color, frontline workers, and those in lower-paying jobs will also be disproportionately affected by the shifts. The jobs in the two lowest wage quintiles (those earning less than $30,800 a year and those earning between $30,800 and $38,200) are disproportionately held by women, workers with less education, and people of color. And the workers in those two wage quintiles are around fourteen times more likely to need to change occupations by 2030 than the highest earners. That is staggering. So, while generative AI will affect higher-wage jobs as well, it will only change parts of these jobs—30 percent of their activities, on average—instead of eliminating them entirely. The much greater impact will be on those jobs that pay less than $38,200 a year.

While these numbers are daunting, there is good news and bad news for affected workers. The good news is that as low-paying roles are declining, the number of jobs in the highest wage quintile (earning more than $68,700) will grow by up to 3.8 million by 2030 in the United States. Medium-wage jobs are set to remain relatively static. These changes represent opportunities for women and other displaced workers to shift into higher-paying roles.

The bad news, of course, is that these higher-paying jobs often require greater levels of education and skills. Reskilling and upskilling yourself and proactively seeking out opportunities across your career will be key to staying in the mix. Your ability to access growth occupations is therefore a way of maximizing your experience capital *and* an indication of the current curve of your experience capital. You can gain in-demand skills by working in thriving occupations. At the same time, you need up-to-date, marketable skills in order to land these jobs.

For instance, while Kristie pursued her DEI work because of her passion and not necessarily because it was a growing occupation, the skills she gained along the way proved to be marketable. Of course, there is a serendipitous element to her story, but maintaining a steep experience capital curve, representing a lifetime of learning, is the best way to have a sustainable, resilient career.

New Occupational Categories

In addition to the growing and shrinking job categories, between now and the end of 2030, technology will help create entirely new occupations, opening up additional opportunities. For each decade in the United States, around 9 percent of jobs are entirely new roles.[9] Examples from the past decade include machine learning and AI experts, ride-hailing drivers, and social media influencers. In the future we will see new jobs emerge, many of which will be high-paying, such as generative AI prompt engineers and machine learning analysts.

Kristie's role in DEI is another new category that has arisen not from the advent of technology per se but rather from a cultural shift. Another example is roles in environmental sustainability, which have been growing steadily since the 1990s. These jobs originally focused on companies' efforts to comply with environmental policies, but they have since become more strategic and more senior. Many publicly traded US companies now have a chief sustainability officer.

While the energy industry is male-dominated, opportunities in sustainable energy are increasing both overall and for women. From 2011 to 2018, the percentage of women chief sustainability officers in the United States grew from 28 percent to 45 percent.[10] The number of sustainability-related occupations is likely to keep growing as environmental issues continue to influence societal and corporate priorities.

Nathalie Oosterlinck's experience speaks to how working in emerging occupations can help maximize experience capital. She did not study STEM at university in her native Belgium, and after graduating she spent years in finance and management roles for energy companies. She was well established in her career when she got a call from a headhunter who was looking to fill a CEO role for a new offshore wind company. When they offered her the job, Nathalie couldn't understand why; she had no experience in offshore wind. But the hiring committee said they saw something in her and felt she was the right person.

Nathalie accepted the role and feels it was one of the best decisions she's ever made. Not only was it the beginning of a long and successful career in renewable energy, but she has learned so much along the way. She says that everything she learned before taking that job is minimal compared with what she gained in that one position. The company was basically a startup, and she quickly grasped how to build an organization from the ground up in addition to the financing, technology, and engineering of offshore wind. Those skills have proven to be marketable in this emerging field, and today Nathalie is the managing executive officer and global head of renewables for JERA, Japan's largest power generation company.

However, outside of DEI work and environmental sustainability, women remain underrepresented in the highest-paying new and emerging job categories. Research by economist David Autor finds that new and emerging occupations in the United States typically fall into three categories: frontier jobs, wealth jobs, and last-mile jobs.

Frontier jobs, such as AI specialists, roboticists, and machine learning engineers, are highly paid and tend to be male-dominated. Women only work 28 percent of the total hours spent in frontier jobs.

Wealth jobs typically involve providing labor-intensive, in-person services to affluent consumers and pay average wages. These roles tend to be dominated by women, who supply 62 percent of the hours devoted to them. Broadly, these roles do not demand technical skills, but they are still increasing in importance as incomes rise, particularly in urban areas. Occupations in this category include nannies, beauty care specialists, baristas, yoga instructors, sommeliers, pet care workers, and exercise coaches.

Finally, last-mile jobs offer lower-than-average pay. Workers in these jobs carry out tasks that have largely been automated but retain a residual human component, such as contact center representatives, order fulfillment workers, data entry clerks, and underground utility cable locators. These jobs are more evenly split between men and women.

Highly paid frontier jobs therefore represent untapped opportunities for women. If women can build the skills to get those roles, they would have access to a much broader set of growing opportunities with a high likelihood of continuing to grow their experience capital.

Occupation Versus Industry

Just like occupations, entire industries shrink or grow or even disappear completely over time, often leaving workers feeling stuck and unable to transition to a new job in a different industry. Yet while some occupations, such as nurses, are industry-specific, others are far more portable, and those tend to be in support functions. Workers in human resources, accounting, and operations, for example, can choose to work across multiple industries over the course of their careers.

Workers often don't realize that it's possible to do a very similar job in a very different industry. But as sectors evolve, it's important to think about your skill set in a broader way instead of as something you use in your current job. If you are in a shrinking occupation, regardless of industry, it is likely that you will need to reskill or upskill in order to move into a growth area. This may be more urgent if you are in a shrinking occupation within a dying industry—a double whammy, so to speak. But if you are in a stable or growing occupation in a shrinking industry, transitioning to a new role will be more about developing a flexible work mindset and thinking creatively and strategically about your next move.

It's similar to—or perhaps even identical to—how you might think about your skills and how to market yourself when making a bold move to a new occupation. You will be taking relevant skills with you. And don't forget that making a big move is one of the best ways to increase your experience capital. So, all is not lost if you find yourself in a shrinking industry. It could be just the push you need to find a bigger opportunity in your career.

This is what happened to Giovanna Fabiano. While studying journalism and communications at Rutgers University with a minor in political science, Giovanna started interning at the *Star-Ledger*, the largest newspaper in New Jersey. She helped find leads and gain intel for a political gossip column, which was the perfect mix of her interests. She loved working at the prestigious, award-winning newspaper. When she graduated and landed a job at a smaller paper, Giovanna always planned to build her résumé until she could find her way back to the *Star-Ledger*.

However, by 2008, after Giovanna had been working at smaller papers for about seven years, it had become painfully clear that this wasn't going to happen. It wasn't necessarily because Giovanna wouldn't be able to return to the *Star-Ledger*, but because she would no longer want to. Its newsroom had shrunk dramatically with layoffs, and the paper had become a shell of what it once was.

Of course, similar things were happening across the newspaper industry. While layoffs hadn't hit her smaller newspaper yet, Giovanna saw the writing on the wall. Every time someone at a New Jersey paper was laid off, their fellow journalists would gather at the same local pub to toast and send them off. When Giovanna found herself at that pub nearly every week, she knew that she had to make a change.

She had no experience in digital media, but it was clear that the field was the new frontier. So, she applied for and received a fellowship from the Knight Foundation to attend a monthlong workshop at the US Berkeley Graduate School of Journalism to learn about podcasting, video editing, and digital journalism. When she returned, she accepted a job as a regional editor for Patch.com, a local journalism site that had been acquired by AOL.

At the time, it felt like a radical move. Online journalism wasn't a respected field, and Giovanna's mentors were concerned that she was flushing her career down the toilet. But she was convinced that she'd be doing herself a disservice by staying at traditional newspapers instead of learning digital skills.

In fact, Giovanna gained more than digital skills in her new role, becoming a manager for the first time and running a staff of eleven and then later twenty-seven. She learned leadership skills and how to run a newsroom.

Patch was growing rapidly, so Giovanna was shocked one day when she and many of her colleagues were asked to join an emergency call, on which they were told via a recording that their positions were being eliminated, effective immediately. Patch was folding. It had grown too fast, and the business model had become unsustainable.

It was the start of an incredibly stressful time. Not only was Giovanna pregnant with her second child, but she and her husband had just made an offer on their first house. Now they were scrambling to see if they would still be approved for their mortgage without Giovanna's income. She immediately reached out to her entire network and took on some freelance work while interviewing for a new job.

One of the companies she interviewed with was SJR, a content marketing firm. Before the interview, Giovanna felt sure that it wouldn't be the right fit for her. She imagined a stuffy corporate environment that wouldn't mesh with her personality. But instead, she entered a funky industrial space filled with high-quality art. The people she met with were smart and creative, and there was a fast-paced energy to the place that Giovanna found exciting.

SJR was among the very first content marketing firms out there. The entire field was so new that many people didn't even understand what it was. SJR was trying to mirror a journalism model, but with the work benefiting companies rather than serving the public. It needed someone who could write quickly and lead a team, and Giovanna knew that she had the right skills to thrive there. Despite the rough ending at Patch, it had been a great stepping stone that helped her move up to this new role.

Soon after taking the job, Giovanna saw that her journalism background had prepared her to write within deadlines and work well with clients. As a senior editor, she put together small teams to align with a company on its content strategy and then create the work. Since the field was new, there were few expectations and the team was able to experiment, which Giovanna loved. She soon moved up to become managing editor and lead a bigger team, and then to her role in the C-suite as the chief content officer.

Shrinking and Growing Industries

While it was clear for some time that the newspaper industry was shrinking as technology and online content expanded, in other cases it's not as obvious. So, which industries are growing and which ones are shrinking?

In addition to health care, growing industries include social assistance, construction, transportation and warehousing, arts, entertainment, recreation, manufacturing, utilities, and professional, scientific, and technical services. Industries that are remaining static include agriculture, forestry, fishing and hunting, and educational services. The top shrinking sectors are accommodation and food services, real estate, wholesale trade, mining, finance and insurance, and retail.

It is also helpful to look at industries and occupations together to get a more specific view of where things are going and areas you may want to target in your job search. While most occupations are either growing or shrinking consistently across industries, there are exceptions. In some industries more than others, specific skill sets are needed, causing occupations in that sector to grow. For example, demand for architects in mining is expected to decrease by 16 percent by 2030, while there will be 18 percent more architect jobs in health care, designing hospitals, nursing homes, and other facilities. Likewise, demand for building engineers is expected to grow by 30 percent in health care and 22 percent in arts and entertainment by 2030, but decrease by 5 percent in transportation and warehousing. In retail and education, these jobs are expected to remain static.[11]

While working in a growing industry can drive experience capital and therefore lifetime earnings, it is important for other reasons too. For one, it is far more pleasant to go to work each day when you are swimming downstream and there are ample opportunities to grow and develop the skills of the future. That same downstream current can either help you along or hold you back.

When your industry is shrinking, people often begin to feel threatened and territorial, and their sharp elbows can come out—not typically a recipe for job satisfaction. On the other hand, when workers feel secure in their jobs and growth is plentiful, they are more likely to support each other in an environment that feels abundant. This will make it more likely that your job will drive personal satisfaction and have other direct career benefits.

In some cases, it may be worth trading salary for a growing occupation in a growth sector. Doing so likely provides some level of job security and often makes for a more satisfying work experience.

If your occupation and/or industry has been discussed in this chapter, then you already know if your field is growing or shrinking. Otherwise, it's important to assess whether you're currently on the right path or may need to consider a change. When it comes to your occupation, ask yourself how many of your regular tasks could potentially be automated. Also think about what unique skills you bring to the table that cannot be replicated by a machine. It's helpful to also look at what is going on within your organization. Is the number of people in your role being reduced? Or has hiring for people in your position stopped or slowed? These are clear signs that your occupation may be shrinking.

When it comes to your industry, it pays to follow the news and the markets to see where things are moving. Also pay attention to the amount of investment in your industry. The idea is to keep your antennae up so that you start to become more and more aware of what is coming. Doing so will allow you to move with the direction of the wind.

Consider Moving Where the Jobs Are

When you think about the trajectory of your career, it's important to consider where you will physically live and work. Location is becoming less important as more and more people are working remotely—a shift that has generally been good for women and workers of color in terms of work flexibility. Ninety-two percent of companies offer remote or hybrid work options and women report working remotely gives them more focused time to get their work done. In addition, women experience fewer microaggressions when working remotely.[12] Yet the majority of jobs are still at least somewhat dependent on geography and require some in-person work—often a few days a week.

Of course, some cities are thriving and offer plentiful job opportunities, while others have more depressed economies. This factor is worth considering when choosing where to live. Your next job and your network will be in that city, so picking an opportunity in a vibrant place can be very helpful. If you are open to moving, look at whether jobs are growing or shrinking in that area.

Unfortunately, location often makes it more difficult for Black women in particular to access opportunities. In the United States, 65 percent of the Black population is concentrated in states that have unfavorable economic and social conditions. There is a mismatch between where they live and where jobs are growing. Some companies have made commitments to open new plants and headquarters in some of these states, which will help, but the mismatch persists.

Black Americans are also more vulnerable to industry changes. Forty percent of the revenues of Black-owned businesses are located in the five most vulnerable sectors, such as hospitality and retail, compared with 25 percent of the revenues of all US businesses. Add in the fact that women are clustered in three of the four occupations that are shrinking the most, and Black women will face a disproportionate number of career obstacles.

Of course, there are many other factors to consider when deciding whether and where to move. When our colleague Hana, who identifies as Asian American, got married, her husband was trying to convince her to move to his home city of Minneapolis. In addition to the fact that dozens of *Fortune* 500 companies are headquartered there, one of his arguments was that it has the highest rate of dual-career couples in the country. That fact is what finally convinced Hana to make the move.

She knew that there would be greater infrastructure and community support in a city where dual-career couples were the norm.

. . .

Ultimately, you are in control of where your career is going in terms of the occupation and industry—as well as the location—you work in. Knowing where you are likely to have greater opportunities to grow and learn is a vital step toward maximizing your experience capital. And if you are making this decision as part of a dual-career couple, which is more likely for working women than working men, balancing both careers will be important.[13]

Next, we will cover the specific skills that will be the most valuable as you navigate the various roles you will hold throughout your career.

PART THREE

BUILD THE MOST VALUABLE SKILLS

CHAPTER 7

The Multiplier Effect

Susanne Prucha, senior director and commercial lead of M&A and disruptive growth at the Hershey Company, credits her network with having a positive impact on her career from the very beginning. After graduating from Indiana University, she worked on strategy development for blue-chip companies at a management consulting firm. On her first project, she was staffed with a man who was a senior partner. Susanne was by far the youngest and most inexperienced person on the team—plus she was the only woman. So, she was surprised when the senior partner consistently elevated her work by putting her front and center.

It would have been typical for someone at Susanne's level to remain in the background, gathering data throughout the project and leaving the presentations to more senior colleagues. But her boss encouraged her early on to present her work to leaders at global banks. This was incredibly intimidating, but Susanne recognized the opportunity that came with it. She had no choice but to learn how to effectively present ideas to clients who were much more experienced than she was. And she had to learn quickly.

Those clients recognized how young Susanne was, not to mention the fact that she was almost always the only woman in the room. Some reacted better than others, pushing her in ways that forced her to be at her best, which helped Susanne learn to be a confident contributor. At other times, there were clients that went too far. During one presentation, a bank executive bristled at what Susanne was saying. "How much could you know?" he asked her. "You're right out of college."

As part of her training, Susanne had learned how to respond when a client challenged her like this. "I may not have all your years of experience," she told him calmly, "but I have done the research and talked to all of the key stakeholders, and I would love to share those findings with you." The meeting improved after this brief interaction, so Susanne was surprised when the senior partner pulled the client aside after the meeting and asked him to be more respectful to the team. That meant the world to Susanne. She saw that he not only supported her and her work but also had her back.

Susanne was grateful for bosses and mentors like this senior partner. Yet as she grew in her career and worked on increasingly big accounts, she was keenly aware that she had no women mentors or role models. She wished there was someone she could see herself in, someone who could show her what was possible for the type of leader she aspired to be.

Then one of the clients Susanne worked for chose a woman to lead a new organization they were creating. Susanne loved watching her in action. She could finally see herself in one of the executives that she regularly came into contact with. One day, the men on the team were leading a presentation, and the woman executive made a point of singling her out by saying, "I'm curious to hear what Susanne has to say."

In her male-dominated world, this was her very first experience of a woman elevating another woman. Susanne sought out that woman executive as a mentor, and over time they developed a close relationship. And since then, Susanne has made a consistent effort to give back to other women in big and small ways.

The Multiplier Effect of Networks on Experience Capital

Susanne's story is just one example of how important professional networks are to a successful career. In fact, nearly every woman we interviewed for this book credited her network as a major contributor to her success.

Workers intuitively recognize the power of networks: 80 percent of professionals consider networking to be vital to career success.[1] As we'll discuss, however, they don't always know how to build as strong a network as possible. They also may not recognize how their network impacts their experience capital. In fact, a strong network can multiply your experience capital by pulling nearly all of the levers we've discussed so far.

It's difficult to learn about job opportunities in the first place without a strong network—at least 70 percent of openings are not even made public. Even if you do find out about a job and apply, the odds are against you unless you have a connection. Professionals who are referred by an employee within the company are nine times more likely to get the job. And 70 percent of professionals are hired at companies where they already have a connection.[2]

This means that having a strong network can make it much easier to find a job at a high-quality organization and open the door to making the type of early job move or bold move that can dramatically boost your experience capital. Even better, your network can help you make those moves faster. An average job search for someone with a strong network is one to three months shorter than it would be otherwise.[3]

As you move through your career, your network remains critical. Those contacts are often sources of knowledge themselves, not just about job opportunities but also about their areas of expertise. A network contributes to your experience capital and helps you see the roles and skills and understand the industry in ways that help you move up in the power alley. Most professionals—85 percent—believe that networking keeps them updated on industry trends. That knowledge is necessary to maximize experience capital.

Your Network Is Your Support System

After graduate school, Susanne pivoted into brand management, starting with an internship at General Mills. She loved the fact that the brand manager was the "hub of the wheel," in the middle of all the action and key decisions. The person in this position led cross-functional teams and was accountable for business results. Susanne says it was like running an entire business that just happened to be a brand within a larger corporation.

At General Mills, Susanne's boss was a woman, and she met many more women mentors who had an impact on her career. During her first year there, she was an associate brand manager for Betty Crocker and had to present an annual plan to the president. Susanne went in with her slide deck ready, but before she could start, the president stopped her. "Before you dive in," she said, "always explain why someone should be excited about your plan."

Off the cuff, Susanne mentioned three things she was excited about that would drive growth for the business. She received such good feedback that she has used this technique ever since—she never starts a presentation with the deck. Instead, she opens with, "These are the things you're going to hear that I'm most excited about." It allows her to intentionally position any conversation.

At the time, marketing employees at General Mills were promoted based on how long they'd been at the company. When Susanne's peers started to get their first promotions, her boss asked what was most important to her. Susanne responded that she wanted the best possible job, even if she had to stay in her current role longer. She was willing to hold out for a top-tier assignment.

That meant Yoplait, the brand with the highest annual media/consumer budget. Susanne's boss made good on her ask and went out of her way to help her land on the Yoplait desk. Susanne was later promoted to lead customer growth strategy for Yoplait's $240 million portfolio, and from there she became the business unit director for the $1 billion Cheerios franchise.

Although this wasn't true of Susanne, most women have weaker networks than men and can benefit significantly from strengthening their own network.[4] In particular, your contacts can play a big role in helping you avoid tripping over a broken rung. Professionals with a strong network are more likely to advance in their careers than those without one.

In addition, the people in your network are likely to act as advocates and speak up on your behalf, not just when there are opportunities at stake but also when you are facing bias or microaggressions. In fact, they can turn negative moments of microaggression into moments of micro-opportunity, such as when Susanne's credibility was questioned. Over time, these micro-opportunities can add up and create real career impact.

Overall, your network is an important part of your support system. However, only one in five employees have a sponsor and two in five employees have a mentor at work. But when they do have either a mentor or a sponsor, employees are twice as likely to be engaged at work, to agree that they have had opportunities to learn and grow at work, to acknowledge that their workplace provides a clear plan for career development, and to recommend their organization as a great place to work.[5] Apparently, work is just a lot more fun with mentors and sponsors.

While serving as brand manager on the kid cereal portfolio at General Mills, Susanne had her first child. When she came back from maternity leave, her boss took her aside. "I want you to take some time to get comfortable with the new you," she told Susanne. "The way you work might be a little different than before, and that's OK. You're going to be the only one judging yourself, and you are going to have to give yourself grace to know when 'good' is good enough." She told Susanne that when things got tough, she should feel free to come to her, and they'd work through it together.

Susanne remembers thinking, *She's crazy.* Of course, she ended up eating those words as her motherhood journey progressed, and Susanne realized then how incredible it had been for her boss to go out of her way to start that dialogue. She now has that same talk with all of the women on her team who go out on maternity leave.

What Makes a Strong Network?

It's clearly important to build a strong network, but what makes it strong? There's more to it than just acquiring as many contacts as possible. It's crucial to have the right relationships with the right people and the right mix of people.

The quality of your network and relationships matters a great deal, but so does quantity. The bigger your network, the greater your access to opportunities, information, and other connections. There is some debate around the ideal number of people, though anthropologist and social psychologist Robin Dunbar claims it is 150. That number is based on the size of our neocortex, he explains, because it's the highest number of relationships that humans can maintain where each party is willing to do favors for the other. We literally cannot fit more than 150 relationships in our brains. After tracking human communities over time, Dunbar has found that the average social group is indeed that size.[6]

But don't just go out and grab the nearest 150 people. The diversity of your network in terms of gender, industry, and level of seniority is also extremely important. A network that includes people from different industries and backgrounds can help you learn about entirely new areas of interest and decide whether you want to pivot. And if you do want to move in a new direction, they can help open the right doors for you.

While having peers and junior colleagues in your network is valuable, more senior leaders have a greater ability to advise, support, and unlock opportunities for you. Remember, these may or may not be people that you identify with personally. When building your network, look for power over role models. Ideally your network will have a mix of both, but to advance in your career you need allies at work above all.

The importance of senior leaders in your network is one reason that having a gender-diverse network is key. Since men are disproportionately represented in senior-level positions, they tend to be in greater positions of power. Without an adequate number of men in your network, you won't be able to access the greatest possible number of opportunities. In addition, the women who have made it to senior roles tend to already be mentoring or sponsoring more people on average than their male peers.[7] Of course, a more diverse network will also provide you with a wider variety of insights, opinions, and experiences.

The specific type of relationship that you have with the people in your network is another important factor. There are three types of contacts: connections, mentors, and sponsors. A connection knows you in a professional or personal context and can be either more or less senior than you. When we talk about having 150 people in your network, most of them will certainly be connections.

A mentor shares knowledge, wisdom, and advice and can act as a sounding board. This person is usually (but not always) more senior than you. Finally, sponsors do what mentors do by understanding and inspiring you, but they take it further and open up real opportunities, such as promotions, project assignments, a specific role in a meeting, or greater visibility. Clearly, sponsors are particularly impactful when it comes to helping you advance. For every new sponsor you have, your chance of being promoted increases by 10 percent. And if you have four or more sponsors, you are five times more likely to be promoted.[8] It is also important to recognize that sponsors typically do not become sponsors immediately. They may start out as a connection or a mentor and then grow into a sponsor over time as the relationship deepens.

Over-mentored and Under-sponsored

Despite widespread knowledge about the importance of networks, women around the world have struggled to make theirs as robust and powerful as men's. The gender network gap is now a global phenomenon, with women being 14 percent to 38 percent less likely than men to have a strong network, as measured by its size and openness, meaning their connections aren't necessarily connected to each other.[9]

On average, women's professional networks are weaker than men's along all dimensions. They are smaller, with the average man's network being double the size of a woman's, and less diverse.[10] Women are also five times more likely to have a network made up mostly of women, likely due to homophily, the tendency to prefer interacting with people who are like us, including when it comes to gender.[11] That might be surprising since the stereotype is that women are more social than men, but building a network is quite different from developing friendships or even having a close-knit group of friends. Networks by design are broader and more relevant to the work environment.

Women also approach networks differently than men. On average, women are less comfortable mixing friendship with work-related favors and often doubt the basis of the friendship if work starts to get mixed in. However, men are, on average, quite comfortable combining the two, often believing that the business elements will go better if they are friends with the other person.[12]

In a world in which men are overrepresented in positions of senior leadership, having smaller and less diverse networks can have a big impact on women's careers. Twenty percent of women are likely to never have a substantive interaction with a senior leader about their work, as compared with 17 percent of men.[13] Because senior leaders are often the ones who create opportunities and open doors, this lack of access puts women at a disadvantage.

In addition, women are often locked out of the formal and informal networks that are important pipelines for promotion and apprenticeship. To some extent, this may be due to senior men's concern about propriety: 30 percent of male managers say they are uncomfortable working alone with a woman. Senior men are 3.5 times more likely to hesitate about having a working dinner with a junior woman, and five times more likely to hesitate about traveling for work with one. And 48 percent of men have lunch with other managers at least once a month, but only 33 percent of women do. It is important to find ways to address these issues that do not leave women at a disadvantage.

Women and people of color tend to be "over-mentored and under-sponsored." They have enough people who offer advice, but not enough who create real opportunities for them. In other words, women may experience a lower conversion rate from mentor to sponsor, which is true even for those who have networks similar in size to men's. Women also consistently report receiving suboptimal sponsorship support, regardless of the size of their networks, which directly limits their access to advancement since, unlike mentors, sponsors create concrete opportunities.[14]

The network gap is even wider for women of color, particularly when it comes to sponsorship. More than half of Asian American workers are lacking a sponsor, for example. And while roughly half of Black employees have at least one mentor, only 38 percent have at least one sponsor, which leaves many Black women lacking valuable career direction and support. Black and Latino frontline employees report the lowest levels of sponsorship: the majority (nearly six in ten) have no sponsor at all.[15]

Vivian Jones, a Black woman who is an information security manager for a large financial company, has experienced the downside of lacking a strong network. Although she recently received a promotion, she has had negative experiences at prior companies.

For instance, several years ago, after earning her MBA, Vivian applied for a role on the leadership team of her former company, which she had been at for seven years. One of her peers was going after the same role, but Vivian knew that he did not have an advanced degree and had been at the company for a shorter amount of time. When she compared herself with her colleague, she felt she was more qualified in every capacity, so she was confident that she had a strong chance of landing the role.

One thing that Vivian didn't account for, however, was her coworker's sponsor, who advocated for him behind the scenes. She also noticed that the coworker had a good rapport with the leadership team; she observed them having casual conversations and going for coffee. Vivian herself lacked that sort of relationship with the leadership team, but she also knew that her peer's relationships didn't make him better for the role.

Vivian was disheartened when her colleague was chosen above her for the job. But she was far more discouraged when leadership explained that she should stay in her current role because that was where her current strengths lay. Vivian felt a complete and total lack of support and belief in her potential. If she was to stay in a role just because she was good at it, how was she supposed to learn and grow? Clearly, staying there would flatten the curve of her experience capital. Vivian felt she had no choice but to leave the organization.

Building and Nurturing Your Network

There is a lot you can do to build a more powerful network. For instance, after two years on the Cheerios desk, Susanne Prucha had been at General Mills for twelve years and felt ready for a new challenge. When weighing different options, one of her mentors told her to create a "personal board of directors" to help her make this type of decision, given its importance. "You need a group of objective people that can act as an advisory group on a range of topics," she told her.

If Susanne could go back, she says she would have recruited that board earlier. While she had intentionally sought out women mentors throughout her career, putting together this board helped her realize that a more diverse group would have been even more beneficial. Further, she found that the right people were already all around her; they were untapped resources. For example, she recruited a neighbor who had retired from a robust career in an entirely different industry and a former professor, in addition to personal friends who knew her well from work.

With the help of her board, Susanne made the leap to the Hershey Company, first as brand director and then as senior director and commercial lead of mergers and acquisitions (M&A) and disruptive growth. In this role, she is responsible for maximizing commercial value creation within M&A.

To this day, Susanne finds herself relying on the advice she's received from her mentors throughout her career—from the storytelling skills she learned in her early days at General Mills to the question that her boss posed when looking ahead to her promotion: "What is most important to you right now?" When things get hectic and overwhelming, Susanne asks herself this same question, and it always helps steer her in the right direction.

Although women may be at a disadvantage when it comes to establishing a strong network, there are many actions you can take to strengthen and nurture your own. In fact, another characteristic of a strong network is that it is well nurtured. Unfortunately, there is a gap between men and women here, too.

Compared with women, men invest more in building and maintaining their networks. They spend more time getting in touch with old contacts, building new relationships, and strengthening existing relationships. In addition to having weaker networks to begin with, women report having less access to or feeling less connected to the people in their networks than men.[16]

Assessing Your Network

To begin strengthening your network, start with a self-assessment. First, think about your main objectives so you can align them with your approach. At this stage of your career, what are your main objectives? What do you want to learn, explore, and be exposed to?

Get a sense of the size of your network. How many connections do you have on LinkedIn, for example? The average is 1,300, although this is another number you would build up to over time. You likely don't know all 1,300 very well, nor is that required. Depending on your industry, that number may or may not be an accurate representation of the size of your network, but it is a good starting place for many workers.

Next, look at how diverse your network is. Are most contacts within your occupation or industry? Is there a good mix of men and women? What about levels of seniority?

Now you know where you are starting from. To expand and diversify your network, push yourself outside of your comfort zone. Reach out to role models and senior executives and make an effort to attend events where influential people will be gathered, even if you may not know anyone. Also recognize the power of *weak links*—people outside of your immediate contacts ("friends of friends"). These links have value too in terms of employment opportunities and promotions.

Finally, think about the structure of your network. How many mentors do you have? Do you have at least one sponsor? If not, it's important to start developing these relationships. While connections can't be forced, it is important to take a structured and systematic approach to building relationships at work. It's not enough to have people in your corner; you want to have the *right* people, which requires you to think about who will make the most effective mentors and sponsors for you.

While sponsor relationships are the most impactful, they are also the most difficult to establish. A sponsor needs to be in a position of power, so they can create opportunities for you. They also have to be someone who enjoys helping others. Finally, a sponsor generally has to know your capabilities and have confidence in your potential, so it helps if you've worked with this person directly.

You can't force relationships to become sponsorships, but you can look for opportunities to develop relationships with people that may evolve into sponsorship. Stay in touch with the people you've worked with as you progress—it might mean a coffee chat or video call every three to six months to stay in touch. These are the people who know you and can speak to the quality of your work. A potential sponsor also has to know what you want to achieve so that they can tailor their advice and opportunity creation to what you care about most. This is one more reason it pays to be vocal about your goals and aspirations.

Map out all the mentors and sponsors you have today on a piece of paper. You may prefer to do this visually, with clusters of related people close together; to simply make a list; or to color-code your mentors and sponsors based on the energy you get from the relationship or the strength of the relationship.

You only need a few sponsors. Even having one or two is a luxury that most people lack. To identify potential sponsors, start by looking at your professional connections, particularly those who are more senior to you. Once you have your list written down, circle anyone that you currently consider a mentor. If you don't have any mentors, circle the people you'd like to have as a mentor. Next, do the same thing with sponsors. If you have any, circle them in a different color. If not, circle your aspirational sponsors, the people you would love to have directly opening up opportunities for you. The circled names are where you'll invest your energy going forward.

Nurturing Relationships with Mentors and Sponsors

Now you should have a good idea of where your network stands today and how you can grow it. While it's a good idea to nurture all of your connections, you should pay particular attention to building relationships with both your current and aspirational mentors and sponsors.

The best way to nurture these relationships is to spend time with people one-on-one. The vast majority of people—95 percent of men and 93 percent of women—find it easiest to give and receive guidance in a personal setting.[17] Also make sure that the relationship is reciprocal, even if the other person is more senior. Make an effort to be of help to them in some way and look for opportunities to work with them directly. And make sure they know about your aspirations so they can help support you along the way.

But these interactions don't have to be or feel transactional. The people in your network are human, and small gestures can make a big difference. Reach out and wish them a happy birthday, congratulate them on a promotion, and show an interest in their projects, passions, families, and so on. The more genuine these relationships are, the more impactful they will be.

Many books have been written with valuable advice on how to network effectively. In the classic *How to Win Friends and Influence People*,

Dale Carnegie teaches readers to be genuinely interested in other people, to encourage others to talk about themselves, to praise any improvement no matter how small, to always remember people's names, and to never criticize, condemn, or complain about others.

Indeed, it's important that your network has an ethos of support that goes both ways. Make an effort to help the other women in your network and to pay it forward. When you have the opportunity, invite them to events and help them build their networks through introductions. This is an important way of nurturing your own network—by putting it to use. Remember, it's a two-way street. When you help others, they will be far more inclined to say yes to a favor or to think of you the next time they hear about an exciting opportunity. You will likely end up getting much more than you give.

And when you do succeed in becoming a more senior leader, consider giving back and mentoring and/or sponsoring other women. You'll be playing an essential role in helping them build their experience capital and advance through the pipeline without being held back by the broken rungs. Mentoring women is a great first step, but it's even better to set a bar for true sponsorship, which will make a much more direct impact on women's career trajectories. Advocate for promotions and stretch assignments and speak up in performance reviews. Actively provide other women with the opportunities they need to grow and reach their full potential.

Next, we will explore the importance of gaining technology skills in today's changing world of work and how you can best build those skills.

CHAPTER 8

Everyone Needs to Be a Technologist

Karlie Kloss and Mojgan Lefebvre are two women who took different paths toward radically different but successful careers, each of them gaining the technology skills that gave them a professional edge in their respective industries and occupations.

Executing on Ideas

Karlie grew up in St. Louis with four sisters and an interest in science and math from a very young age. She idolized her father, a doctor who always encouraged her to pursue a career in science like his. This was the plan until Karlie's life took a surprising turn at the age of thirteen, when she was approached at the mall about becoming a model.

The world of fashion and modeling was not one that Karlie had ever fathomed being a part of. Yet she soon found herself as a young teen attending a midwestern high school in between traveling the globe, appearing on magazine covers, and walking in international shows. By the time she was seventeen, *Vogue Paris* had declared her one of the top thirty models of the 2000s.

All along, Karlie knew that she would ultimately want to stretch herself beyond modeling. So when she was able to meet with leaders in the fashion, music, and technology industries, she was determined to make the most of these learning opportunities. When Karlie met with technology startup founders in particular, she was blown away by the fact that these people, who were transforming entire industries, not only had big ideas but also possessed the technology skills to execute on them. Karlie asked herself what they knew that she didn't, and one simple answer was that they knew how to code.

In 2015 Karlie signed up for a coding boot camp in New York, and she was shocked by how simple it really was. Learning to code and other ways of using technology helped her expand her professional career far beyond modeling. She eventually became an investor as well as the owner and CEO of the British fashion magazine *i-D*.

Karlie realized that these skills could be learned by anyone—so why weren't they being taught to young girls? She decided to underwrite twenty scholarships for girls to take the same boot camp she had. Her goal was to make the process less intimidating while providing access to those who would not otherwise be able to learn the skills.

When she received thousands of applicants for the scholarships, Karlie realized how big the need really was. She went on to found Kode with Klossy, a nonprofit organization that cultivates a technology skills–based community for young women and gender-expansive youth. The organization fosters lifelong connection for its participants though coding education programs that include summer camps, year-round coding workshops, and coding challenges with corporate partners.

By providing technology learning experiences and curated opportunities, Kode with Klossy creates path-changing impact for its alumni across their education and career milestones. In fact, 78 percent of Kode with Klossy alumni who are in college have chosen to pursue majors or minors in computer science or engineering.

Unique Expertise in Business and Technology

Now compare Karlie's unique story with that of Mojgan Lefebvre, who also grew up dreaming of becoming a doctor, this time in Iran. As a young adult, Mojgan came to the United States with only a few dollars to pursue a medical degree. However, she quickly realized how difficult it would be to pay for medical school, and she began considering other options.

Everyone Mojgan spoke to insisted that computer science was the future. In school, she had always been very strong in math, but there was one problem—she had never even seen a computer. Regardless, Mojgan applied to and then enrolled at the Georgia Institute of Technology with no technology skills to speak of.

But she was pleased to learn that her rigorous math education in Iran had put her ahead of the curve in some areas. She started trading calculus lessons with her peers in exchange for their help with programming. The plan worked out well, and after a lot of hard work and late nights to catch up in learning to code, she ended up graduating as class valedictorian.

Mojgan landed a job at telecom firm BellSouth as a program developer. She loved the fact that she was using technology to solve business problems, but after a few years she realized that staying exclusively in technology roles would limit the opportunities that were available to her. She wanted to be actively involved in the business decisions that were being made with the use of technology.

Four years after graduating, Mojgan applied to business school, which completely opened up her career trajectory. She spent a few years running her own company before meeting a headhunter who was looking to fill a chief information officer role at a French company called bioMérieux, whose specialty was in vitro diagnostics.

Mojgan was living in Boston with her husband and two young children at the time. Taking this role meant that she would have to spend at least one week each month in France. The following few years were extremely hard on Mojgan and her family, but they paid off when she received an opportunity to become the CIO of a large division of Liberty Mutual, an insurance company based in Boston. She stayed there for eight years, expanding her responsibilities to include global risk solutions. Then came the opportunity she had been waiting for, one that allowed her to bring her technology and business expertise together as the chief technology and operations officer at Travelers, an insurance company.

Mojgan says the beauty of technology today is that it no longer exists in a silo—instead, it is at the center of every business function. Early in her career at BellSouth, she observed this synergy between technology and business operations, and she proactively built the necessary skills to establish herself at that intersection. Now she is able to do what she has always wanted, which is to use technology to create better experiences for customers and employees.

Technology Skills and Experience Capital

Karlie and Mojgan both stress how important it is for all women to gain tech skills, regardless of their industry or occupation. The research clearly proves them right. Interacting with technology is becoming a bigger and bigger part of nearly every occupation and industry, so it is becoming increasingly difficult to build experience capital without those skills. These trends also mean that women will miss out on opportunities to maximize their experience capital if they remain underrepresented in tech roles and in the field overall.

In order to make the necessary job moves to keep up with the changing future of work, women will need to gain new skills of varying types. Employers estimate that 44 percent of their workers' skills will be disrupted in the next five years.[1] Time spent at work using physical and manual skills and basic cognitive skills will decrease as related activities are more automated, and nearly all workers will spend more time interacting with technology—not just coding, but also using technology or apps to do their jobs more efficiently and effectively.

For example, workers will need to use tools to do the first draft of a design or follow the instructions on an app to replace a part in a machine. In order to thrive in a changing world, we all need basic tech skills. Without them, many opportunities will be inaccessible, and it will be impossible to maximize experience capital.

The Impact of Automation Technologies

The biggest factor in the changing demand for technology skills is automation, from industrial robots, to machine learning algorithms, to text-drafting tools, to digital document processing systems. Generative AI and a basket of automation technologies are both accelerating automation and extending its use to an entirely new set of occupations. The total economic potential of these technologies is an additional $4.4 trillion in GDP—or larger than the total economy of the United Kingdom today.[2] In the United States, our research estimates that by 30 percent of hours currently worked could be automated by 2030.[3]

We all need to build the skills to use gen AI and automation more broadly and to think through the risks and business implications of these technologies. They are not necessarily replacing jobs, but are augmenting them and shaping the tasks, activities, and how work gets done. As Erik Brynjolfsson, the director of the Stanford Digital Economy Lab, said, "AI won't replace managers, but managers who use AI will replace those who don't."[4]

For women, and frankly all workers, what will distinguish them is understanding how to incorporate these technologies into their jobs to create "superpowers," or new ways to accomplish tasks. At their best, these technologies take the toil away from our daily activities, leaving more time for people to spend time with people—engaging, learning, and connecting. But using the tools is not just a matter of willingness; it also requires new skills and training. While many of the new skills will be things like coding or analytics, not all the new skills will be technical in nature. With generative AI for example, one critical skill is the ability to prompt the large language models, which is essentially the skill of designing and asking good questions.

Increasing Jobs Related to Technology Trends

While we are seeing an overall decrease in jobs globally, there is a simultaneous increase in jobs related to tech trends. From 2021 to 2022, global job postings overall decreased by 13 percent, but increased by 15 percent in fields related to technology. Next-generation software development had the most significant growth, followed by applied AI.[5]

These higher-wage jobs of the future require greater tech skills than lower-paying roles. Workers in the highest wage quintile will spend more time using technology skills than those in any other quintile—a full 26 percent of their working hours. That means by gaining the right skills, women can position themselves to move into higher-paying roles. The key is how to build the skills that are the right fit for those higher-quality jobs. When women have the necessary capabilities to work alongside and collaborate with technology, automation can enhance and often improve the way they work instead of threatening their livelihoods.

As machines increasingly handle routine physical and cognitive tasks, workers will be able to spend more time managing people, applying expertise, and interacting with stakeholders. For instance, nurses could experience the automation of activities that take up about 30 percent of their time, which could have a disproportionate impact on women as they represent the majority of nursing professionals. These automatable activities include maintaining medical facility records, ordering equipment, and testing biological specimens. Even managing the preparation of special meals and maintaining an inventory of supplies can be automated. However, activities such as explaining medical procedures to patients and collaborating with other health care professionals to plan or

How Organizations Can Support Women to Meet the Demands of the Future

Long-established barriers will make it harder for women around the globe to gain the skills they need to keep up with the changing world of work. They have less time to reskill or search for employment because they spend much more time than men on unpaid care work (shopping, cooking, cleaning, taking care of kids, taking care of parents, taking care of in-laws, etc.); they are less mobile due to physical safety, infrastructure, and legal challenges; and they have less access to digital technology and lower participation in STEM fields than men.

When Mojgan took on her role at Travelers, one of her initial focus areas was upskilling and reskilling the technology team. But she also felt strongly that everyone in the company—from the CEO to the contact center—should have a fundamental understanding of technology. Her team developed a digital fluency program and made it available to all employees. They also created a course to teach people about the importance of data. While plenty of employees have taken these courses and then continued on in their current roles, many have also continued their learning on their own and/or moved into different positions requiring additional technology skills.

This is a great example of the kind of reskilling and upskilling that can help employees keep up with in-demand skills and maximize their experience capital. There are many additional actions that employers can take to help women gain the necessary abilities to thrive in a changing world. You can look for the following when choosing an organization or push for these changes in your company when possible:

(continued)

Expand Talent Pools

With women underrepresented in the entire technology pipeline, from education to leadership, employers have a shallow pool to draw from when recruiting female technology talent. One solution is to hire high-potential women who are not currently in a technology role but have adjacent skills, and then help these candidates gain the additional skills they need to thrive in their new jobs.

For example, Microsoft has an apprenticeship program that targets reskilling and upskilling "unconventional talent" ranging in age from nineteen to seventy-three. The immersive program offers a mix of in-classroom learning and hands-on engineering projects to upskill participants into roles such as cloud solution architect, data analyst, cybersecurity engineer, software engineer, product manager, and user experience designer. Out of the first seventeen cohorts across North America and Africa, 98 percent of participants are employed full-time at the company. The program has also increased the diversity at the organization.

Invest in Changing Skills

Organizations can support workers by building targeted education and apprenticeship pipelines. It's important to focus on growing occupations and to invest in upskilling and reskilling programs.

For example, Disney created the CODE: Rosie program to train select women employees across divisions in software engineering. The highly selective initiative chooses twenty participants from diverse backgrounds to receive computer science training, two six-month apprenticeships, and the opportunity to then take a technology job at the company or return to their previous role. In the first year of the program, more than 80 percent of the participants stayed with the company and ended up working in a technology role.

Embrace Changing Workforce Preferences

Employers should continue to explore new working models that meet the changing needs of workers (such as independent and hybrid jobs). Offering more flexible work while managing its downsides will allow organizations to attract a broader set of talent, which will help more of the workforce participate in higher-wage jobs.

For example, after the Covid-19 pandemic, Spotify implemented a work-from-anywhere policy for its more than 6,500 employees. Workers were able to choose how often they were at home versus in the office, or if they wanted to be fully remote. Spotify also adjusted salary bands to countries instead of cities, widening employee options. Not only did the attrition rate drop by 15 percent, but the company also saw a 5 percent increase in ethnic diversity among its staff. Due to this and a number of other actions, women's representation in leadership went from 25 percent in 2019 to 42 percent in 2023.

provide treatment are less likely to be automated. Nurses may therefore be able to fill the time freed up by automation by building stronger relationships with patients and spending more time interacting with people throughout their care.

Similarly, in education, another female-dominated field, up to 40 percent of activities could be automated. These activities include maintaining student records, ordering instructional materials, and designing lesson plans. Time could then be freed up for tasks that cannot be automated, such as building relationships and encouraging students, advising students on academic matters, discussing students' progress with parents or guardians, assisting students with special needs, and developing instructional objectives.

Using Technology to Enable Human Outcomes

Ursula Soritsch-Renier has always been passionate, curious, and willing to put herself out there to take opportunities and at times even create them for herself. As the CIO of Saint-Gobain, a manufacturer of construction and other materials, Ursula credits these characteristics—and her willingness to experiment, grow, and learn from both successes and failures—for her successful career.

Earlier in life, when Ursula was enrolled in a two-year program in economics in her native city of Vienna, a professor told the class that two journalists were looking for students to help them test and review different types of accounting software for their magazine. Ursula was thrilled to have an opportunity to gain experience outside of the classroom, and she immediately stepped forward.

Over the course of the project, Ursula was intrigued by everything she was learning—so intrigued that after it was complete, she decided to go after a job at a startup that had been named as having the best software. It was an exciting environment for Ursula, who stepped far beyond her role to learn as much about the company and its technology as possible.

Before then, she had never considered a career in technology, but she realized that the field had a bad rap. It wasn't just about coding and computer science. To the contrary, Ursula was excited to find that technology was really all about humans. After all, technology by itself is not the answer. Every type of tool requires humans to decide why and how it is used; even AI and gen AI need humans to copilot. Ultimately, technology only works as well as humans mold and implement it for results.

Ursula went back to school to finish her degree and decided to study philosophy and computer science. This combination may sound odd at first, but she says that today she uses her philosophy degree more than her education in computer science. For one thing, specific tech skills quickly become outdated. More important, Ursula explains, the tech field is really about integrating the human aspect into technology by navigating between options and tools and applying them for the purposes of the business. Technology is about putting yourself in other people's shoes, whether that is to understand customers' experiences, the needs of business units in order to expand, or how to make employees' lives easier.

When Ursula tells people that she is a CIO, some assume that she spends her days coding in the corner, but this is far from the truth. In fact, a very small number of the people in her organization are coders. In order to attract a greater diversity of workers in the field, Ursula is passionate about educating people on its full breadth of opportunities. Fascinating careers in business analysis, change management, user experience, and cybersecurity all fall under the umbrella of technology. Ursula encourages women to overcome their potential discomfort with the technical parts of "technology" to take part in this exciting and thriving industry that is creating real human impact.

Biases in Technology

With technology increasingly being utilized in every company in every sector, women will not be able to maximize their experience capital until they are better represented both in specific roles and within the industry as a whole. Further, with technology being used to solve business problems, women are missing out on opportunities to help shape these outcomes.

Generative AI in particular is poised to be a transformative force, so it is especially important for women to gain relevant skills in using it. Their contributions can help provide a diverse set of inputs for AI algorithms—which may help minimize gender bias being built into digital tools.

The same thing goes for all types of technology. These products affect huge portions of our environments and lives, and when they are designed and created primarily by men, they can strengthen inequalities and biases. Women should have a seat at every table where decisions are being made, and that includes decisions around the creation and use of technology.

Yet women remain absent from many of these tables. While they made progress in several male-dominated fields in the late twentieth century, their representation in computer science has not risen in recent years; rather, it has plateaued after rapidly rising in the 1970s. In 1995 women represented 37 percent of computer science workers in the United States, but the number dropped precipitously at the turn of the century. By 2017 women represented only 26 percent of computer science workers, and in 2022 that number decreased to 27 percent in the United States.[6]

The Technology Gender Gap

Of course, if you don't have a passion for technology, there is no reason to force yourself into one of these roles. Unfortunately, however, many women assume they have no interest in technology without ever giving it a chance or fully understanding the full breadth of roles that are possible. For instance, math is a critical skill for computer scientists, and there is a stereotype that boys outperform girls in math. Their performance, though, is closer to equal.[7] In addition, globally, across education levels and income groups, girls outperform boys in reading; in middle- and high-income countries they also outperform boys in science. But if girls are deterred from pursuing technology roles because of stereotypes, women will continue to be underrepresented in technology.

Much has been written about the subtle and overt ways that women are discouraged from pursuing technology roles. Norms in socialization, toys, media, and clothing all keep girls from imagining themselves in tech jobs.

In addition, lower expectations for girls to succeed in tech courses can lead to self-fulfilling prophecies. Both teachers and parents are likely to encourage boys to pursue technology activities and courses over girls. They also often attribute girls' success in math to effort while attributing boys' success to their innate ability.[8]

We see a huge drop-off of girls in computer science between the ages of thirteen and seventeen, and another drop-off upon entering university. When selecting a major, undergraduate students often compare themselves with people currently in the field. That's a problem because in the United States in 2022, according to data from the American Society for Engineering Education, women were only 19.6 percent of engineering faculty members, including even fewer of the full professors: 14.6.[9]

These gaps leave women vastly underrepresented in STEM across industries and functions. In Europe, women make up 37 percent of workers in any type of role at a tech or tech-adjacent company, such as a business development manager at a social media company. This number drops to 22 percent for women in tech roles in nontech companies, such as a software engineer for a traditional bank. And when it comes to tech or tech-adjacent companies, women represent only 25 percent of workers in technology roles, such as a product developer for a software company.[10]

When they do enter the field, many women end up feeling isolated due to a lack of women colleagues, mentors, and role models.[11] As a result, women in tech roles are twice as likely as women overall to say they are frequently the only woman in the room at work.[12]

Anita Leung experienced this firsthand. When she was a sophomore in high school, she happened to see a flyer about the need for more women in technology, and she was interested in learning more. She signed up for a class in Cisco, the peer-networking software. Out of thirty students in the class, she was the only girl. When they had to pick partners to work with, she was always chosen last. This pattern repeated itself every semester, yet she continued taking classes because she enjoyed what she was learning.

After doing some research, Anita felt confident that a career in computer science was a good fit for her. It was clearly where the future was going, and she felt passionate about the topic. She found it thrilling to build something and bring it to fruition.

Before she finished high school, Anita landed an internship at Amazon, where she was the only female on the team. It was intimidating, but she had already gotten used to being an "only." Anita pressed on, and after graduating from a computer science program at the University of Washington, she got a job as a software engineer at Google.

The underrepresentation of women was not as apparent at Google as it was in many other organizations, Anita says. There is a focus on DEI, the company has a women's engineering networking group that has been a source of support and information, and there are some women in senior leadership roles. Interestingly, however, she has noticed that there do not seem to be as many women in the middle rungs of leadership. When she thinks about the career that lies ahead of her, Anita wishes that there were more accessible women whom she could talk to about what it's like to be a leader in tech. Although she has a supportive manager, with so few women managers to look up to, she feels like she is on her own in somewhat uncharted waters.

The numbers support Anita's observations. Overall, more than half of women in technology leave the industry by the midpoint of their careers.[13] Out of these women, 23 percent cite a lack of management support and opportunity as the reason, while 75 percent of women who stay in technology credit their role models for helping them thrive.

It's especially important as a woman in tech to have sponsors. With male sponsorship, female talent is 70 percent more likely to have their ideas endorsed, 119 percent more likely to see their ideas developed, and 200 percent more likely to have their ideas implemented, compared with women who don't have a male sponsor.[14] Hopefully, with more examples of women who have women sponsors in the future, we can better understand the impact of such sponsors on their careers.

Technology leaders like Mojgan are working to change this. About ten years ago she got involved in Girls Who Code, an international nonprofit organization that aims to support and increase the number of women in computer science. Its goal is to close the gender gap in entry-level tech jobs by 2030. Among women who have gone through its programs and can be tracked in the workplace, more than half are working in tech-related jobs. Mojgan has mentored some of the girls who have participated in their courses, and initiated Travelers' sponsorship of the program.

In-demand Technology Skills and How to Build Them

Technology skills do not comprise just one simple skill set. There are various and diverse abilities that will be in demand in the future. They include:

- *Digital skills.* First and foremost, we all need to develop basic digital skills, which include being able to use computers, phones, or tablets to execute a limited set of predefined tasks, such as operating basic applications and communicating. The most frequently used activity requiring basic digital skills is programming equipment to perform production tasks. The need for workers to have basic digital skills will increase 69 percent in the United States and 65 percent in Europe by 2030.[15]

- *Programming.* The need for advanced IT and programming skills—installing and maintaining computer software and hardware and using programming to automate repetitive tasks or enable new ones—is growing, potentially by as much as 90 percent in the United States by 2030, as AI and automation become a core part of each sector. The top activity requiring these skills is installing programs onto computers. While generative AI has reduced the demand for computer science majors, people with programming skills will inevitably be an in-demand minority in the future.

- *Analytics.* Advanced data analysis and mathematical skills are also increasing in demand. These skills include being able to apply advanced methods of data analysis (statistics, machine learning) to extract insights from large amounts of quantitative data. Companies are making big investments in training their employees in these skills; organizations with more than fifty thousand employees are investing in them more than in anything else. Clearly, executives believe that they will need more employees with these skills in the future, so it is a smart bet to start building them now.

- *Technology design.* To develop business or financial information systems, skills to design, develop, and maintain technology are needed.

- *Research.* Finally, scientific research and development skills involve developing and testing specific hypotheses to conduct research.

Regardless of your role or industry, it's important to invest in gaining some of these new skills to maximize your experience capital. In today's world, part of building your overall career must include at least some of the skills listed above.

A simple benchmark is to set aside 10 percent of your workweek and spend that time investing in yourself; this comes to about four or five hours a week. Ideally, you can find ways to invest in yourself that count twice—methods that build your experience capital and are part of your role, even broadly defined.

For example, start by taking advantage of continuous learning or online courses offered by your current organization. Doing so could count as part of your day job but will also give you knowledge that you'll take with you into the next role or company. If your organization does not offer any such courses, look for external ones with recognizable names or topics so that others will understand their value.

In addition, find out about the technology or tech-adjacent roles in your organization or others. Ask people with interesting jobs or those who work for exciting companies to meet with you, and learn about their day-to-day work. You may find that some of these roles are a good fit for you. Then, you can ask about the exact skills you need in order to be qualified for them.

If, however, you already have basic tech skills and find that a technology career is not a good fit for you, that's not a problem. The approaches we've described here are just one way to boost your experience capital. Next, we'll cover the other types of skills that will also be in greater demand in the future, primarily social and emotional skills.

CHAPTER 9

Treat Soft Skills Like Hard Skills

Julie Morgenstern says that when she was growing up and entering early adulthood, she was one of the most disorganized people the world has ever seen. She was always late, left everything to the last minute, and spent half of her days looking for things she had lost. As a creative theater person, part of her identity was wrapped up in being spontaneous and in the moment, never planning ahead. Despite the chaos, Julie always managed to pull off excellent work, but the stress and anxiety leading up to it was as draining as it was predictable.

Between her lack of organization and the fact that she didn't attend a top-tier university, Julie says that she started her career feeling at a bit of a disadvantage. She decided that she would make an effort to focus on learning from everyone she encountered at any level, believing that everyone has a unique set of skills, talents, and perspectives that she could find value in. Along the way, Julie would try to see the world from their unique point of view. This, she says, is how she has navigated her career and gained nearly every skill she has.

Julie was still learning—and still extremely disorganized—when she became a mom. One day, she decided to take her newborn daughter for a walk. The baby had just woken up from a nap, so the timing was perfect. Spontaneous as always, Julie started grabbing a few things the baby would need, but of course she couldn't find half of them. Once she found something, she'd think of something else and couldn't find that. Two hours later, the baby had fallen back to sleep, and they'd missed the walk entirely.

Looking down at her child, Julie realized that something had to change. Previously, the only victim of her chaos had been her, but now someone else was being impacted as well. In Julie's mind, she flashed forward and saw her daughter missing doctor appointments, showing up late to school, and never having what she needed when she needed it. That didn't seem fair. Julie sat down on the nursery floor and organized her diaper bag for future outings. From there, she slowly began to organize everything else in her life.

At first, Julie worried that being organized would make her boring and subtract from her identity as a creative person, but in time she found that the opposite was true. Having immediate access to everything she needed fueled her creativity. The change she experienced was so profound that Julie decided to start a business to help other people bridge the gap from chaos to order. Having experienced the shift in her own life, she felt that she was uniquely positioned to understand people's needs and address them in a nonjudgmental, empathetic way.

When starting the business, Julie knew that her success was completely dependent on whether the solutions she offered to her clients would be effective in the long term. In order to ensure that this happened, she created a list of questions that would help her fully comprehend every client's individual needs. Then she listened astutely to their answers before taking time to create systems that she knew would work for them.

As the business grew and Julie began hiring additional coaches, she taught them how to replicate this process, which she says can also work with managers, clients, or during negotiations. To become an astute listener, Julie says, you need to ask great questions and aim to speak only 20 percent of the time—the rest of it should be spent listening, documenting the person's answers, and clarifying anything that you don't understand.

Most important, don't offer any recommendations or insights before taking some time to process what the other person said. Your single function during the conversation is to fully take in their goals, their frustrations, the problems they are trying to solve, and what success would look like to them. Processing information and offering suggestions are separate steps. If you try to do them both at the same time, you'll miss something and won't be fully present and truly listening.

Put simply, Julie says not to try to add value too soon. By listening and asking good questions, you're giving the other person an opportunity to be heard. This is valuable in and of itself.

In the more than thirty years since she started her business, Julie has branched out to become a renowned organization and productivity expert, keynote speaker, executive coach, and *New York Times* bestselling author. She's accomplished all of this by leveraging her ability to listen to, empathize with, and understand people, and she teaches women how to utilize the same skills to enhance their own careers.

Her work has given Julie unique insight into the pitfalls that many women tend to fall into because of our instincts and our societal training. One is the tendency to take care of others before ourselves, both emotionally and physically. Julie has worked with countless high-level women who burn themselves out by prioritizing work over their health and well-being.

She insists that women must take care of themselves, too, to perform at their best. She recommends a mindset shift about self-care: it's not stealing time from your work life; it's in service of your career. Then, force yourself to pause to replenish your energy. Once you feel the payoff, the experience will be self-reinforcing.

Julie has seen how women's attunement and impulse to care for others can work for or against them in their jobs. On the one hand, it can manifest as struggling to make decisions because of concerns about how people will feel about those choices. On the other, women can harness their empathy to paint inspiring and compelling cases for where the company or team is going and what they are trying to achieve—which is how the world's most powerful leaders get buy-in and motivate their teams to succeed.

Soft Versus Hard Skills

Did you notice when reading about Julie's impressive career—built on listening, empathy, and inspiring others—that it's all about soft skills? When most of us hear that term, or the similar "social and emotional skills," we imagine someone who is simply good with people; they're the type who connects easily to others, is sociable, and can talk to anyone.

Ironically, we typically think of these skills as being important in our personal lives but not necessarily so at work. As Julie's story clearly shows, however, this is false. Soft skills are incredibly valuable in the workplace, especially as you advance in your career, and they're critical for maximizing your experience capital.

Further, soft skills are not limited to chatting at parties. In fact, they encompass a wide range of complex abilities that fall within five broader categories.

- *Self-awareness and self-management.* Understanding your emotions and triggers, self-control and regulation, understanding your strengths, integrity, self-motivation, and self-confidence

- *Entrepreneurship.* Courage and risk-taking, driving change and innovation, energy, passion and optimism, and breaking limiting beliefs

- *Mobilizing systems.* Role-modeling, creating win-win negotiations, and crafting an inspiring vision

- *Developing relationships.* Empathy, trust, humility, and sociability

- *Teamwork effectiveness.* Fostering inclusiveness, motivating different personalities, resolving conflict, collaboration, coaching, and empowering others

One look at these skills makes it easy to see how valuable they are for all workers, especially leaders. However, they have historically been underrated and undervalued in the workplace. Even the term "soft skills" implies that they are less important and less complex than so-called hard skills.

Hard skills are the technical abilities that are required for a job. They are learned, as none of us are born knowing how to code or solve algebra equations, and they are measurable. Unlike soft skills, hard skills tend to be occupation- and/or industry-specific. For instance, an architect would need a very different set of hard skills than a surgeon. But some hard skills are valuable across industries and occupations, such as writing and basic technology capabilities.

It's interesting to note where the terms "soft skills" and "hard skills" came from. The United States Continental Army Command (CONARC) coined and distinguished between the two when it sponsored a Soft Skills Training Conference in 1972. Its goal was to clearly define the army's use of soft skills so it could standardize military school courses. Ironically, CONARC actually concluded that there should be no distinction between the two, and that the term "soft skills" should be eliminated from the army's terminology. However, the terms stuck, and so have the many things we associate with them.[1]

Stereotypes about Hard and Soft Skills

The word "soft" is often connected to the concept of femininity. In fact, "feminine" is listed as a synonym for "soft" in the thesaurus, and indeed, soft skills have historically been considered more feminine skills. According to stereotypes, women are naturally better than men at listening, communicating, connecting, and exhibiting empathy. The word "hard," on the other hand, is considered more masculine, and men dominate many of the fields that rely most heavily on hard skills, such as parts of STEM. Men are also stereotypically less emotional and empathetic and less effective connectors and communicators than women.

These stereotypes leave women (and men) in a difficult and confining position. First and foremost, the stereotype of women having naturally strong soft skills perpetuates the myth that women have weaker technical skills than men, which can keep them from being hired for STEM roles.[2]

The assumption that women have stronger soft skills perpetuates additional stereotypes that can paint them as overly emotional and irrational. It also implies that women lack hard skills both inside and outside of STEM. That faulty assumption is important because hard skills are what are most often listed in job requirements and used to make hiring decisions—especially for certain high-paying jobs. An analysis of over ten million job postings showed that jobs requiring hard skills, such as specific programming languages, paid twice as much as jobs requiring soft skills, such as communication and teamwork.[3]

In addition, the association between women and soft skills may encourage women to pursue career paths that typically lie outside of the power alley. For example, the assumption that they are naturally good with people may push them to pursue careers in HR, where people skills are needed. Likewise, the stereotype that women are good communicators may steer them toward jobs in communications and public relations. And while these are all worthy professions, it is often more difficult to land a seat at the table from these roles than from those requiring hard skills, which lie more squarely in the power alley.

These stereotypes can be even more complex for women of color. Soft skills are more subjective than hard ones and are difficult to objectively measure, so it's easier for employers to use a supposed lack of them as a reason to avoid hiring certain people and even to justify discriminatory hiring processes. Multiple studies have shown that many hiring managers subconsciously believe that soft skills vary with race.[4] In one study, employers in the hotel industry used a supposed lack of soft skills to justify a preference for Latina over Black workers.[5]

There is also a common misconception that soft skills are innate and cannot be learned. The misconception can lead employers to discount soft skills as unimportant and to focus their training programs on hard ones instead. But the truth is that soft skills indeed can be taught. Just look at how Julie taught herself and trains her coaches to become more astute listeners. Some soft skills, such as advanced communication, can actually be taught more easily than certain hard ones.

Further, training employees in soft skills often has a bigger payoff in the long run because they're evergreen. Empathy, negotiation, and collaboration will never be outdated, while specific hard skills, especially those required in the STEM fields, can quickly become obsolete. Without the support to master soft skills, though, it is difficult for workers to move into senior leadership positions.

The Increasing Importance of Soft Skills

The truth is that soft skills will only grow in value as you progress throughout your career. This is true for two reasons: First, soft skills are going to be more valuable in the future for workers at all levels. Second, they are required for managerial roles and advancing in your career. Let's look at both reasons in more depth.

After technology, soft skills are going to be the most critical growing skill category in the future, which is part of an ongoing trend. Interpersonal tasks at work have been rising over the past fifty years, as the need for routine manual and cognitive tasks (simple rules-based judgments, for example) have declined. This trend is now being accelerated by AI. As advanced technologies are increasingly utilized in the workplace to automate activities, there is a greater need for workers with finely tuned social and emotional skills to power human-to-human interactions that technology cannot easily replace.

Demand for workers with social and emotional skills is increasing. By 2030 workers in the United States and Europe will spend an average of 24 percent more hours using those skills. Specifically, there will be the greatest rise in demand for entrepreneurship and initiative-taking.[6]

These changes may also provide opportunities for those with less formal education. A survey of eighteen thousand people across fifteen countries reveals that while soft skills can be learned, they are not as directly tied to formal education as hard skills. And although job listings may not reflect the importance of soft skills, workers who are most proficient in them have higher rates of employment, higher salaries, and greater job satisfaction than those who aren't.[7]

A significant portion of the workforce will need to further develop their soft skills within the next five to ten years. In particular, tens of millions of midcareer, middle-aged workers in advanced economies will require reskilling.[8] Employers are catching on to this trend and are beginning to recognize the importance of soft skills. In fact, 80 percent of C-suite executives worldwide say that reskilling at scale—including soft skills and hard ones—is a concern and a priority.[9]

Soft skills will also be more important in the future because no matter what role you start out in, advancing almost always includes managing others. And soft skills are essential for good leaders, who must rely on their relationships and the ability to motivate their teams to succeed. Early in your career, your value may be more tied to your hard skills and/or specific subject area expertise. As you rise, though, it is more about your ability to lead, inspire, and collaborate with other people.

Christina Gaw, managing principal at private equity fund Gaw Capital Partners, has experienced this shift in her career. Growing up in China, Christina was the youngest in her family and the only girl. She felt very protected and had a happy childhood, but she was not encouraged to have academic or professional ambitions. When she went to the United States for college, she wasn't sure what to study and ended up choosing hospitality management, partially because she enjoyed working with people.

Approaching graduation, Christina started to apply for hotel jobs. But fate stepped in when one of her older brothers, who was working at investment bank Goldman Sachs, recommended her for a job. She had no experience in finance, but Goldman was starting a new equities analyst program and the roles involved a lot of sales.

Christina's brother knew that she would thrive in a predominantly sales role, but she still doubted that the company would hire her among the many qualified candidates. As luck would have it, during the interview process Christina met a senior partner who had also studied hospitality management. He knew that with this degree, Christina was likely to have strong people skills, and he recommended her for the role.

Much like Julie, Christina suffered from self-doubt at the beginning of her career. She didn't have an Ivy League degree or any background in finance, unlike the majority of her peers. So, she more than compensated by making sure that she was the hardest-working analyst in the program.

Her effort paid off, but as Christina advanced throughout her career, she suspected that she was not being treated the same as her male peers. She received timely raises and promotions, but she knew that external hires at her level were receiving bigger bumps. Since she was "home-grown," as she puts it, her salary increased more modestly.

So, when Christina received an offer from another investment bank, UBS, she took it. At that point she already had two children, and while working her way up to become managing director she had two more, becoming a mother of four. She had just stepped into this role when her brothers started Gaw Capital back in Hong Kong. Christina thought about going to work for them, but she didn't feel right leaving UBS so soon after taking her new job. But when her brothers approached her again two years later, she felt the time was right to make the move.

Progressing to her current role as managing principal and global head of capital markets, Christina recognized that her success relied on two key soft skills: talent management and empathy, both of which have little to do with the hard skills that are valued for entry-level jobs in finance. She says that your IQ may get you a job early in your career, but it's your EQ, or emotional intelligence, that will get you much further. As a leader, she understands that her primary role is to identify, empower, grow, and retain talent.

On the client side, Christina believes that her competitive advantage comes down to communication and empathy. She spends a lot of time thinking about how things will affect her clients. She listens carefully so that she knows what is important to them, and then she only presents options that are likely to work for them. This approach lets them know that she understands their needs, making them more likely to trust her with their assets. Although her hospitality management training seems to have very little crossover with her career in finance, Christina is, ironically, now using skills she learned in college more than ever.

Redefining Leadership

Increasing numbers of executives like Christina are embracing collaboration and empathy as key aspects of their leadership models, and we are beginning to see proof that delivering results and exhibiting this type of positive, inclusive leadership are not mutually exclusive. It helps to broaden the definition of leadership so that many different styles are viewed as successful, as opposed to strictly a stereotypical hard-charging approach.

In fact, a leadership model that includes a focus on soft skills has proven to be good for business and for company culture and morale, which is key to attracting and retaining talent. The younger generations of workers in particular want to work for leaders who are empathetic, humble, and self-aware. And 89 percent of employees say they are satisfied when their company has great leaders who are inspirational, supportive, empowering, and focused on their development.[10]

Jessica Sibley, the CEO of *Time* magazine, has exemplified this broader definition of leadership throughout her career in media. She started in sales and had always been in external, customer-facing roles, even early on as an individual contributor. Jessica says that in sales she was in the business of changing people's minds. To do this, she relied on the power of persuasion, which, in fact, is a critical soft skill.

At the same time, Jessica wanted to start her career in sales because she felt it gave her some level of control over her destiny. As she says, you can't fake math. In sales, there is little subjectivity, and you receive real-time feedback and proof of how your performance compares with that of your peers. This has served her well in male-dominated companies. Eventually, though, she hit the ceiling as an individual contributor and moved into management roles.

Jessica says that she has shown up at work as her authentic self since day one, simply because she didn't know how to be any different. But it wasn't until she became a leader that she recognized how important and meaningful doing so really was—because it was important to the people who worked for her.

Out of all the feedback you receive, Jessica says it's the opinions of the people who work for you that are the most important. It's their happiness that allows you to retain talent and help others feel they are working on something that matters beyond the day-to-day business goals of the company. She also notes that younger employees are not only hungry for this sense of fulfillment but increasingly expect it.

Becoming this type of leader requires bringing your best and most positive self to every interaction, even in the face of conflict and tension. If Jessica is the recipient of disrespectful communication, she tries to summon inner calm and not overreact. It's important to note that when Jessica has been unable to do this and has gotten defensive or offended, it has not led to the best results. But when she is able to remain positive, respectful, and professional, she is best able to persuade the other person and change their mind.

Negotiation as a Soft Skill

Somewhat surprisingly, Alex Carter, a clinical professor of law and the director of the Mediation Clinic at Columbia Law School, considers the type of positive persuasion that Jessica talks about to be a form of negotiation, and she offers a unique perspective on this critically important soft skill. Negotiation is commonly misunderstood; although most people think of it as what happens when you sit down to make a deal, Alex says that the act of negotiating also includes everything you do beforehand to build your relationship with the other person and ultimately make that deal possible.

Alex adds that the goal of a negotiation is never to win—it is to advance yourself toward your unique objectives, which is why you need to be clear on what those objectives are before beginning any negotiation process. What you want may be different from what your colleague wants and what you will want in the future.

So, the first step of any negotiation, Alex says, is to negotiate with yourself. Sit down and ask yourself some important questions, such as, "What problems am I trying to solve in my life and within my company? What support do I need to solve them? What do I need from my company to get to the next stage of my career?" With these answers, you have data against which you can measure any offer that comes your way.

The next step of a negotiation is to engage the other person with questions. Don't ask a question that they can say no to. Instead, compel them to give you information. Like Julie says, you should be listening 80 percent of the time.

This process is important for a few reasons. First of all, listening well and asking the right questions are valuable soft skills in and of themselves. Second, the information you will gain through listening to the answers is power. It will allow you to craft a pitch that is grounded in everything that person has already told you is important to them. Your goal here is to write that person's victory speech—in the context, of course, of getting exactly what you want. Asking the right questions and listening carefully to the answers will tell you exactly what that person would want in their speech.

Clearly, this type of negotiation is not a one-day endeavor. It's a year-round process of using your words to teach people to trust you and understand your unique value. In other words, you are painting a picture that will justify the role or salary or whatever it is you want. You can also think of this as a way of signaling your experience capital.

Alex explains a simple three-step process for effective persuasion:

1. *Help people understand specifically what you do that no one else does.* For example, are you a connector or a researcher or a rapport builder? If you're not sure, notice the moments when you feel the most joy and connection at work and take note of what you're doing during those moments.

2. *Communicate whom you do those things for.* The audience may be internal or external. Whom do you love to serve?

3. *Identify your specific impact.* What can other people do as a result of working with you that they couldn't do before?

You should start this process long before you get to your ask. That way, by the time you do get there, the other person will be far more likely to want to help you advance toward your objectives or to be influenced and inspired by you.

Harnessing Emotions and Building Soft Skills

Although stereotypes imply that women have naturally stronger soft skills than men, some women may not naturally excel in these areas and need to build them, just as they would learn any new skill.

An important piece of building your soft skills is learning to appropriately express your emotions. Leadership coach Natacha Catalino works with leaders to develop their soft skills, and the journey of learning them has been much of her own life's work. At the age of eight, she began attending an old-fashioned boarding school in the United Kingdom. She says it was the kind of place where students thrived by appearing strong; those who showed signs of weakness were often bullied. It was a tough environment, and from a young age Natacha learned to put up a veneer and suppress her true emotions. Doing so appeared to serve her well throughout her education, but that all changed as she entered the workforce.

Like most people, Natacha faced challenges at work, but she didn't have the tools to properly manage or express her emotions. She says it was a muscle she had never used, and she found herself crying in the bathroom and even tearing up in meetings when her suppressed emotions bubbled up at the most inconvenient times.

Through her leadership training, Natacha began to understand that emotions can be harnessed instead of suppressed and ignored. She learned how to name what she was feeling, identify the sensations that those emotions created in her body, and then express that emotion constructively. Over time, she was able to manage her emotions so they no longer controlled her.

For example, say Natacha received a stressful email right before going into an unrelated meeting. Before developing the necessary awareness to harness her emotions, she would have likely brought the frustration or fear she was feeling as a result of that email with her to the meeting. It would affect how she performed and engaged with the people around her, even though it had nothing to do with them.

With greater awareness, Natacha is able to read such an email, pause, and notice: *My heart is racing. I am feeling really anxious.* Then she takes a few deep breaths to calm her nervous system before heading into the meeting. This approach doesn't solve the problem, of course, but it helps release the grip that her emotions have on her. She is able to be present and engaged during the meeting without any unrelated emotions bubbling up.

Julie explains this same principle a bit differently. She encourages women to recognize their power and the fact that moods and energy are incredibly contagious. When women leaders express negative emotions, their teams may feel the urge to take care of them, which can diminish performance. Julie encourages everyone, and particularly women leaders, to be responsible for the energy they bring into every room.

Although there is clearly a double standard against women showing emotion at work, the truth is that learning to harness and manage your emotions is a powerful leadership skill. The stereotype of an overly emotional woman is someone who does not take responsibility for her energy or have control of her emotions. It is frustrating that women are told they have to moderate their emotions. But the truth is that when we learn to harness them and take responsibility for our energy in a positive way, we become more effective and powerful leaders—the kind that will be in even greater demand in the future.

While many people think of entrepreneurship as an occupation, it is actually considered a social and emotional skill. Next, we'll discuss how you can gain and leverage this skill to build experience capital.

CHAPTER 10

Entrepreneurship Is a Skill, Not a Profession

All of Caterina Fake's childhood drawings include a unique feature—a price listed in the bottom right-hand corner. Most of them were marked at only five or ten cents, but Caterina realized that she had a small but very loyal market of consumers (her parents) and that she might as well sell instead of giving away her drawings.

Caterina's innate entrepreneurial skills were encouraged from a young age. Her father always told her that she should run her own business one day and be her own boss. That eventually happened, but there wasn't a direct line from selling her drawings to being one of the first women tech founders in the world. First, she received an undergraduate degree in literature and moved to Berkeley, California, to attend graduate school for Renaissance literature. Once she was there, however, everything changed.

It was the 1990s in Northern California. The internet was in its infancy, and Caterina was enraptured by the palpable energy in the city. She says that it felt like you were a part of inventing the future, and it was a great fortune to be there during that unique moment in history. She quickly decided that Renaissance literature wasn't going anywhere; she could return to it at some point. For now, she wanted to join the exciting movement to develop the internet.

Caterina's first job in tech was designing CD-ROMs before she later moved to a web design company. There was no training or establishment—they were inventing and learning everything as they went. She took on more tech jobs at community websites, bouncing from being a product person to a designer and community builder. She also learned to write code so that she could understand that aspect of the technology.

Although she put her graduate degree on hold permanently, Caterina never stopped reading. Even now, she reads every single day on a wide variety of topics. She credits this habit with much of her success, as she says that people who are constantly exposed to different ideas end up synthesizing those concepts and coming up with something new.

In the early 2000s Caterina was synthesizing a few things that happened in the same year. One, the social networking site Friendster launched, and people were starting to feel comfortable putting profiles of themselves online. Two, bandwidth was no longer dial-up, so it became much easier to download photos. And three, for the first time, more than half of all new cell phones had a built-in camera. Meanwhile, Caterina was well versed in online communities, and she saw an opportunity for an online photo-sharing community. The insight ultimately led to the creation and growth of Flickr, which she cofounded with Stewart Butterfield.

Along the way, she faced many obstacles as a woman founder in tech. She says that she experienced all of the #MeToo moments, all of the discrimination, and all of the being discounted for having a "cute idea." In addition, there was no road map back then for founding a company. There were no blogs or podcasts hosting founders and sharing their stories. And there were certainly no woman founders that Caterina could learn from—she was among the first.

Caterina relied on the lessons she'd received from her parents as a child to persevere through this time. With a Filipino mother, Caterina was the only nonwhite student in her elementary school. When kids made nasty or ignorant comments, her parents encouraged her to refuse to give them another thought, to not let them take up any of her mental or emotional energy. Although it was certainly difficult, Caterina learned to ruthlessly ignore any sexism or racism that she experienced.

After Flickr was sold to Yahoo in 2008, the founders of Etsy reached out to Caterina asking if she would contribute to the front page of its site, which was brand-new and a shell of what it is today. But Caterina saw Etsy's potential right away and decided to become an investor. From there, she continued supporting many other successful startups and enjoyed giving back to the entrepreneurial world that she knew.

As an angel investor, Caterina was offered jobs at some of the big venture capital firms in Silicon Valley, but she was quick to turn them down. They were open about the fact that they were looking to add one female partner after being all male for many years. To Caterina, this was clear tokenism; if they really wanted to transform their fund, they would add an equal number of women partners, not just one. She knew that she wouldn't be able to make a big enough impact as the only woman, so Caterina decided to cofound her own venture capital fund with equal representation of women from the very beginning.

Entrepreneurship Is an Increasingly Valuable Soft Skill

When we think of an entrepreneur, most of us imagine someone like Caterina who has struck out on their own and started a company. While this is of course one common and visible form of entrepreneurship, there are also many others. Within a role in an existing organization, entrepreneurship can look like taking initiative, starting a new project, identifying fresh opportunities for impact, or creating a team. It can also look like becoming an independent worker or contractor or taking over an existing business.

In fact, it is more accurate to think of entrepreneurship as a set of skills that you can use across a variety of roles, rather than as a specific job. Those skills include courage and risk-taking, driving change and innovation, energy, passion, optimism, and breaking orthodoxies. These are required for a founder, but the truth is that regardless of your role, they are also critical for advancing your career. Since it is not measurable or directly tied to education, being entrepreneurial falls under the umbrella of soft skills—and it will be in even greater demand in the future, as discussed in chapter 9. Like other soft skills, entrepreneurship is not easy for technology to master. We still need humans to identify opportunities and come up with new ideas, even if they rely on technological tools to help carry out some of those plans.

The ongoing increase in independent workers is another reason that entrepreneurial skills will be in greater demand. In McKinsey's American Opportunity Survey, 37 percent of employed respondents identify as independent workers; this is the equivalent of fifty-eight million Americans, and they represent all ages, education levels, and incomes.[1]

More and more people are turning to independent work, for a variety of reasons. One is the increasing desire for flexibility—25 percent of the survey's respondents cite autonomy and flexibility as the primary reason for choosing independent work. Meanwhile, 26 percent choose it out of the necessity to support themselves and their families, 20 percent as a way of earning additional discretionary income, and 25 percent simply because they enjoy this way of working.

Interestingly, independent workers also tend to lead with an optimistic mindset. The most optimistic of all are the ones who choose this type of work either because they enjoy it or for the autonomy and flexibility it offers. Of course, we can't assume independent work simply makes people more optimistic—correlation is not the same as causation. It's possible that people who are already more optimistic tend to choose this type of work. After all, every type of entrepreneurship involves some level of risk. The willingness to take on that risk requires a sense of hope and optimism. It's also possible that people who feel in control of their destinies as independent workers end up feeling more optimistic about the future.

However, independent work does come with its downsides. Without the benefits of an organization, independent workers often have more problems accessing health insurance, quality health care, nutritious food, convenient housing, transportation, and childcare than full-time employees. These workers also have to balance the tasks they do with the constant pressure to find new opportunities and in some cases negotiate their fees, all without the safety net of a consistent, reliable income. To do all of this successfully, independent workers need to develop strong entrepreneurial skills.

Entrepreneurship and Experience Capital

Regardless of your current or future career plans, developing entrepreneurial skills is key to maximizing your experience capital since it can help you demonstrate leadership and progress more quickly. Senior leaders with stellar entrepreneurial skills are often candidates for the top jobs.

Despite the risks, starting or running your own company can be an effective path to maximizing your lifetime earnings. Not every founder is going to become the next Caterina Fake, but if you have the skills and risk appetite, entrepreneurship can be a highly gratifying and financially rewarding path.

An analysis of US entrepreneurs reveals that the entrepreneurs with the highest average salaries are actually small-business owners who run professional services firms, including highly specialized experts such as lawyers, accountants, and web developers.[2] In other words, starting a company in your area of expertise is a great way of maximizing your experience capital.

Rachael Johanson is one of these entrepreneurs. As a child, her parents worked for a large corporation. She observed their anxiety about the future and the lack of agency they seemed to have over their careers, and she decided that she wanted something different for herself. While some teenagers pursue sports or the arts, Rachael says that her hobby was professional development. Before she even started college, she had already held a few internships and knew her way around a résumé and a job application.

Once she was studying entrepreneurship and home furnishings at High Point University, Rachael noticed that many of her friends were not in the same position as her. These other women were smart and talented and had great leadership skills, but they downplayed their qualifications and didn't know how to market themselves to land the jobs they wanted. So Rachael started helping her friends craft their résumés differently.

As soon as these friends started getting hired for highly sought-after jobs and internships, Rachael realized that she was onto something. She had a secret sauce that helped people go from qualified to hired. Rachael continued honing this skill throughout college, often trading her services for sandwiches at Panera Bread. By the time she graduated, Rachael had helped thirty of her peers land their dream jobs.

After graduating, Rachael started her own coaching business called the Brand Girls—and she no longer accepted sandwiches as a form of payment. Recognizing the huge need in the market, and feeling passionate about closing the confidence gap in her generation of women, Rachael moved fast, and the next few years were a whirlwind. In addition to her coaching clients, Rachael was hired to speak at seventy-five universities, consulted with corporations about Millennials in the workplace, and was often featured in the media. She was working one hundred hours a week, though, and was completely exhausted. Soon, she taught her methodology to seven coaches to continue scaling her business.

Many fellow young women entrepreneurs observed her success and reached out, asking how she was managing to book all of these speaking events, media placements, and brand partnerships. This opened Rachael's eyes to another need in the market: these women could use help marketing and branding themselves, too. Rachael sold off the assets associated with the Brand Girls and started a new company to coach women entrepreneurs on how to brand themselves in the luxury marketplace.

With a personal passion for fashion and design, Rachael feels that she has found the work that she was born to do. Each year, she coaches a small handful of high-achieving women, typically doubling their opportunities and sales within two years. Best of all, as an entrepreneur with a professional services company, she has maximized her experience capital by helping other entrepreneurs maximize and signal their own experience capital, and this work is both emotionally and financially rewarding.

The Gender Entrepreneur Gap

One reason that Rachael is so passionate about serving women entrepreneurs is the gender gap in entrepreneurship. Although one in three businesses around the world are owned by women, the gap exists globally at every stage of the entrepreneurial funnel and grows increasingly wider from formulating a business concept to establishing and growing a company.

At the initial stage of entrepreneurship, where opportunities are merely being identified and developed, women's participation compared with men's is 90 percent, but this number drops to 80 percent when it comes to the intention to create a business. At the early stage of actually founding a company, women's representation goes down to 73 percent, and at the point of a business being created, it bottoms out at only 60 percent.[3] The gap extends to scaling businesses, too. Many more male-founded companies grow to become unicorns, meaning they achieve over $1 billion in value.

When women do found businesses, they tend to be very different from the ones created by men. For instance, women are 1.5 times more likely to be solo entrepreneurs, meaning they have zero employees.[4] While small professional services businesses that fall into this category can be quite lucrative, to close the entrepreneurship gap we need more women founding and running larger companies. Globally, only 1.8 percent of women entrepreneurs run a business with twenty or more employees, compared with 6.1 percent of men.

In addition, women entrepreneurs are overrepresented in industries that tend to have low profit margins and where there is already a lot of businesses and competition, such as retail and hospitality. Globally, half of all women entrepreneurs work in retail. Women are also underrepresented in the highly profitable tech and business services space, with even greater representation gaps than we see in tech as a whole.[5]

This is yet another reason it's so important to increase women's numbers in tech overall. Eighty-five percent of entrepreneurs found their companies in a field that's closely related to one they worked in previously, and the length of time they worked in it has a positive impact on their company's success.[6] C-suite executives and board members are the most likely to found their own companies, so increasing the number of women leaders in tech could help encourage more women tech entrepreneurs.

Funding Women Entrepreneurs

Inside and outside of technology, women entrepreneurs experience a severe lack of funding. In 2020 only 2.3 percent of venture capital (VC) funding across the globe went to women-led businesses. In the United States, roughly half of startups are founded by women, but startups with all-women teams receive only 1.9 percent of VC funding. In terms of overall fundraising, women founders raise $0.38 for every dollar raised by a male founder. The number is far lower for Black women: For every dollar raised by a man, Black women raise only $0.02.[7] Yes, you read that right—two cents.

Further, when potential investors meet with women entrepreneurs, they treat them very differently than they do men. A study from the Wharton School showed that venture capitalists tend to ask men and women different sets of questions. They are more likely to ask male founders questions such as, "How do you want to acquire customers? How do you plan to monetize? Do you think this is a growing market? What major milestones are you targeting this year? What's the brand mission? Can you tell us a little about yourself?" These are considered "promotion" questions.

Women, however, are more likely to face questions such as, "How many daily and active users do you have? How long will it take you to break even? Is this a definable business where others can't come in and take share? How predictable are your future cash flows? How much of this are you actually doing in-house?" These are called "prevention" questions and are more focused on the business's potential downsides than its upsides.[8]

Another issue is the profound lack of women investors. In the United States, women represent only 8 percent of VC partners and hold only

7 percent of board seats in VC firms.[9] As Caterina points out, adding one woman partner to a firm will not make enough of a difference—we need to reach a tipping point to create significant change. To get close to equity in venture capital, we'll need many more women in decision-making positions.

An analysis of VC partner roles suggests that there are three primary pathways to them: having a background in engineering or tech; having a graduate school education, typically an MBA; or having attended Stanford University or Harvard University. Unfortunately, having a background in tech is the number one pathway, which means women's underrepresentation in tech contributes to the lack of women in venture capital.

But the problem is broader than VC firms. Women are severely under-represented in every type of asset management business, including private equity, where women make up only 23 percent of all investing roles and 12 percent at the managing director level.[10] Women are also far less likely than men to make personal investments in businesses. Globally, the ratio of women to men who have invested in a business is 70 percent, and the amount they invest on average also tends to be lower. When looking at the actual amount of money that women personally invest in businesses compared with men, it is only 50 percent as much.[11]

The Benefits of Closing the Gender Entrepreneur Gap

Although biases lead investors to view companies that are founded or led by women as risky, the data shows that the exact opposite is true. In fact, women's companies are often more profitable than those led by men. Women-owned startups generate $0.78 in revenue for every $1 of investment, compared with $0.31 generated by men-owned businesses.[12] So it's not just women entrepreneurs who are missing out due to a lack of funding—investors themselves are overlooking valuable business opportunities.

Indeed, closing the gender entrepreneurship gap would benefit com-panies as well as women. Employees with entrepreneurial skills are incredibly valuable: They drive change and help the firm innovate and stay ahead of industry trends. They are also key to building a culture that is creative, inspiring, and innovative.

On a greater scale, entrepreneurs who start their own companies are good for the economy and for society as a whole. Of course, these new businesses create additional jobs that are an important engine for the economy. In fact, new and young businesses are a key source of job creation—they create 20 percent of the new roles in the United States in an average year. They also boost productivity throughout industries by creating competition.

New companies are disproportionately responsible for innovations that disrupt existing markets or that spark the beginnings of entirely new ones. When businesses are started to compete against, support, or complement existing goods and services, there are ripple effects that lead to more jobs, more competition, and on and on in a virtuous cycle. The gender entrepreneurship gap keeps us from maximizing this growth—closing it could add up to $2.3 trillion to the global economy and create up to 433 million new jobs.[13]

Perhaps most important, by breaking through real or perceived constraints and innovating, entrepreneurs often introduce products and solutions that change the ways in which we play, work, learn, and interact. It's not an exaggeration to say that entrepreneurs have the power to change the world. As a society, we rely on innovation to lead us forward, and we rely on entrepreneurs to provide those innovations. Yet the International Labor Organization estimates that 50 percent of women's entrepreneurial potential is underused, as compared with 22 percent for men. With so many untapped women entrepreneurs, we are missing out on new ideas that can help shape our future and the economy.[14]

Leveraging Your Expertise as an Entrepreneur

As mentioned earlier, the most successful entrepreneurs, like Caterina, tend to start companies that are closely connected to their previous industries and roles. Interestingly, this is in contrast to some of the other methods we've discussed of maximizing experience capital. While making bold moves across roles is often a smart strategy overall to grow your skills and experience capital more quickly, the opposite is true for entrepreneurs. They find the most success when developing and then using deep industry-specific expertise. So, jump far and boldly if you are making a job change, but stay closer to home and to what you know if you are becoming an entrepreneur.

Christa Pitts exemplifies this idea. Early in her career, she was working in a sales role for a window and door manufacturing company when her mother-in-law convinced her to attend an open audition for on-air hosts at the shopping channel QVC. Christa thought the idea was ridiculous, but she played along and was shocked when she was called back and eventually landed the job.

Christa says that working at QVC was like receiving a master's degree in retail. She learned about data analytics, statistics, business principles, and merchandising, as well as receiving training on the psychology of sales. She learned how to engage a potential buyer's "romance factor" by helping them imagine how a product would make them look and feel, while at the same time engaging their left brain with technical specs and price considerations. Then there was the real-time feedback from customer callers, which Christa found tremendously helpful.

In addition, she had the opportunity to sit down with the entrepreneurs who were behind the products she was selling on-air. She always made sure to ask them about the choices they'd made that had paid off and the things they wished they had done differently. For her, these conversations were an invaluable education in how to successfully launch a business and what pitfalls to avoid.

Christa loved being at QVC, but as a host she worked long hours, often overnight. Meanwhile, back home in Atlanta, her mom and sister were working on a passion project that they never expected to become anything more than a hobby or a side hustle—it was a book about a family tradition called Elf on the Shelf.

Going back generations, Christa's family on her mother's side had a toy elf that they put out before Christmas. They told the children that the elf worked for Santa and would report back on their behavior. The tradition was sacred in their family, and Christa decided that if she was going to keep working as hard as she was at QVC, she was going to do it to help her mom and sister share their project with the world.

Christa's sister was a teacher and became the creative force behind the business, while Christa managed all of the operations. Drawing on every aspect of the deep knowledge in retail that she had gained at QVC, they founded the Lumistella Company. It is now home not only to the beloved book *The Elf on the Shelf*, but also to 150 additional products that are sold in 23 countries. More than 19 million people worldwide have bought their own Elf on the Shelf, a stuffed toy that parents move to new locations overnight so their children will think that the elf is watching them for Santa Claus. The Lumistella Company now employs 110 people and has brand partnerships with HarperCollins, Netflix, and the Food Network.

Building Your Entrepreneurial Skills

Whether you intend to found, run, or work for a company, building your entrepreneurial skills is an essential way of maximizing your experience capital. Here are a few of the skills you should focus on and how to strengthen them:

- *Foresight.* Entrepreneurs are good at looking ahead and seeing how the future is unfolding and which trends are accelerating. This enables them to imagine and develop products and services that will be in demand. One way to build this capability is to start identifying patterns. Look for trends in cash flow statements, market sales data, and how users engage with your company's products. Then think about what is likely to happen based on these patterns. Are there additional features, services, or products you can develop to meet future needs?

- *Networking.* You already know how important networking is for building your experience capital, but it is even more important for entrepreneurs, who must excel at meeting people. Making connections will not only introduce your business to potential investors or support your in-house entrepreneurial efforts; it can also help you understand the needs of a diverse group of people and create products or services to meet those needs.

- *Financial literacy.* Anytime you are thinking about introducing a new product or service, you must consider the related financials. Basic skills such as budgeting and preparing and analyzing financial statements are therefore essential for entrepreneurs. And if you are founding or running a business, these skills become even more important, as does a thorough understanding of capital investments.

- *Public speaking.* As an entrepreneur of any kind, you have to spend a lot of time pitching your ideas to others. It's extremely important to learn how to confidently communicate why your idea is a good one, what problem it is going to solve, and why you are the right person to create this product or service. If public speaking is a weak spot for you, it might be worth working with a coach or taking a class—it's a valuable skill for everyone.

- *Curiosity.* Like Caterina says, you need to receive a constant flow of thoughts and concepts to open your mind to new ideas. This flow can come from other people, podcasts, or Caterina's favorite—reading. The more of these inputs you have, the more connections you'll start to see between different topics. Caterina recommends reading every day and writing your biggest thoughts and ideas in a journal to keep over time. When you revisit those notes, you will begin to see ideas coming together.

- *Resilience.* The path to entrepreneurship is rarely straight and can be riddled with failures and risks. Entrepreneurs must know how to adapt, react to feedback, and persevere without giving up. Persistence is key. Talk to others about their journeys, and try to maintain a growth mindset in which you believe that you can learn whatever you need to know. Entrepreneurial skills are not fixed. Anyone can build them in order to be a better employee, start or run a company, or simply maximize their experience capital and keep up with the changing skill demands of the future.

You now know which types of skills and experiences will likely provide the most value as you progress through your career, and you can make a plan to build a strong network along with the right mix of technical and soft skills, including entrepreneurial skills. However, even those of us with the most well-plotted road maps often run into obstacles. The next section will help ensure that your career is protected against some all-too-common headwinds. In any work environment, biases are unfortunately a fact of life. Next, we will explore the different biases that exist in the workplace and how you can best counteract them.

PART FOUR

PREPARE FOR THE INEVITABLE

CHAPTER 11

Confront Bias Head-On

Yeimy Báez grew up in Colombia, where many, including her parents, lacked access to higher education. Yeimy's father came from a poor family that struggled to put food on the table. At fourteen, he moved from a rural area to the city and worked various low-paying jobs to support himself. Eventually he saved enough money to return to school and received a degree in mathematics.

Reflecting on her upbringing, Yeimy recognizes that her strongest skills came from her parents: resilience and the ability to challenge societal expectations. Throughout her career she has embraced these values. When she became the vice president of low emissions solutions for Ecopetrol, the largest company in Colombia and among the top two energy conglomerates in Latin America, she knew that her journey was unexpected. Her determination to challenge stereotypes has been instrumental in pursuing her dreams.

Twenty-five years back, when Yeimy was deciding what to study in university, she chose a field that seemed like a safe bet—engineering—due to her proficiency in mathematics. However, she was unaware of the stereotypes about STEM fields and had no idea she would be one of the few women in the program. Frequently being the only woman in the room was challenging. Nevertheless, she persevered and graduated with a degree in petroleum engineering. With high grades and a completed training program at British Petroleum (BP), she felt well prepared to start her engineering career and secure a job quickly.

However, reality differed from her expectations. For an entire year, Yeimy applied to numerous jobs but received no offers. She could not understand why. Although she'd done everything right, no one seemed willing to give her a chance.

The reason soon became clear during an interview for a field engineer position. The hiring manager repeatedly asked Yeimy if she was sure she would be able to handle the job, which included driving a truck and working with large equipment. Despite her assurances of being trained and capable of doing all this and more, Yeimy was not offered the job. It was evident to her that some people were uncomfortable assigning such physically demanding tasks to a woman.

Conscious and Unconscious Biases

It's no secret that women like Yeimy encounter gender biases in the workplace. Unfortunately, they are one of the biggest obstacles women face in advancing their careers. While we may not be able to fully eliminate bias in the workplace, women can better understand what challenges they will likely face and learn from other women who have successfully navigated these headwinds.

Bias is a preconceived notion or prejudice for or against a certain person, group, thing, idea, or belief, often based on stereotypes. While many women encounter biases in the workplace, it's crucial to recognize that members of minority groups, such as women of color, LGBTQ+ women, and differently abled women may face an even tougher environment. Intersecting biases can significantly impact well-being and progression. Negative biases can also impact men who identify with minority groups.

There are two main types of bias: *conscious*, when someone is aware of their prejudice and intentionally acts upon it, and *unconscious*, when prejudices are present without our awareness. We all have unconscious biases, which manifest as assumptions and quick judgments that can disadvantage certain groups. They are often deeply ingrained and can go unnoticed.

Throughout the day, our brains process an overwhelming amount of information, leading them to seek patterns and create shortcuts to interpret it. While this is a natural process, it can lead unconscious biases to influence our behavior and decision-making, often to the detriment of certain groups. When theses biases become systematic, they can result in discrimination.

Bias and Experience Capital

Women often experience higher volumes of conscious and unconscious biases in the workplace compared with their male counterparts.[1] And these biases can also slow down or inhibit gaining experience capital. For example, bias can limit access to job rotations, promotions, raises, mentors, sponsors, or even the constructive manager feedback essential for building your expertise.

This is exemplified in Yeimy's story. During the year she struggled to secure her first engineering job, opportunities to grow or learn new skills were limited. Like many recent graduates, she faced the dilemma of finding a source of income while also seeking personal and professional development. Despite this challenge, she continued to interview for engineering positions while also taking on freelance work to teach computers skills and programming. After several rejections, she found herself in another interview, where she was finally given the opportunity she had been seeking. That chance, while unexpected, would prove to be transformative.

Upon starting her job, Yeimy was determined to defy the stereotypes against women in engineering. At first she hid behind a mask of self-protection, concealing her emotions, appearing tough, and avoiding asking for help. She did this under the false belief that the path to success was to blend in, to be like everyone else, and to belong. Many people who try similar approaches don't even realize all of the ways they're self-shielding by dressing the part, keeping their voices down, or putting forward a false persona. For Yeimy, it was a daily struggle to hide her true self, and after a while she realized she couldn't uphold this facade and began to embrace her true self at work, recognizing that her unique value came from being different.

Gradually, Yeimy began to embrace and reveal her authentic self. The transition involved adapting her approach to working with colleagues. While there were instances where her peers had to undertake additional physical tasks, Yeimy's unique contributions were significant, particularly her skill in building connections with people. Being a native of Colombia, she could directly communicate with the communities the company served, which proved to be an asset.

It was eye-opening for Yeimy to see that she didn't have to conform or blend in to be valuable. Instead, by being transparent about her strengths and weaknesses, she and her colleagues could complement each other effectively, enhancing their teamwork and overall effectiveness. It could be said that companies that overlooked Yeimy during the hiring process missed out on the full extent of her capabilities.

Indeed, numerous studies have highlighted how unconscious bias influences decision-making, often creating a barrier to recruiting and hiring qualified candidates. The Harvard Implicit Association Test (IAT) has been completed by over 20 million people since it was introduced in 1998, and it is used to measure unconscious bias. The results are revealing about social behaviors and judgments. For instance, individuals who strongly associate "female" and "family" are more likely to favor a male candidate for a job over an equally qualified female candidate. The IAT is available for free online (https://implicit.harvard.edu/implicit/takeatest .html), and we recommend taking it to gain insights into your thinking. We all have prejudices that can impact our perceptions and actions, and therefore, recognizing and addressing them is essential.

Biases can also contribute to women receiving fewer opportunities to get jobs or interviews. In one study in Spain, fake résumés that were identical except for the implied gender of the name at the top were sent to real job offers in eighteen occupational categories across Madrid and Barcelona. The "women" were 30 percent less likely to be called for a job interview than the "men," whose résumés showed the exact same bullet points, qualifications, and other characteristics.[2] Studies of this type have been replicated in many countries around the world, and the results are consistent and clear: both men *and* women tend to ascribe greater leadership and higher future potential to men than to women.

The biases carry across other categories, too. When a similar US study that used "John" and "Jane" to measure gender bias was repeated using "John" and "Jamal" (or other white- and Black-sounding names), the Black candidate was 50 percent less likely to get called in for an interview. A Muslim-sounding name like "Mohammed" was four times less likely to be called than "John."[3]

That disparity has also held in studies where Black candidates "whitened" their résumés by changing their names and other characteristics so that, on paper, they appeared to be white. With their original résumés, 10 percent of Black candidates received callbacks for interviews, but 25 percent of the same candidates did when using a "whitened" résumé. There was a similar impact for Asian American candidates: 21 percent received a callback with a "whitened" résumé, versus 11.5 percent with their true details. These findings are particularly shocking since so many leaders say they are looking for a diversity of talent. However, the studies show that we often can't see talent—even when it is staring us in the face with identical résumés—because of our prejudices.[4]

It is important to note that biases—both conscious and unconscious—are not held just by men or even white men; they are a part of *all* of us. Women can exhibit negative conscious or unconscious bias against each other. Examples of some unconscious biases are that women are more emotional and more associated with family, and that men are stronger and more associated with high ambition.

The Most Common Biases Women Face in the Workplace

While there are many different types of prejudices, we'll focus here on gender-related ones in the workplace, the most common being performance bias, attribution bias, affinity bias, likability bias, loyalty bias, intersectionality bias, and motherhood bias. Unfortunately, these are all still common, even in gender-balanced and female-dominated industries.[5]

Performance bias

This bias leads to men being hired and promoted based on their future potential, while women are hired and promoted based on their past accomplishments. It is particularly damaging to women's experience capital and ability to be promoted early in their careers, because early on, neither men nor women have extensive track records; they have far more potential than experience. So, if men but not women are being hired and promoted based on potential, men are at a significant advantage.[6]

Attribution bias

Directly related to performance bias is attribution bias. Because of the prejudice that women are less competent than men, women receive less credit for their accomplishments and more blame for their mistakes. When two people experience the same failure, it may harm the reputation of a woman more than that of a man, for whom others may be more willing to explain it away by the "context and circumstances."

Affinity bias

While prejudices against certain groups are important to address, another reason we see so much hiring discrimination is a preference *for* people in the same social group. This is an affinity bias, which causes people to gravitate toward those who are similar to them and often to avoid people whom they see as very different. Affinity bias can drive a desire to hire similar profiles of people for a job (athletes in sales roles, for example) or to prefer candidates with a similar background or from the same school or city as the hiring manager. The prejudice is one reason that men and women tend to have gender-imbalanced networks and that women hiring managers are more likely to hire other women than male hiring managers are. Since men hold the majority of leadership positions, this bias puts women at a significant disadvantage when applying for jobs.[7]

Likability bias

Women often face a trade-off between being seen as a competent leader and being considered likable. They tend to be judged as less likable when they do not conform to gender stereotypes and instead are confident and assertive, traits that are stereotypically ascribed to men. Meanwhile, if women act too stereotypically feminine—caring, warm, modest, deferential—they are considered more likable but not as strong of a leader. This phenomenon has been referred to as the *double bind*, describing how being both liked and respected is extremely challenging.

The double bind can hold women back from being hired or promoted.[8] In one experiment, people were asked to evaluate the performance and rate the competency and effectiveness of a candidate. One group was told that the candidate's name was Howard, and the other was told that their name was Heidi. As in the résumé studies, all other facts and details between the two candidates were exactly the same.

Tellingly, Howard and Heidi were rated very differently. Howard was considered likable, and the evaluators said they would be willing to hire or work with him. On the other hand, Heidi was considered competent and effective, but the evaluators said they did not like her and did not want to work with her.[9]

The likability bias can also be a factor during salary talks. Women who negotiate for higher pay are often judged more harshly than men, especially when the evaluator is male. Interestingly, some women seem to understand this implicitly: when negotiating with a man, they are far less likely to ask for a higher salary, compared with when they are negotiating with another woman.[10]

Women also tend to avoid self-promotion for fear that they'll be seen as less likable and it will be held against them. Women who are seen as self-promoting are considered less likable than those who downplay their achievements, and they often act modestly as a form of self-protection.[11] Yet a certain amount of self-promotion and visibility is needed in order to reach senior leadership positions.[12]

Loyalty bias

Another stereotype that can hold women back is the assumption that they will favor relationships and loyalty to their organization over their career advancement. Even exceptionally qualified women are expected to stay at their employer regardless of whether they have better opportunities elsewhere—which can lead them to be taken for granted.

Intersectionality bias

Women of color, LGBTQ+ women, and differently abled women face overlapping biases, which is called intersectionality bias.[13] Notably, the likability bias and others can be even more complex for Black women, who tend to be seen as less likable the more senior they become in their careers. This unfortunate reality can cause people who act as mentors and sponsors to Black women early on to turn their backs as those women advance. In one study, a full 50 percent of people of color said that a white mentor or sponsor who supported them early in their careers undermined them later.[14]

Motherhood bias

The main stereotypes against working mothers are that they are less committed to their careers and less competent than nonmothers. When comparing parents who work, 75 percent of working Americans believe that fathers are more dedicated to their careers than mothers, and 77 percent believe that fathers are better than mothers at managing their career responsibilities without being stretched too thin.[15]

Around the world, these biases tend to be especially prevalent in the STEM fields. Researchers in Brazil, where women represent 50 percent of scientific researchers, surveyed nine hundred scientists about whether they have equal access to professional opportunities compared with their peers. Seventy-two percent of fathers, but only 43 percent of mothers, said they did. In addition, 71 percent of mothers and 50 percent of fathers said they have to constantly prove their competence in order to earn the same level of respect and recognition as their peers.[16]

Internal Bias

So far we have been talking about subconscious *external* biases, which are the implicit judgments we make about others or that are made about us. It is also possible to have an *internal* subconscious bias, meaning that we are biased against a group to which we belong. Women often experience this when they have internalized messaging about how they "should" act or what women are typically good at.

In studies, women consistently evaluate their own abilities and performance less favorably than equally performing men. This finding is especially true when it comes to stereotypically male skills and fields. For instance, on their résumés women are less likely to say they are proficient or skilled in programming than equally qualified men.[17]

Job applicants in one study completed a math and science test and then evaluated their own performance. They were told that their self-evaluations would be used when deciding whom to hire and how much to pay them. There was a significant gap in how women and men evaluated their performance. On one question that asked them to indicate from zero to one hundred how much they agreed with the statement "I performed well on the test," women's average scores were thirteen points lower than those of equally performing men.[18]

Similarly, MBA students were asked to rate their own performance as compared with their peers'. Seventy percent of the women surveyed rated their performance as equivalent to that of their peers. Meanwhile,

70 percent of the men rated their own performance as higher than their peers'.[19] In study after study, we see that women tend to underestimate their own value and skills while men tend to overestimate theirs. This not only affects women and men's own perceptions of themselves but also how others—say, interviewers or senior leaders—look at them, which may implicitly give an advantage to men.

This internalized bias extends to expectations about the future as well. On average, women tend to have more modest expectations for their career trajectories and salaries. When women and men graduating from university in the United Kingdom were asked to predict their salaries both one and five years after graduation, the men's expectations were 27 percent higher than the women's.[20]

Ja'Nay Hawkins is a Black leader and the chief partnerships officer at MAKERS, an organization that aims to advance women in the workplace. She says that she has experienced internal biases and has seen them affect others, and believes that dismantling internal biases is the key to keeping external ones from holding you back.

Ja'Nay's journey to dissolve her internal biases started in the honors college class in foundational leadership at Tennessee State University, a historically Black university. There she began to connect to her story, strengths, and purpose—which she calls her "why"—and over time she developed this connection through coaching, therapy, and spending time alone asking herself some hard questions.

Doing the work to understand herself has helped Ja'Nay battle the internal biases she held. When you're locked in on your why, she says, you no longer feel the need to play to stereotypes, which helps you dismantle internal prejudices that others may hold against you. You are simply too busy focusing on your path.

For instance, once Ja'Nay was going to a job interview and a friend encouraged her to straighten her hair. After sitting with the advice and asking herself questions to reconnect to her why, Ja'Nay was able to release the internal bias telling her that she had to present herself as someone that others might want her to be. She showed up at the interview as herself—with naturally curly hair. And she's confident that if she had succumbed to the bias and shown up in any other way, her heart and mind would not have been aligned, and she would not have been able to get the job.

Microaggressions: Small Actions with Big Impact

Microaggressions are comments and actions that demean or dismiss someone based on their gender, race, or other aspects of their identity. While unchecked biases can hold women back in overt ways, women are also more likely than men to experience belittling microaggressions. Any single negative comment will likely not change the course of a career, but when the comments add up over time, they can become painful, exhausting, and cause individuals to feel differently about their work environment. Seventy-eight percent of women who experience microaggressions at work say that they self-shield, or protect themselves by presenting themselves differently.[21]

Common microaggressions that women face include being interrupted, having their ideas repeated by others without being given credit, hearing demeaning remarks about their appearance, having their judgment questioned, and being mistaken for someone more junior. All of these undermine women's authority and signal that it will be harder for them to advance. The microaggressions are also stressful and negatively affect women's mental health and well-being.

Intersectionality compounds women's experience. In the United States, where microaggressions have been studied deeply through McKinsey's Women in the Workplace and LeanIn.org, 6 percent of male leaders, 12 percent of women leaders, and 20 percent of Black women leaders have experienced someone saying or implying that they're not qualified for their role. In addition, 10 percent of male employees, 18 percent of women employees, and 17 percent of Black women employees have been mistaken for someone at a lower level, and 26 percent of men, 38 percent of women, and 38 percent of Black women have had their judgment questioned in their area of expertise.[22]

Microaggressions may be subtle, but they can have a big impact. Women who experience them are less likely than others to feel psychologically safe, meaning they fear punishment or humiliation and are not as comfortable making a mistake, leading them to contribute less and take fewer risks. They may fear that if they make a mistake at work and others notice, they are representing all others who look like them; it then becomes an uphill battle for these women to propose new ideas or raise concerns—behaviors that contribute to being seen as a leader.

More than any other group of women, LGBTQ+ women feel the need to hide important parts of their identities to fit in at work. They are also 2.5 times more likely to feel pressured to change their appearance in order to be perceived as more professional. This type of self-shielding comes at a cost: Women who do it are three times more likely to think about quitting their jobs and four times more likely to say they are always or almost always burned out. They are also 3.8 times more likely to feel that they don't have an equal opportunity to advance.[23] It takes psychological work to hide your true self and present as someone who is not authentically you. If you are spending mental energy on it, you are likely not at your best to contribute in other ways.

Combating Bias with Microinclusions

Wendy Taccetta, who identifies as Black, plus-size, and Caribbean, has experienced her share of microaggressions at work. She is engaged, positive, and inspiring, but she also has had to learn to navigate headwinds in her career. Success does not come without challenges, and there are some unique ones that Wendy has faced.

She started her career at Verizon in the United States as a temporary employee more than twenty years ago. In fact, she is a generational employee: her father worked at Verizon for thirty-five years, and the company has been good to Wendy and her family. During her time there, she worked her way through a variety of roles in sales and operations to become the senior vice president of sales planning and operations for the US consumer business.

Yet every time she moved into a new role, Wendy heard from what she calls the "welcome wagon." There are a few different types of people on the wagon: those who genuinely want to congratulate you, those who want to see how their connection to you will be impacted by your move, those who want to tell you what other people are saying about you, and those who want to tell you that you're not the right fit for your new job. Sometimes these comments are overt and other times they are subtle. Regardless, they are types of microaggressions.

It took Wendy a long time to accept the fact that while people would always talk, it didn't mean she had to listen or try to convince them she deserved to be there. Earlier in her career, she self-shielded from these slights by trying to fit into the box of what she thought was expected of her. When she moved into her first sales role, she went out and bought a Coach briefcase and a Jones New York suit. But after a while she realized that the company had hired *her*, not a caricature of what she thought a sales executive should be.

At the same time, Wendy acknowledges the fact that you do often have to adapt to your environment. Saying, "I'm just going to be me" is often lip service. But that doesn't have to mean hiding key aspects of your identity.

To strike this balance, Wendy has found people whose feedback she trusts because she knows they are cheering her on for the right reasons. She focuses on those who have supported her and who have been willing to give constructive and actionable feedback. It's not about curating an environment that is only positive. Rather, she has strived to create one that is supportive. Sometimes, the best support comes from someone who cares enough to tell you the hard things.

The trick is to learn who truly has your best interests at heart. Finding that out takes trial and error, and there were times when Wendy trusted the wrong person and suffered the consequences. But, she says, that's just a part of the process.

After getting a seat at the table, Wendy now focuses on making that table more welcoming and comfortable for the people who come after her. She says that sometimes we hold the door open for others but forget to make the room more hospitable for them—which means we are setting them up to fail. Wendy, by contrast, talks openly about the things that make her different so that those differences become more normal for others and hopefully helps them feel that they are not alone.

We can think of Wendy's actions as *microinclusions*, which signal receptivity and supportiveness and bolster a sense of fit. A study of microinclusions showed that they are especially impactful for women in STEM and increase their commitment to their company. Women's sense of inclusion increased when experiencing a microinclusion, and even when observing another woman experiencing one.[24]

Wendy still encounters microaggressions on a regular basis. When she's not smiling, people ask if she's OK. When she's not in full makeup, people ask if she's feeling run down. But at this point in her career, she has gotten better at ignoring those comments and embracing what she brings to the table that is unique.

Of course, Wendy is also more than who she is at work. She's focused on being her best at home as well, requiring her to set boundaries. For a person who cares deeply about others, it's hard to say no or to not answer the phone. But over time she has learned that she can only be at her best for others when she takes good care of herself.

Lack of Support from Leadership

Another type of headwind that women may face at work is a lack of support from some managers and members of senior leadership. Much of this is due to unconscious biases. For example, women often get very different types of performance evaluations and feedback than men. In some companies where analytics have been run on formal performance reviews, we see that women are much more likely to receive feedback on their personal style and how they look and dress than men. Women also tend to receive vague feedback such as, "You're doing great," and are far less likely than men to receive specific comments that are tied to their job outcomes, what they are doing well, and exactly what they need to do to improve. Of course, this lack of feedback keeps them from growing as much as possible.[25]

Research from Australia shows exactly how these dynamics can hinder growth in your experience capital. In a survey of nearly five thousand employees across a range of organizations, women were 30 percent more likely than men to be told they needed more experience to be qualified for a promotion, but only half of these women were given specific feedback on what experience to build or were given the opportunity to gain experience. On the other hand, men were 50 percent more likely to receive clear feedback about how to improve.[26]

The likability bias also shows up in performance reviews. In one study in the United Kingdom and Ireland, 66 percent of women received negative feedback for acting "too abrasive," compared with only 1 percent of men.[27]

On average, women of color say they get even less managerial support than white women. Latinas and Black women are less likely than others to say their manager shows interest in their career development. And Asian American and Black women are less likely to feel that they have allies on their teams, and less likely than white women to say that senior leaders have publicly praised their skills or advocated on their behalf.[28]

Women also receive fewer opportunities to get coaching from their employers, despite being more likely than men to say they want a coach and being willing to devote more time to working with one. In a US study of eighteen thousand full-time employees across industries, occupations, and job levels, 22 percent of men and only 16 percent of women had access to coaching through their employer.[29]

When women receive coaching, they are often asked to focus on changes that reflect workplace biases. For instance, Black women may be asked to work on their executive presence or on being "nicer" at higher rates than others.[30] Yet these kinds of goals can perpetuate the problem by encouraging women to play to stereotypes and by reinforcing both internal and external biases.

Taking Action against Bias

After ten years in various engineering roles, Yeimy Báez sought a new challenge and set her sights on transitioning into strategy and finance. While in engineering, she had provided information to support decision-making by others. The prospect of being in finance thrilled her, as it represented a potential opportunity to advance into leadership positions and take on more decision-making responsibilities. However, Yeimy was pregnant, making it a challenging time to pursue a career move. Despite this, during an interview with Equion Energia Limited, a company specializing in oil gas exploration, development, and production, she encountered a female CEO who empathized with her situation and was willing to offer her an opportunity.

Finding such support was transformative. Despite facing a steep learning curve, Yeimy gained significant experience capital by taking a bold step into a new industry. After a few years, she was able to transition to Ecopetrol, where she managed the entire investment portfolio of more than $4 billion annually, eventually became the youngest member of the executive committee, and started working in a field she was passionate about—reducing emissions and fighting energy poverty.

As she has flourished in her career, Yeimy took leadership in diversity seriously to combat bias whenever possible. She used a proactive approach in raising the topic of bias and providing examples with her superiors and colleagues. Frequently, these discussions were uncomfortable, as her bringing up the topics often left those around her feeling taken aback. However, rather than marginalizing her, Yeimy's courage had positive consequences by allowing her voice to be heard.

There is one experience she will always remember when it comes to advocating for diversity and making tough decisions between family and work. The company was in the midst of planning a two-day trip for senior leadership to review strategy. Following a conversation with Yeimy, the CEO decided to invite some women, including her. Professionally, Yeimy was thrilled, but personally, she was torn. Attending the trip would be a great opportunity for her and the company, but it coincided with her son's birthday. To Yeimy, her son's birthday held more significance than any work opportunity, but she feared that declining might label her as not committed and could be held against her.

Despite these concerns, Yeimy knew she had to prioritize her family, and she also wanted to set an example of prioritizing family across her team. So, she decided to graciously decline the invitation. When the CEO inquired about her decision, she explained honestly, albeit somewhat fearfully, that it was her son's birthday. She was pleasantly surprised when the CEO expressed understanding. He suggested Yeimy join for the first day and then return home in time for the party. She was relieved to see that her family priorities were respected, and not long after, the same CEO promoted her to vice president.

As a leader, Yeimy now encourages her team to speak up about their priorities, even when it isn't easy. She understands that revealing your true self can sometimes lead to criticism, but she has learned that taking this chance repeatedly throughout your career will ultimately bring more benefits than drawbacks.

Yeimy has pushed against many boundaries, but she is aware that millions of women worldwide face even greater challenges related to poverty and violence, particularly in Colombia, her home country. That's why her work in female leadership also encompasses combating energy poverty as a means to assist more women in need.

Unfortunately, not all leaders are as brave as Yeimy. Despite how common workplace biases are, only one in three employees, including managers, challenge biased behavior when they see it.[31] While companies must fix the structural issues that are allowing biases to hold women back, it is also essential for all of us to act as allies. As you become a leader, you can choose to lead in a way that is more open, less biased, and true to who you are. And while right now you may not have the seniority to drive structural change, you can act as an ally regardless of your role.

Ja'Nay believes that the best way to be an ally at work is to listen to and understand someone in need, rather than trying to respond right away. Most women, including women of color, need a safe space to be heard. And doing the work to dismantle your internal biases will make you a better ally, as it's more difficult to listen to someone when you're battling your judgments and doubts.

In addition, as Wendy says, it's essential to make the rooms we enter more hospitable for all. One way to do this is by acting as a role model for diversity and inclusion. Always introduce yourself when you start a meeting if there are people you don't know, and ask how to pronounce their names. While the customs for it differ around the world, in some environments it is helpful to share your pronouns when you introduce yourself, to normalize others sharing their own.

In meetings, be mindful of who is being interrupted or talked over. When it happens, you can respond as an ally by saying something like, "I want to hear what Juliana was saying." Make sure to give the right person credit for their ideas and speak up if someone else is getting credit by saying something like, "Yes, that goes back to what Lucia was suggesting earlier."

If you find yourself experiencing a bias, such as someone mistaking you for a receptionist or assistant, try, "I'd love to get the coffee. Why don't you come with me and we can have a pre-meeting huddle?" Or if you are being mistaken for someone much less experienced than you are, address it. Try something like, "One of the people that I mentor is passionate about that topic you mentioned earlier . . ." You can use these or come up with your own responses when you witness others experiencing these biases.

Of course, whenever you have an inkling that you might be having a biased reaction, take the time to explore it more. Make sure you are also paying attention to moments when you may be experiencing an internal bias, and pause for a moment to think about why. As Ja'Nay says, work to connect to your purpose and your why to keep yourself focused and aligned.

Standing Out and Using It to Your Advantage

While we have described a number of both conscious and unconscious biases that systematically disadvantage women, there are ways in which standing out at work can be an advantage. When you are the only person who looks like you, you can be sure that others will remember you and what you have to say. Fight any internal biases, speak up, and advocate for yourself.

It may help to spend a little extra time preparing before a meeting for what you want to say and considering when it might fit best in the discussion. A little preparation can often go a long way toward helping you feel more comfortable speaking up, even in large groups or situations where you know few people. Over time, hopefully both you and others can learn to see your unique position as an asset.

Victoria Ossadnik, the chief operating officer of E.ON, a German electric utility multinational, experienced bias that was both positive and negative in her career. She studied physics at Ludwig Maximilian University in Germany, and she says it was there that she fell in love with lasers. After receiving a PhD, she worked at a startup for laser technology. As a woman working in STEM in the early 2000s, Victoria certainly stood out and experienced her share of biases. For instance, long after she'd left the startup and advanced in her career, a man she passed in the hallway asked her to make him some photocopies, assuming that she was far more junior than she actually was. A few days later, he saw her making a presentation and was mortified, but she didn't take offense. She figured that now he would never forget her or her work.

Plus, Victoria already knew by then that standing out could be to her benefit. Back when she was at the startup, she was tasked with hosting its booth at a big trade fair in Tokyo. At first, people assumed that she was someone junior, but once she started speaking to them about the lasers, they recognized her expertise and started listening.

On the second day of the fair, Victoria arrived at the booth and was surprised to find a huge line of people waiting for her. Then they told her they had heard there was a woman from Germany who knew all about lasers, and they were excited to meet her. Victoria seized that opportunity to tell them about the company's products. It was a moment that she—and likely the attendees—would never forget.

In addition to biases, the choice to become a mother can—but doesn't have to—disrupt the growth of experience capital. Next, we will explore how motherhood can potentially impact your career and highlight strategies for continuing to build experience capital during this important time.

CHAPTER 12

Motherhood as an Experience Capital Disrupter—or Escalator

Delphine Maisonneuve has always wanted to make an impact, continue trying new things, and never allow herself to get bored. Those goals drove her through twenty years of professional growth at AXA, a French multinational insurance company, from an entry-level sales job in her native France to roles in Spain, Brazil, and many other locations. It's further allowed her to later become the CEO of VYV Group, France's leading mutual health care, insurance, housing, and support services company. She also happens to be the mother of four children.

Starting her career, Delphine knew that she wanted the opportunity to live and work abroad. But she also wanted a family. So, she and her husband made a deal: they would both get jobs at global companies, which would hopefully make it easier for them to move around. Whenever one of them had a good opportunity, the other would look for a job in the same location. As much as possible, they would alternate, taking turns moving for the other.

For the most part, this plan has worked, and although Delphine has stayed at one company for nearly her entire career, it has not inhibited her from growing her experience capital. If anything, she has been able to more easily balance work and family while continuously relocating because she developed such deep relationships within the company and built up so much trust. When her husband moved to Spain for a job, for example, the Spanish division of AXA was willing to take a chance on her. And when one of her daughters was ill, her bosses understood that she needed a break from traveling to be home every night.

Throughout her various roles, Delphine followed her curiosity and willingness to take risks to build her experience capital. A few years ago, after working solely in developed economies, Delphine wanted a chance to work in less developed economies, where she could experience rapid growth. She was given the opportunity to become the CEO of AXA Brazil.

By then, Delphine's three oldest children were young adults, and her youngest daughter was ten. This time, she wanted to bring her youngest daughter with her and leave the rest of the family in France. She negotiated with the company to provide travel so that Delphine and her daughter could spend a week with her husband every six weeks. Then they went off to have a wonderful adventure, and Delphine was able to completely turn the company around. As her daughter adapted to and came to love life in Brazil, Delphine was able to witness firsthand how much her career adventures had allowed her children to grow and thrive.

The Motherhood Penalty

Although Delphine's story shows that motherhood does not always have to interrupt career progression, choosing to become a parent remains the biggest potential disrupter of experience capital growth for most women. Our aim in this chapter is to arm you with the facts on the impact that motherhood can have on your experience capital and provide tactics to help you minimize the disruption—and leverage motherhood as an escalator instead.

Much progress has been made to help women avoid being penalized at work for having children. In fact, Delphine recalls receiving a lower raise than a male colleague early in her career when she was in sales. In this role success was easily quantifiable, and she knew that she was doing better than her peer. When she asked her boss about the lower raise, he explained that Delphine had a spouse who worked, while the other employee did not. Delphine refused to accept this answer as valid, but she believes that her income remained lower than her male peers' throughout much of her career. The good news is that she was able to catch up over the last ten years or so as diversity, equity, and inclusion (DEI) efforts have increased and decisions of this kind are less accepted.

However, many women still experience the *motherhood penalty*, a term used to describe the disadvantages they often face when becoming a parent. These disadvantages range from fewer job offers to lower recommended salaries and reduced opportunities for advancement and high-profile assignments. To the contrary, men often have a *fatherhood boost* and benefit from becoming parents instead of being penalized.[1]

Professor Claudia Goldin won the 2023 Nobel Prize in Economic Sciences for her work studying the history of women in the labor market. Interestingly, she was the first woman to win a Nobel Prize in economics solo (not as part of a team). Her research found that in developed economies, the gender pay gap is driven by motherhood more than by any other factor. While many experts previously believed that the gap occurred directly after a child's birth and evened out soon after, Goldin's work shows instead that the gap actually begins to widen a year or two after a woman has her first child.[2]

Indeed, it is harder for working mothers to be hired or to be considered for hire. Based on Goldin's research on the United States, equally qualified mothers are six times less likely than childless women and 3.35 times less likely than childless men to be recommended for hire. They are also rated as 10 percent less competent than equally qualified nonmothers. Women without children receive more than two times as many callbacks as equally qualified mothers.

Once they have a job, it is difficult for working mothers to achieve equal pay and to rise in their careers. Mothers are offered a starting salary that is on average 7.9 percent lower than those offered to other equally qualified women. Once hired, women without children are 8.2 times more likely to be recommended for a promotion than mothers.[3]

While the motherhood penalty is unfortunately a global phenomenon, its magnitude does vary from country to country. There are some consistent trends, however. Universally, women tend to experience a significant drop in earnings immediately after the birth of their first child. Ten years later, the vast majority of women's careers have not recovered.

The size of the remaining gap, however, does vary—and it tends to widen with each subsequent child. For example, in many European countries, having one child has only a small negative effect on a mother's overall wages, but women with two and especially three children experience a significant and lasting wage impact. A mother's wage penalty ten years after her child's birth ranges from 21 percent in Denmark to about 40 percent in the United States or the United Kingdom and up to 61 percent in Germany. This includes the nonexistent earnings of women who give up work entirely. Men's earnings in all countries are largely unaffected by parenthood.[4]

These kinds of effects can perhaps be seen most clearly in a study that used two résumés that were identical except for a one-phrase difference: "membership in the Parent Teacher Association (PTA)," which implies that the person is an active and involved parent. The résumé that mentioned the PTA was 79 percent less likely to be recommended for hire and was offered $11,000 less in salary.[5]

Eynat Guez experienced the motherhood penalty even as a well-established and successful entrepreneur. After losing her mother when she was very young, Eynat knew that she never wanted to be financially dependent on anyone. She wanted to have her own money and her own business—her goal, which she reached, was to start a company in her native country of Israel before she turned thirty. In fact, by her mid-thirties, Eynat had founded two successful companies. Both were service-related and were therefore reliant on her as an individual, so she decided to start something based on a product as well. She began developing a global payroll platform, which she named Papaya Global.

By the time Papaya was raising Series A funding, its metrics were strong and Eynat felt good about the company's future. So did potential investors. After a first round of Zoom meetings, several of them enthusiastically asked her to fly out to meet with them. Eynat was thrilled. Surely, one of the many interested parties would end up being the right fit.

However, when these almost exclusively male investors met with Eynat in person, they realized something that wasn't visible over Zoom—she was five months pregnant. Eynat says that as soon as they saw her, the investors' interest completely dissolved. No one acknowledged it, but in every meeting, she says, there was an elephant in the room; her pregnancy had clearly given them pause.

For her last meeting, Eynat did something different. She made sure to arrive before anyone else and sat down at the conference table with her belly hidden. When the investors entered the room, she stayed seated. It was impossible not to notice that the tenor of that meeting was completely different from the others'. This group exhibited the same level of enthusiasm they'd had over Zoom—until, that is, Eynat got up at the end of the meeting, and the elephant was back. Once again, the enthusiasm immediately dissipated.

Returning home, Eynat was devastated. She felt like she had let her employees down and worried that she would have to lay them off if she couldn't find a way to secure funding. Desperate, she reached out to her early investors. They weren't at the same level as those she'd gone to for the Series A, but they might still be able to help. One of them offered Eynat a bridge loan that allowed the company to temporarily stay afloat. A few months later, Eynat gave birth, and the very next month she was able to successfully close a round of funding.

A few years later, the company was raising its second round of funding, and as luck would have it, Eynat was pregnant with her second child. This time, she only met with investors over Zoom. And after securing funding, she waited to tell her investors that she was pregnant until just a week before giving birth.

While it is important for leaders to set an example and normalize motherhood, some situations may require more extreme measures. In terms of her pregnancy, Eynat decided that it simply wasn't her investors' business. After all, if a male founder was about to have a child, it wouldn't be held against him. If people's biases were going to keep them from investing in or supporting her, Eynat figured that she had no choice but to keep her private life private. Like Delphine, she knew that she would continue to deliver results, and that's what really mattered.

The Decision to Return to Work

Between the motherhood penalty and the burden of most household and caretaking work falling to them, many women choose to take a step back in their careers after having children. Women have a lower workforce participation rate than men overall, and the gap is particularly large between mothers and fathers with children under six years old: 68.9 percent of mothers with children under age 6 participated in the workforce, compared with 77.8 percent of mothers with children between six and seventeen years old. Fathers had a high workforce participation rate throughout, even higher for those with younger children: 94.6 percent of fathers with children under age six versus 92.4 percent of fathers with children ages six though seventeen participated in the workforce.[6]

Across the Organisation for Economic Co-Operation and Development (OECD) countries, roughly 60 percent of women between the ages of fifteen and sixty-four with at least one child are employed (including both full-time and part-time work), compared with 73 percent of women in the same age range without children.[7] A study that looked specifically at the UK workforce, meanwhile, revealed that just 28 percent of mothers work full-time three years after having a child, compared with 90 percent of fathers.[8] And 17 percent of UK mothers leave the workforce completely within five years of childbirth, compared with only 4 percent of men.[9]

Staying home to care for children is a personal choice; there is no one right path for all parents. But for a woman considering leaving the workforce for a medium or extended period of time, it is important to consider the long-term impact on her overall career trajectory, experience capital, and lifetime earnings.

Delphine's advice for overcoming the motherhood penalty is to refuse to accept it in your head and in the heads of others. This means speaking up and fighting for the role and salary you want as if biases against mothers do not exist. She also focuses on maintaining high performance, knowing that she will deliver. The attitude she brings forward in interviews is, *If you want someone who delivers, choose me.*

However, many women who want to have children understandably worry about their careers as this life experience approaches. In fact, 61 percent of US women feel fear and anxiety around planning a family, which impacts their career and life goals. Sixty percent of US women are willing to delay starting a family until they have reached a certain level in their career or earned a specific job title. Sixty percent of US women also delay having children for financial reasons.[10]

Yet the expectation that motherhood will interrupt careers may have a ripple effect, causing women to hold themselves back, organizations to overlook them for leadership roles, and even women's partners to assume their own careers will be the priority within the family. By making decisions that anticipate the negative impacts of motherhood, women are likely to find themselves in less rewarding roles when and if they do become mothers.

If you plan to become a working mother, it is a better strategy to focus on building your experience capital before, during, and after the moment arrives. In fact, there are numerous opportunities to build experience capital as a mother. Many do it without even realizing it.

Building Experience Capital as a Mother

One afternoon, Anette Lippert was at the playground with her young son, who was with another child in the sandbox. She noticed that the child had a toy truck. When she looked over a moment later, her son was holding the truck, and the other boy was crying. Anette went over and facilitated a negotiation between the two children. Soon they were happily playing together, sharing the toy.

The next day Anette was in a meeting with two department heads, who were quarreling about a project. In her head, she thought, "Just give him the truck back!" Then she realized what an interesting thought that was. She proceeded to facilitate a conversation between the department heads, once again finding a solution that worked for everyone.

Anette walked away from that experience fascinated by the idea of transferring skills she had gained as a mother to the workplace. She wondered if it was something that other mothers were able to do and if she could show women how to signal these skills to bosses and potential employers. Anette went on to interview seventy women leaders in different sectors to find out what leadership skills they had developed as mothers. She found consistent themes and organized them into five categories: consistency and project management, empathy, resilience, advancement and development, and vision. This work became the basis for her book, *Leading Mothers.*

We often focus on the motherhood penalty, but what if we reframed this as the motherhood bonus? There are skills you may get extra practice refining as a mother that can also be an asset to your leadership capabilities—just like Anette found.

A common challenge mothers face is rebounding to work after a parental leave. Even more challenging can be returning to office work after choosing to make work in the home a full-time commitment. Reentering the corporate world full-time is exactly what Dina To was able to do. After graduating from law school, Dina worked at an international law firm in litigation before moving to the US Department of Justice and then to Yahoo to become an in-house counsel. When she wanted to have children, she was grateful to be in a position to stay home and decided to temporarily step out of the workforce.

Dina ended up having three sons and staying at home for fourteen years before she went back to practicing law full-time. But during those fourteen years, the curve of her experience capital remained far from flat. She had known all along that she would want to return to work someday and that she needed to keep growing and evolving in order to successfully do so.

One of the biggest boosts to Dina's experience capital during her time away came from starting a cookie company with a friend. She had no expectation that she would make money from the endeavor but wanted to experience what it was like to be an entrepreneur. She also spent a tremendous amount of time volunteering for her kids' schools, especially around fundraising. Both of these efforts helped her build many new skills that were broadly applicable.

When she started thinking about going back to work full-time, Dina realized that she had built up her soft skills over the past several years but needed to sharpen her hard skills. New laws had been passed while she wasn't practicing, especially around technology and privacy, so she did her homework and studied them.

Once she started interviewing for roles, Dina signaled all of her skills, just as Anette suggests. She explained to potential employers that while she was trained in the law, what she had that was harder to learn was a set of skills that included collaboration, delivering guidance in a diplomatic way, and resilience. After joining a returnship program at LinkedIn, Dina is now a senior leader at the company and says that she was able to leapfrog her peers because of those valuable soft skills.

Step Back, Build Back, Comeback

As Delphine's, Anette's, and Dina's stories all show, despite the challenges, becoming a mother is an opportunity to not only survive but thrive and perhaps revitalize your career and broaden your skills. Certainly there are potential negative impacts that motherhood can have on your professional momentum, but if you plan well for your maternity leave and eventual return to work, the following tactics should help minimize the penalty and even help you increase your leadership skills.

It may be helpful to focus on three stages: the step back, the build back, and the comeback. The step back is when you are preparing well for your leave and taking a moment to consider the best path forward. The build back includes continuing to connect with your network and potentially building a new network of working parents, while investing in yourself and your experience capital. Finally, the comeback is when you find a new operating model that works for you and your family. During this time, you can also seek out additional mentors and sponsors, as well as participate in reboarding programs to further build your experience capital.

The following tips can help you through these three stages:

The step back

First and foremost, make sure you have a round-trip ticket, if that is what you want: plan for your leave and return, and discuss your plans with your mentors, sponsors, and personal board of directors. If you haven't already made a plan, now is a good time to start. Make sure to do so even if you are not sure how long of a career break you may take. Dina says that before stepping away from her career, building relationships was extremely important. When you're getting ready to step out, make sure you leave on a positive note and that people understand your circumstances; you'll likely end up relying on these relationships again in the future. In fact, when she heard about the returnship program at LinkedIn, Dina reached out to a former colleague who was working there to find out if she might be a good fit. Learn all the details of your company's benefits and resources, too. There may be programs you might not know about that could help create a smooth on-ramp for your return.

You should also set boundaries for your leave. Some women enjoy touching base with clients and colleagues during their maternity leaves; others want more of a clean break. If you've having your first child, it may be a more intense period than you anticipate, and a clean break may be easiest so you can focus on your new family member. Think about what will make the most sense for you—perhaps there are specific issues that you want to be contacted about, for example. Come up with a list and share it with your colleagues and team. Communication is key.

Examine whether you can use this leave as an opportunity to step away from any projects or clients that aren't giving you energy and reshape your responsibilities so they are more in line with your areas of interest. Doing so will likely require you to put yourself out there and ask for what you want. No one is going to hand you the perfect situation on a silver platter, but you may be surprised by how many people want to help you if you ask.

The build back

Above all else, do everything you can to be present and enjoy this precious time. While you focus on your health and your new child, new priorities will naturally emerge. Pay attention as this happens and don't think too far ahead or make too many changes right away.

Once you have settled into life as a mother a bit, think about what parts of your operating model or lifestyle will need to change when you return to work. Be honest with yourself without judgment; every woman is different. As Delphine says, ask yourself what is essential to you. For some moms, it's most important to be home for bedtime each night. For others, weekends are sacrosanct and they don't mind traveling or working late during the week. Remember that your priorities will also change over time. For now, think about what will work best for you and your family in the near term.

Consider staying in touch with your team and colleagues, even informally. Sending periodic messages or photos during your leave works for some. Others who have a close relationship with their team enjoy bringing their new baby to the office to meet their colleagues.

If your leave is long enough, consider taking this opportunity to expand your capabilities. It might be as simple as reading up on the latest technology trends, or as involved as taking an online course. Or, in the case of a multiyear leave like Dina's, consider pursuing passions that help you build new skills. For a leave on the shorter side, however, don't put pressure on yourself to do anything but heal and figure out how you want to be a mother.

And start building the pillars of your support system. Don't wait until you are ready to go back to work to figure out your childcare plans and discuss the details of how you will coparent with your partner, if you have one. As you think about childcare solutions, leave as much time as possible for trial and error. Delphine suggests making your partner a part of plan A from the very beginning. For a long time her husband was the backup—plan B—and she had to think of plans C and D on her own. Once she started considering him an equal part of plan A and therefore responsible for coming up with plans B and beyond, she freed up her schedule and mental load tremendously.

Likewise, keep in mind that the childcare patterns you start now will shape the next few years. For example, if you are always the "expert" who knows how and what to feed the baby or how to change diapers, then you will become the default parent. If you share that more equally with a partner, the "unpaid care work" will be shared more equally over time.

If you don't have a partner, figuring out the network of family, friends, caregivers, and service providers who can help you balance childcare with work will be key.

The comeback

Regardless of the circumstances, returning to your job will require you to adapt. You may need to transition back slowly and experiment with new daily routines until you find something that works. Prepare yourself ahead of time for plans to potentially be derailed. Since the Covid-19 pandemic, remote work has been more acceptable in many roles, which may make a flexible operating model more accessible. Many working mothers see this as a benefit—in fact, US women with childcare responsibilities who are able to work remotely are 32 percent less likely to report intending to leave their jobs, compared with similar women who cannot work remotely.[11]

Go easy on yourself, especially during your first few months back. It tends to be an emotional time. You may doubt yourself or even feel conflicted about returning to work at all. Try to hold off on making any permanent decisions until you have given yourself a chance to adapt. Doing all this may require you to intentionally practice optimism and to develop a growth mindset. It might help to speak to other working moms who have been through it and can show you what is possible. Hopefully the stories in this chapter can do that as well!

Clearly define what success will look like during your first year back, and make sure you have a plan in place to get there. Some companies make this a part of their on-ramp process, but even if yours doesn't, you can replicate it by creating an informal contract with your manager. Don't be shy about working with your sponsors too and asking for help to get there. Sponsorship is increasingly important during this time. Many women, like Delphine, have thrived as mothers thanks to their support. Make sure to nurture and secure these relationships as much as you can.

Remember, all of the capabilities that new mothers develop can be applied to your job. When you find yourself leaning on these skills in order to adjust, remind yourself that you have a valuable opportunity to grow your experience capital.

Next, we'll explore how taking care of your financial, physical, and mental health can help bulletproof your career so you can use all of the tools in this book.

CHAPTER 13

The Foundations of Your Experience Capital

Regardless of what tactics you use to rise in your career and build your experience capital, it will be impossible to reach your full earning potential or achieve your ambitions without taking care of your mental, physical, and financial health. This chapter is about these foundational elements and how to make them work for you so you can maximize the benefits of your experience capital across your career.

A Healthy Bedrock for Your Career

When Alex Mahon took over as CEO of Channel 4, a publicly owned and commercially funded UK public service broadcaster, she sat down one by one with each of the employee resource groups (ERGs). She admits that when the women's ERG, 4Womxn, told her that it was important for the organization to address menopause, her initial response was, "Is it?" But once Alex learned that menopause symptoms interfered with many women's ability to work and even caused some to leave the workforce, she was determined to help make a change.

Symptoms of menopause can directly impact someone's performance and productivity at work, yet their significance has been overlooked for decades. In a survey of 1,000 people who currently are or recently were going through menopause, 54 percent of respondents had dealt with menopause-driven work challenges and 70 percent had considered at least one type of major employment-based change due to their symptoms.[1] These realities struck Alex as terribly unfair. So many women had worked so hard and for so long to rise and build experience capital throughout their careers. They had overcome obstacles in an environment with even fewer women in leadership positions than there are today, and many of them had found a way to balance their careers and parenthood. Yet now they were stepping aside right at the time when they should have been reaching their peak and really going after the top jobs—and all because of a temporary situation that could be addressed through proper medical care.

Part of Channel 4's public service remit is to be the voice of the unheard, and Alex was determined to weave that into everything she did as CEO. Now that she knew how many women were silently suffering, she decided that she would be their voice, too.

Under Alex's leadership, Channel 4 put in place one of the world's first menopause policies, which included simple things such as access to private, quiet, cool rooms in the office, flexible working arrangements, and paid leave to manage symptoms. The organization's top mission was to stop menopause from being taboo in the workplace, so it also created menopause awareness briefings for leadership teams.

When the policy launched, it blew up in the media. Alex couldn't believe that a simple HR policy was getting global press coverage. But she also realized that Channel 4 was in a unique position to influence both the industry and the public. So, her team made their policy available to other companies, and more than eight thousand of them—including some very large organizations—quickly adopted it.

Then Channel 4 turned to creating programs targeted at consumers. After a documentary about menopause aired, twenty-two thousand doctors and nurses signed up to complete a course on it. The next year, prescriptions for hormone replacement therapy (HRT), the most effective treatment for menopause symptoms, went up 42 percent in the United Kingdom. It led to a national shortage of HRT and a campaign for change in Parliament, so the government changed the law so that HRT would be covered by government subsidies.

However, Alex is perhaps most proud of the ways this work has impacted her employees. A 2022 staff survey showed that 84 percent of employees who identified as women were exceptionally engaged and proud to work for Channel 4. In addition, the number of women employees over the age of forty-five has gone up by more than one-third, and women now represent 54 percent of the one hundred top-paid staff.

The Gender Health Gap

While it is common knowledge that women on average live longer than men, their average health spans are shorter. In other words, women spend more time in poor health. On average around the world, women spend eleven years in debilitating health, compared with eight years for men. This disparity—which we call the *gender health gap*—is even larger for women of color and the LGBTQ+ population.[2]

Why are we talking about health in this book about navigating your career? Simply put, your health is foundational to your career success and your ability to grow your experience capital. Any time spent in poor or even moderate health is time when the curve of your experience capital is likely to be flattened or interrupted, and when striving to reach your potential will be more difficult. In addition, over half of women's health burdens affect those of working age, with some of the most common issues—such as infertility, pregnancy or birth complications, and menopause—coinciding with pivotal career moments.

The gender health gap is much broader than just sexual and reproductive health, which roughly accounts for just 5 percent of the gender health gap. Another 4 percent of it is related to conditions that affect women differently than men, including atrial fibrillation (heart attacks) and colon cancer. The biggest piece of the gender health gap (48 percent), however, is related to conditions that affect women *disproportionately.* These include autoimmune diseases, headache disorders such as migraines, and certain mental health conditions.

The remaining 43 percent of the gender health gap is related to conditions that affect women and men at similar rates, such as ischemic heart disease and tuberculosis. In these cases, the gap can be attributed to differences in care and diagnoses.

For example, women are seven times more likely than men to have a heart condition misdiagnosed. That is because the symptoms of a heart attack are different in women than in men, and doctors and hospital triage teams are not always trained on those differences, which often delays treatment for women and/or makes it less effective. Women are more likely to experience overall fatigue and feeling a bit "off" instead of acute chest pain, which is more common for men. For this and similar reasons, approximately two-thirds of the time that women spend in debilitating health can be addressed with existing solutions through improvements in access and care delivery.

Closing the gender health gap by 2040 could add $1 trillion in global GDP, or the equivalent of seven days of life per woman per year. It is equivalent to having 137 million more women in the workforce in full-time positions. In addition, having more women in the talent pipeline for longer—particularly at more senior levels—would go a long way toward improving women's representation. Although knowledge about the gender health gap can't necessarily save you from its impact, it can help you successfully navigate issues at work while advocating for yourself with medical professionals. As broader awareness grows, access and care gaps will shrink.

The Gender Mental Health and Wellness Gap

No element of wellness exists in a vacuum, and women's mental health can be just as critical as physical wellness for a successful and rewarding career. Good mental health is not just the absence of disease or a consistent state of happiness; it's what women experience when they have good overall cognitive functioning, resilience, and a state of well-being that allows them to cope with the stresses of life, contribute at work and home, and realize their full potential.

Women around the world seem to be aware of the critical importance of their mental health and overall wellness. In a survey of more than ten thousand women of working age, 85 percent said that their mental health was very important or extremely important. Roughly 20 percent said that school, work, or their careers negatively impacted their mental health. These findings highlight how important it is for organizations to support all their employees' wellness needs.

Yet mental health conditions affect women more often and differently than men. Women are 1.6 times more likely to experience a mental illness, such as an anxiety or a depressive disorder.[3] They are also at a 40 percent higher risk of experiencing insomnia, and insomnia is predictive of depression and other mental health disorders.[4]

Women also experience unique mental health challenges that evolve with time over the course of their careers. For instance, they may struggle with postpartum depression or anxiety, premenstrual syndrome or premenstrual dysphoric disorder, and/or mental health symptoms of menopause.

While there are certainly some mental health conditions that require medication and other interventions, all women can benefit from a holistic approach to their health. Some nonmedical interventions have proven to make a difference for many people. For example, developing a growth mindset—seeing intelligence and abilities as learnable and capable of being improved through effort—has been shown to have a lasting and positive effect on mental health.[5]

Exercise and meditation are two additional powerful tools. Vigorous exercise in adolescence and adulthood is inversely related to depression in adulthood.[6] And studies suggest that exercise may be 1.5 times more effective than counseling or some medications at reducing mental health symptoms, with some of the largest benefits seen in pregnant and postpartum women.[7] Yet from as early as preschool and young childhood, women fall behind their male counterparts in minutes per day of physical activity, a trend that continues into adulthood.[8]

Many studies have focused on the connection between meditation and mental health. Meditation can improve overall brain function and help address various issues like social anxiety disorder, post-traumatic stress disorder, anxiety, and depression. It is also good for physical health, since it can improve immune system function, decrease inflammation, bring down cholesterol levels, and improve diastolic blood pressure.[9]

To start taking control of your mental health and overall wellness, the first step is to recognize its importance and make it a priority. As women move through their professional and personal lives, it can be difficult to juggle work and family along with mental health. And seeing a physician to treat a medical condition may feel like a necessity, while taking time to meditate, practice yoga, or see a therapist may feel like a luxury. Yet you cannot reach your potential without taking care of your mind and body and all of the intricate ways they are connected.

Tactics for Building a Healthy Foundation for Your Career

Let's look at a few strategies to set yourself up for long-term health, drawing on the points we've covered so far.

Focus on the basics

Invest in yourself by getting adequate sleep, exercise, and nutrition. Sleeping for at least seven hours a night, and ideally going to bed at a similar time each night, can make a big difference in your health and mood. Regular exercise—at least thirty minutes a day—helps people live longer. Eating more healthful food—fewer processed and fried foods, less alcohol, and more fruits and vegetables—will help as well. You may consider starting a meditation practice if you don't already have one. Your lifestyle habits have a big impact on your physical and mental health and your ability to grow and thrive.

Get regular screenings

It's easy to let these slide as life gets busy, but it's critical to ensure that you are getting all of your regular screenings. At a minimum they include a yearly physical, OB/GYN visits, Pap smears, mammograms, and colonoscopies once you reach the appropriate age, and dental visits. Especially important is developing a relationship with a primary care doctor, who can help you navigate the health care system and find the right specialists as needed. Preparing and writing down any questions before your appointments is also a good idea.

Maximize your insurance benefits

Ensure that you fully understand your current benefits and take advantage of those offerings. When you are starting your career, it may seem appealing to save money by opting out of life insurance and disability insurance that you are unlikely to need, but in the rare instance that you experience a health crisis, they can make all the difference. The quality of health benefits is just one reason it's so important to choose your employer carefully.

Learn about your health and educate others

Understand the gender health gap and how it might affect you. As we were interviewing women and doing research for this book, we heard so many examples of people whose symptoms were not taken seriously or who had to push hard to advocate for their health. As you progress in your career, you may be in situations where you can bring broader awareness to this issue and help improve things. Like Alex Mahon, you can implement and advocate for real change. If you are more junior, you can still be a part of the change by refusing to allow women's health or mental health issues to be taboo and by speaking openly about your experiences. Doing so will make the workplace a more inclusive and healthier place for you and other women who come behind you.

Making the Most of Your Lifetime Earnings

When Beth Smith was growing up, her family didn't have a lot of money. Though her father owned his own small business, he struggled to make ends meet, and once he was diagnosed with cancer, the business eventually went under. Sadly, he passed away shortly after. Beth's mother, who had chosen to stay at home to raise Beth and her three siblings, suddenly had to return to work to support the family.

To make the most of her earnings, Beth's mom joined a ladies' investing group. This was back in the 1990s, and it was rare for a group of women to gather and talk about money, not to mention investing it. Largely out of necessity, Beth's mother learned a lot that she passed on to her children. Whether Beth listened to her advice was another story.

Meanwhile, Beth started working at the age of twelve. Even then, she knew that she never wanted to be reliant on anyone else for her financial needs. By the time she was in high school, she had saved $6,000, which felt like a lot of money. Her mother helped Beth open an account with Morgan Stanley, and after putting her savings in the market, it quickly doubled. Beth was overjoyed. Then the market crashed, and Beth's account was reduced to its initial balance—and luckily not any lower.

The experience was enough to scare Beth off of personal investing. Fearing that she'd lose it all, she pulled her money out of the market. And although her mother encouraged her to reconsider and open a retirement account to start building savings early, Beth didn't listen. She was too concerned about the risk and didn't want to invest money that could potentially just disappear when she had worked so hard to earn it.

After she graduated from the University of Michigan, Beth was a diligent saver and always maximized her 401(k) contributions, ensuring that she got the full value of her employer's match. That was an easy decision for Beth and one that her mother always encouraged so that she would never leave free money on the table. But Beth was still too nervous to invest her savings in the financial markets.

It wasn't until she'd spent nearly a decade in consulting, serving several major financial institutions, that Beth began to reconsider investing her savings. Learning more about the markets and how they work, she finally opened her own investing account and IRA, and once she became more educated on the clear benefits of compound interest, she wished she had listened to her mom so many years ago.

Beth eventually started working for a large financial company and became further intrigued by investing. One year she set a New Year's resolution to learn more about how to maximize her earnings. She got a subscription to *Money* magazine and started studying everything from the markets, to different types of funds, to savings accounts, to how to take advantage of her credit score. She was surprised by how much she was able to learn just by reading the information that was available in magazines and online.

Beth also set some long-term financial goals. It had always saddened her that her father never made it to retirement, which was one reason she wanted to put herself in a position to retire early. She started looking at all of her accounts on a monthly basis and carefully assessing her income coming in, where it was being spent, and where it was growing. Then she was able to make more informed decisions.

As she continued in her career, she kept focusing on her life and retirement goals. At the age of forty-two, Beth has succeeded in making the most of her lifetime earnings. Between saving more than many peers and getting numerous promotions in her career, she is now in a position to retire in the near future if she so chooses.

Meanwhile, Beth's close friend recently went through a divorce and turned to her for support, and she was able to see firsthand how their different approaches to managing their money had led to very different outcomes. Although the friend and her ex-husband both had good jobs, Beth learned that they had been living with limited savings and had accumulated some debt throughout their marriage. In addition, her friend didn't have a credit card or a high-yield savings account. All of her money went straight in and out of her checking account. This left her friend with a lower credit score, which made it more difficult and expensive to get a loan for a car, a mortgage, and a credit card.

Beth, on the other hand, had opened multiple credit cards as soon as she turned eighteen, knowing that it would help her build her credit as long as she paid off the balance every month—which she always did. Beth also used a high-yield savings account to maximize interest on the money in her account.

There are some things that Beth wishes she had done earlier. For one, she wishes she had taken her mother's advice and opened a Roth IRA (a US tax-advantaged individual retirement account) when she was eligible and traditional IRAs thereafter. Beth missed out on fifteen years of IRA contributions where her money could have grown tax-deferred. She also wishes she had been more open to talking about finances with her friends and coworkers, like her mother did with her investing group. Beth always thought that talking about money meant exposing yourself, but she realized later that it didn't have to be that way. She didn't have to reveal anything about her personal financial situation in order to gain valuable insights and perspectives from other people.

Ultimately, Beth wishes she had gotten interested in finances earlier, period. When she started working, she thought that good money management simply meant being diligent and saving as much as possible. Now she knows that there is so much more you can do to make your money work for you. Learning this sooner would have given her a bigger head start toward reaching her personal goals.

The Gender Wealth Gap

It's common knowledge that there is a gender wage gap. Women in the United States earn 27 percent less than men on average. Men and women start their careers in very different occupations, but first jobs ultimately account for only 3 percent of the gender pay gap. Different occupational and role choices after the first job by gender are the primary driver, contributing to 10 percent of the pay gap. In addition to occupational choices, the gender wage gap is due to women having more part-time jobs versus full-time ones (around the world, women have the majority of part-time and the minority of full-time jobs), and the number of years of experience women bring to the job. For every 10 years of experience a man in the United States accumulates, the average woman accumulates 8.6 years due to more frequent and longer leaves. After accounting for the differences of part-time roles and years of experience, however, there is a remaining gender wage gap of 7 percent that is likely due to industry- and firm-level variations, work conditions, as well as bias.

However, even if we closed the wage gap, a gender *wealth* gap would persist. Unlike wages, which are simply a measure of earnings, wealth is a balance of assets versus debts. For example, think of looking at a person's balance sheet (their assets or wealth) versus their income statement (the money they make). Globally, men have accumulated $105 trillion more wealth than women.[10]

Several factors contribute to the wealth gap. The wage gap is just one of them. With women earning less than men, they are less able to save or invest, and this investing disparity compounds the wage gap. When women earn less and invest less, they end up with far reduced net wealth because their money does not grow over time.

To make the issue worse, because women on average live longer than men but spend more years in poor health, they have higher average health care costs. Eighty-one percent of people over the age of eighty-five are women, which means that most women will end up having to take care of themselves financially in their later years.[11] In addition to the greater health care costs, their savings and retirement benefits also need to stretch out longer.

However, women's average retirement savings significantly lag behind men's. In the United States, 62 percent of working women have less than they should in retirement savings based on calculations of how much is required to comfortably retire, compared with just 48 percent of men. In fact, 41 percent of women are significantly behind, compared with 30 percent of men.[12]

For all of these reasons, it is especially important for women to learn about and be actively involved in their personal finances. Unless you do, you will not be able to make the most of your lifetime earnings, no matter how much experience capital you gain. And even if you have a significant other or a partner who is taking care of the finances for you, you need to be involved and aware—which brings us to another gap to be aware of.

The Gender Financial Literacy Gap

Around the world, there is a significant difference between men and women in financial literacy, or the ability to process economic information and make informed decisions about financial planning, wealth accumulation, debt, and retirement. Globally, 16 percent more men are financially literate than women (35 percent of men versus 30 percent of women). This gap exists across countries with different income levels, age, education levels, and socioeconomic characteristics.[13]

In addition to this disparity in knowledge, there is a gap when it comes to how confident men and women are in their financial knowledge. When tested on their financial literacy, women are far more likely than men to answer "I don't know" when presented with that option, which results in lower scores. However, when "I don't know" is not an option, women's scores are much closer to men's, effectively shrinking the financial literacy gap by half.[14] However, if lower confidence results in lack of action, then women are missing out on financial opportunities.

This lack of confidence in their financial know-how can be a slippery slope. Women who feel less sure of their knowledge are less willing to learn about finances, which widens the gap even further.[15] It also makes them more likely to delay making financial decisions, often with negative consequences. Due to the cost of inflation, failing to make a financial decision can be a costly decision in and of itself. Money that remains stagnant is actually shrinking in value in real terms.[16]

Women also tend to participate in the stock market less than men. This appears to be linked to their relatively lower financial literacy, perhaps more than an inherent aversion to risk. In a simulated exercise in which the financial literacy gap was closed, stock market participation between men and women was far more equal.[17] Unfortunately, as Beth learned, the tendency to shy away from participation in financial systems most often results in leaving money on the table.

The financial literacy gap also has real-world consequences when it comes to women's credit scores, retirement savings, mortgages, and overall financial health.[18] Financial health is defined as the state and stability of one's personal finances, including the amount of savings and debt you have, how much money you are putting away for retirement, and the percentage of your income that you spend on fixed expenses. It's an indication of one's overall financial resilience.

Keep in mind that women do not all need to become financial experts. Even slight gains in literacy can have big results, especially for those starting out at a low level. People with average and high levels of financial literacy see almost identical financial outcomes over the long term. It is those with low financial literacy who tend to fall behind.[19]

In addition to all of these consequences, the financial literacy gap also affects women's experience capital. As discussed previously, financial knowledge is a valuable skill in and of itself. Closing the literacy gap can therefore help women boost their lifetime earnings in two ways—by helping them learn an important skill to increase their experience capital and by making the money they earn work for them.

Tactics to Protect Your Financial Health

Here are a few important steps to consider as you increase your financial literacy and aim to improve your financial health:

- *Never hand over control of your finances.* If you get married, consider keeping at least one savings or checking account in your name only. Always be involved and fully aware of what is happening and of the key financial decisions that need to be made. If you are not already involved, pick one area at a time to get educated on. Ask questions, and be aware of the confidence gaps and the typical pitfalls that women fall into.

- *Set goals to help you stay focused.* What do you want to achieve financially in the next year, in the next five years, and over the long term? Who and what can help you achieve those goals?

- *Build emergency savings for yourself.* Early in your career, it is a good goal to be able to cover two or more months of your expenses without any income. That amount can grow as you progress in your career to provide up to six months of expenses. Having that amount of money set aside will protect you from a financial shock and give you the flexibility to quit your job and find a new one if you really need to. These savings are also known as an "F-U fund," since they can help you walk away from a bad job or situation if necessary.

- *Commit to savings in advance.* If you decide before you get a bonus that you will save a certain percentage of it, saving larger amounts over time becomes easier. For example, if you do not have significant debt, you could commit in advance to saving 60 percent of any bonus toward your retirement or a large investment like a house. An amount like that would make a significant difference. Given that people do not typically expect or budget for bonuses, saving a higher share of it should be easier.

- *Spend at least ten minutes a week reading a financial magazine or website.* You'll be surprised by how quickly you learn the basics and pick up valuable tips.

- *Pay attention to credit scores.* If it's relevant where you live, figure out how you can build your credit score. For example, open up a credit card, but only if you can make sure to pay off the balance every month. Some people purposefully charge a small amount on their credit card every month and pay it off to build a credit history.

- *Find a high-yield savings account.* Remember, if your money is not growing, it is actually shrinking in real terms.

- *Open a retirement account as early as possible.* Contribute as much as you can, especially in a tax-advantaged way if possible, and take advantage of all employer matches and contributions. "Pay yourself first" by investing in your retirement as early and as much as you can; the power of compound growth is key to maximizing your lifetime income. And try hard to avoid borrowing from your retirement accounts, since there are sometimes financial penalties for doing so, and you may also miss out on the tax advantages of retirement savings. Even a bank loan is often a better bet.

- *Protect yourself and your family.* Ensure that you have a will in place and also insurance for yourself and your family, if you have one. While everyone who has a car or house in the United States has insurance (given it is legally required), many people are underinsured in other areas. Disability insurance and life insurance are important for protecting your finances and spouse, partner, or children should anything happen to you.

Now that you have a good sense of the career pitfalls to avoid across bias, motherhood, physical health, and financial health, we will pull it all together with some key questions to reflect on as you chart your own career.

CONCLUSION

Realizing Your Full Potential

Although some of the facts that we've brought to light in this book may seem dire, we hope that the stories we've shared have given you the confidence you need to move forward with a sense of optimism. Your career path will be unique, so hopefully you've been inspired by the accomplishments of the dozens of trailblazing, courageous women we've described. Maybe you will connect the dots to found the next big company, like Caterina Fake, land a job that didn't exist a few years ago, like Kristie Lazenberry, or embrace your roots and challenge societal expectations and stereotypes, like Yeimy Báez.

You now have the two main tools you need to do these things and much more. The first is an understanding of the challenges you'll face in the workplace, so they don't catch you by surprise. And while we absolutely should and do expect organizations to make systemic changes toward creating more inclusive and diverse workplaces, we cannot simply wait. So, the second thing you now have is a set of strategies to navigate the speed bumps, such as making lateral and diagonal moves to the C-suite, like Rachel Robboy, traversing a great skill distance for greater fulfilment, like Holland Morris, or building a powerful network in all areas of life, like Susanne Prucha.

As you embark on your journey or seek to accelerate your progress, we would like to leave you with six questions to reflect on and to potentially discuss with your sponsors, mentors, and those closest to you. They will help you understand where you are on your journey toward accelerating your career and building your experience capital, and what you need to do if you choose to change course or pick up the pace.

What is my ambition and how can I embrace it?

The first step is to think through what your ambition is. It may have been clear to you for a long time, or you may be trying to clarify it now. Keep in mind that your ambition does not have to stay the same throughout your career. Reflecting on where your passion lies and what gives you the most energy can help point you in the right direction.

Whether you want to be promoted, to become CEO, or to make your mark on society, don't shy away from your goals. Women are just as ambitious as men—and often more so—yet they avoid voicing it out of fear that it will be held against them. While this fear may sometimes be valid, it is extremely challenging for us to achieve our goals if the people around us don't know what we want to achieve.

Think about the women in this book who boldly fought to achieve their aspirations, like Fuen Clemares, who wanted a specific role and asked her boss two all-important questions: "What are the gaps you see in my skill set and performance that I need to address? And how can I make sure that when the time comes, the decision-makers know me and feel comfortable putting me in the role?"

With your ambition in mind, it's never too early to start thinking about what's next and what you need to do to get there. Your company may or may not have a formal promotions structure. Either way, find out about the next logical role for someone in your position. See if you can talk to someone who is currently in that role and get a sense of how they spend their days, what they like and don't like about their jobs, and what skills help them thrive. Then ask yourself if this is a role you'd be excited about taking.

If the answer is yes, find out what others have done to get there, especially those who moved up quickly—what set them apart? If the answer is no, start talking to people in adjacent jobs, and keep expanding that circle until you find something that excites you.

At the same time, keep looking ahead to your bigger goals and to the paths that might lead there. Who is in the candidate pool for that dream job? How can you best position yourself to be in that pool? And who can you reach out to for support along the way?

Am I strategically building a portfolio of experiences to help me meet my ambitions?

Having excellent performance at work is critical for any level of advancement—it's table stakes. But it's not enough to complete the tasks that are assigned to you and expect a promotion—even if you complete those tasks exceptionally well.

Rather, combating the broken rungs and building experience capital require a shift in mindset, from focusing on doing your job to doing it while investing in building your career. Your job is simply the role and tasks assigned to you today. Your career, however, is the full trajectory of what you will accomplish throughout your professional life. To maximize your experience capital, you have to focus on both.

To build your career while doing your job, try to have bifocal vision. Think about the different experiences that will best position you for advancement, which may include a combination of P&L roles, leadership roles, and roles within companies that will provide opportunities for growth. And don't forget that the path that leads to your goal may not be straight. It may include lateral moves, diagonal moves, or even steps down. Don't fear these, but make sure they are keeping the curve of your experience capital steep.

Here, you may draw inspiration from women like Amy Weaver, who took not one but two steps down to move to a bigger company, where she proved herself as a leader and became the chief financial officer of one of the biggest tech companies in the world. Amy never could have predicted her path, and you can't see from your current position where your path is going, either. You can, however, look at the big picture of your career and make sure you are setting yourself up for future success.

What investments am I making in myself that will increase my chances of success?

Based on everything you've read, think about the specific skills you need to build in order to reach your goals. These may include hard skills that are required for a job, soft skills that are especially important in leaders, and entrepreneurial skills. It's also essential to invest in growing your network to multiply your experience capital. In fact, one of the best investments you can make in your future is to start strengthening your network on the first day of the job.

Once you know what types of skills and opportunities you need to invest in, make a plan to do so. A good goal is to spend 10 percent of your workweek investing in yourself and your career; this should come to about four or five hours a week. How can you best spend this time? You may want to look into enrolling in additional trainings, hiring a coach, attending conferences or networking events, or asking colleagues out for coffee. If possible, find opportunities to gain valuable skills that also count as part of your job, broadly defined. For instance, taking a negotiating course may make you more effective in your current role, plus you'll bring those new skills wherever your path may lead.

Karlie Kloss invested in herself by signing up for a coding class, not knowing that it would inspire her to start an organization that teaches tech skills to girls. Karlie has also used these skills to become a CEO and entrepreneur. Likewise, the skills you gain may take you to unexpected places, but betting on yourself and your potential is always a worthy investment.

Do I have the right short- and long-term habits in place to ensure my career longevity?

Your career encompasses so much more than just one specific role. That's why your long-term success depends on the big and small things you do, and don't do, each day and each year that keep you mentally, emotionally, physically, and financially healthy. Over time, these actions can add up to fuel your success, or they can keep the curve of your experience capital flattened.

Like Ja'Nay Hawkins, do you have a practice in place to connect with your story, your power, and your purpose? Do you make time to listen to the women in your world and act as an ally? Like Wendy Taccetta, are you intentional about where you put your limited energy? Do you have a habit of battling microaggressions with microinclusions?

While health and financial crises can happen, the habits that you establish in these areas can also set you up for long-term success or failure. Listen to Beth Smith's mother, and open high-yield savings and retirement accounts as soon as possible. Educate yourself about finances, and never hand complete control of your money over to someone else. Likewise, advocate for your health while taking care of your mind and body. Making sure you are getting adequate sleep, exercise, and nutrition will literally fuel your rise.

Am I asking for help?

One of the best investments you can make in your career is to focus on building a strong and supportive network that includes mentors and sponsors who can provide support, insights, feedback, and concrete opportunities. The importance of this in maximizing your experience capital cannot be overstated. But having a strong network is not enough. You also must leverage the network by asking for help when you need it and telling your mentors and sponsors exactly how they can support your growth.

Like Susanne Prucha, have you put together a personal board of directors to help you make important decisions? Are you sharing your ambitions with your manager so they can tell you exactly what you need to get there? And are you nurturing your network by creating an ethos of support that goes both ways? These steps will not only help you grow throughout your career but also make your work life far more satisfying and enjoyable.

Am I giving back to my communities and lifting others around me?

As we have discussed, you can begin to lift others around you at any stage of your career, but once you become a leader, you are in an ideal position to reach your hand back down the ladder and help other women avoid common pitfalls.

Think about what you are doing to help the women on your team build their experience capital. Put them on high-profile projects, invite them to important meetings, ask them to weigh in, and create space for them to present their work. Perhaps most important of all, sponsor more junior women, who are often over-mentored and under-sponsored.

At the same time, consider whether you are helping other women combat and reduce bias and microaggressions. If a male colleague (intentionally or not) tries to take credit for a woman's idea, you can make a comment like, "Yes, Jada was suggesting the same thing. That's a great idea." And when someone assumes that a woman is more junior than she is, which happens twice as often to women as it does to men, you can point out, "Mei is actually a manager. She did a lot of the research that you'll be hearing about today."

Make sure to call out women's successes to ensure that their work is visible to other leaders. You can send an email to share news about the win or announce it in a meeting. Doing so will help shape perceptions and open up more opportunities to advance.

Talk to the women on your team about their ambitions and career aspirations, and encourage them to bet on themselves and go after the next stretch opportunity. Make sure they know that you believe in them and in their ability to reach their goals. Offer frequent and direct feedback. As we discussed earlier, women and people of color often receive less challenging feedback than white men, which can keep them from improving in the ways they need in order to advance.

For now, we'd like to leave you with one last story that highlights the importance of giving back and lifting up the women who are coming behind you.

Raphaella Gomes is the CEO of New Gaia Strategies, an investment and consulting firm dedicated to spearheading the global shift toward sustainable energy practices and decarbonization. After graduating from law school, she worked at a firm where her boss specialized in mergers and acquisitions (M&A). When she started her job, she didn't even know what M&A meant. But she joined as many meetings as she could and took notes that served as her study guide so she could learn as much as possible.

One day, Raphaella's boss was negotiating a major deal and lost track of where they were on one of the key points. She referenced her notes, which held the answers, and her boss was grateful. After that, he began giving her more and more space to get involved in closing that deal.

Then, on the day they were set to close, Raphaella's boss called her early in the morning. "I'm sick," he told her. "I need you to go to the signing and fill in for me." She was surprised and nervous. "I can't do that," Raphaella told him. "No, no, you've got this," he assured her. "You worked hard on this deal, and you know as much about it as anyone. Besides, I need your help."

It took Raphaella many years to realize that her boss had not actually been sick that day. Instead, he had wanted to make her visible and give her an opportunity to feel what it was like to sign a deal that she had spent so much time on. As CEO many years later, she credits this moment as being pivotal for her career.

. . .

Remember that your ability to acquire experience capital is limitless. You can choose to carve out a career for yourself that fits your ambitions, your passions, and your individual goals. Your career path, choices, and the precise combination of your innate talents, education, skills, and experiences are unique to you. Now you have the tools to reach your full potential. While women may still be underrepresented in leadership, we can learn, draw from, and be uplifted by the experiences of the brilliant women whose stories we have shared of making it against the odds. And with your leadership, we can break the cycle by adding our stories and our voices to their ranks.

NOTES

Introduction

1. Alexis Krivkovich, Rachel Thomas, and Lareina Yee et al., "Women in the Workplace 2024: The 10th-Anniversary Report," McKinsey & Company and LeanIn.org, September 17, 2024, https://www.mckinsey.com/featured-insights/diversity-and-inclusion/women-in-the-workplace.

2. Alexis Krivkovich, Rachel Thomas, and Lareina Yee et al., "Women in the Workplace 2024."

3. Anu Madgavkar et al., "Human Capital at Work: The Value of Experience," McKinsey Global Institute, June 2, 2022, https://www.mckinsey.com/capabilities/people-and-organizational-performance/our-insights/human-capital-at-work-the-value-of-experience.

Chapter 1

1. Marilyn Loden, "100 Women: 'Why I Invented the Glass Ceiling Phrase,'" BBC, December 13, 2017, https://www.bbc.com/news/world-42026266.

2. "Good for Business: Making Full Use of the Nation's Human Capital," Glass Ceiling Commission, March 1995, https://ecommons.cornell.edu/handle/1813/79348.

3. Emma Hinchcliffe and Joey Abrams, "The Share of *Fortune* 500 Businesses Run by Women Can't Seem to Budge Beyond 10%," *Fortune*, June 4, 2024, https://fortune.com/2024/06/04/share-of-fortune-500-businesses-run-by-women/.

4. Alexis Krivkovich, Rachel Thomas, and Lareina Yee et al., "Women in the Workplace Report 2024: The 10th-Anniversary Report," McKinsey & Company and LeanIn.org, September 17, 2024, https://www.mckinsey.com/featured-insights/diversity-and-inclusion/women-in-the-workplace.

5. Alexis Krivkovich, Rachel Thomas, and Lareina Yee et al., "Women in the Workplace 2024."

6. Vivian Hunt et al., "Diversity Matters Even More: The Case for Holistic Impact," McKinsey & Company, December 5, 2023, https://www.mckinsey.com/featured-insights/diversity-and-inclusion/diversity-matters-even-more-the-case-for-holistic-impact; Alexis Krivkovich, Rachel Thomas, and Lareina Yee et al., "Women in the Workplace Report 2023," McKinsey & Company and LeanIn.org, 2023, https://www.mckinsey.com/featured-insights/diversity-and-inclusion/women-in-the-workplace-2023.

7. Alexis Krivkovich, Rachel Thomas, and Lareina Yee et al., "Women in the Workplace 2019," McKinsey & Company and LeanIn.Org, 2019, https://www.mckinsey.com/featured-insights/diversity-and-inclusion/women-in-the-workplace-archive#section-header-2019.

8. "The Sustainable Development Goals Report 2024," The United Nations, 2024, https://unstats.un.org/sdgs/report/2024/The-Sustainable-Development-Goals-Report-2024.pdf.

9. Lareina Yee et al., "Race in the Workplace: The Frontline Experience," McKinsey & Company, July 2022, https://www.mckinsey.com/featured-insights/diversity-and-inclusion/race-in-the-workplace-the-frontline-experience.

10. Lareina Yee et al., "Race in the Workplace."

11. Alexis Krivkovich, Rachel Thomas, and Lareina Yee et al., "Women in the Workplace Report 2024: The 10th-Anniversary Report," McKinsey & Company and LeanIn.org, September 17, 2024, https://www.mckinsey.com/featured-insights/diversity-and-inclusion/women-in-the-workplace.

12. Anu Madgavkar et al., "Human Capital at Work: The Value of Experience," McKinsey Global Institute, June 2, 2022, https://www.mckinsey.com/capabilities/people-and-organizational-performance/our-insights/human-capital-at-work-the-value-of-experience.

13. Alexis Krivkovich, Rachel Thomas, and Lareina Yee et al., "Women in the Workplace Report 2022," McKinsey & Company and LeanIn.org, 2022, https://www.mckinsey.com/featured-insights/diversity-and-inclusion/women-in-the-workplace.

14. Alexis Krivkovich, Rachel Thomas, and Lareina Yee et al., "Women in the Workplace 2022."

15. "Essential Elements of Employee Retention," Lynchburg Regional SHRM, October 29, 2017, https://lrshrm.shrm.org/blog/2017/10/essential-elements-employee-retention.

16. Vivian Hunt, "Diversity Matters Even More," 24.

17. Alexis Krivkovich, Rachel Thomas, and Lareina Yee et al., "Women in the Workplace 2022."

18. "State of the Global Workplace: 2022 Report," Gallup, May 2, 2023, https://www.cca-global.com/content/latest/article/2023/05/state-of-the-global-workplace-2022-report-346/.

19. Ken Moon et al., "The Hidden Cost of Worker Turnover: Attributing Product Reliability to the Turnover of Factory Workers," *Management Science* 68, no. 5 (2022): 3755–3767, https://doi.org/10.1287/mnsc.2022.4311.

Chapter 2

1. "43% of EU's 25–34-Year-Olds Have Tertiary Education," May 27, 2024, https://ec.europa.eu/eurostat/web/products-eurostat-news/w/ddn-20240527-1.

2. National Center for Education Statistics, "Table 318.10, Degrees Conferred by Postsecondary Institutions, by Level of Degree and Sex of Student: Selected Years, 1869–70 through 2031–32," https://nces.ed.gov/programs/digest/d23/tables/dt23_318.10.asp.

3. "Progress toward Gender Parity in Education Is Undeniable: 2020 Gender Report," UNESCO, https://gem-report-2020.unesco.org/gender-report/progress-towards-gender-parity-in-education-is-undeniable/; National Coalition for Women and Girls in Education, *Title IX at 45: Advancing Opportunity through Equity in Education* (Washington, DC: NCWGE, 2017), https://www.ncwge.org/TitleIX45/Title%20IX%20at%2045-Advancing%20Opportunity%20through%20Equity%20in%20Education.pdf; National Center for Education Statistics, "Table 318.10."

4. Anu Madgavkar et al., "Human Capital at Work: The Value of Experience," McKinsey Global Institute, June 2, 2022, https://www.mckinsey.com/capabilities

/people-and-organizational-performance/our-insights/human-capital-at-work-the
-value-of-experience.

5. Alexis Krivkovich, Rachel Thomas, and Lareina Yee et al., "Women in the
Workplace 2024: The 10th-Anniversary Report," McKinsey & Company and LeanIn
.org, September 17, 2024, https://www.mckinsey.com/featured-insights/diversity-and
-inclusion/women-in-the-workplace

6. Anu Madgavkar et al., "Human Capital at Work."

7. Anu Madgavkar et al., "Human Capital at Work."

8. Anu Madgavkar et al., "Human Capital at Work."

Chapter 3

1. Anu Madgavkar et al., "Human Capital at Work: The Value of Experience,"
McKinsey Global Institute, June 2, 2022, https://www.mckinsey.com/capabilities
/people-and-organizational-performance/our-insights/human-capital-at-work-the
-value-of-experience.

2. Anu Madgavkar et al., "Human Capital at Work."

3. Anu Madgavkar et al., "Human Capital at Work."

4. Peter Senge, *The Fifth Discipline: The Art and Practice of the Learning
Organization* (New York: Doubleday/Currency, 1990).

5. "Becoming Irresistible: A New Model for Employee Engagement," *Deloitte
Review*, no. 16, January 27, 2015, https://www2.deloitte.com/us/en/insights/deloitte
-review/issue-16/employee-engagement-strategies.html.

6. Paul Ashcroft, Simon Brown, and Garrick Jones, *The Curious Advantage*
(Laïki Publishing, 2020).

7. Chris Gagnon et al., "Organizational Health: A Fast Track to Performance
Improvement," McKinsey & Company, September 7, 2017, https://www.mckinsey
.com/capabilities/people-and-organizational-performance/our-insights/organizational
-health-a-fast-track-to-performance-improvement.

8. "About Six Sigma," Six Sigma, n.d., https://www.6sigma.us/six-sigma.php,
accessed September 4, 2024.

9. Jeffrey K. Liker, *The Toyota Way* (New York: McGraw-Hill, 2004).

10. Michael Timmes, "Internal Mobility: The Missing Piece of 2023 Business
Strategy," *Forbes*, February 17, 2023, https://www.forbes.com/sites/forbescoaches
council/2023/02/17/internal-mobility-the-missing-piece-of-2023-business
-strategy/.

11. Erica Volini et al., "Leading the Social Enterprise: Reinvent with a Human
Focus," Deloitte, 2019, https://www2.deloitte.com/content/dam/insights/us
/collections/HC-Trends2019/DI_HC-Trends-2019.pdf.

12. Vivian Hunt et al., "Diversity Matters Even More: The Case for Holistic
Impact," McKinsey & Company, December 5, 2023, exhibit 1, https://www.mckinsey
.com/featured-insights/diversity-and-inclusion/diversity-matters-even-more-the-case
-for-holistic-impact; David Rock and Heidi Grant, "Why Diverse Teams Are
Smarter," hbr.org, November 4, 2016, https://hbr.org/2016/11/why-diverse-teams-are
-smarter.

13. Vivian Hunt et al., "Diversity Matters Even More."

14. David Rock and Heidi Grant, "Why Diverse Teams Are Smarter."

15. Samuel R. Sommers, "On Racial Diversity and Group Decision Making:
Identifying Multiple Effects of Racial Composition on Jury Deliberations," *Journal of*

Personality and Social Psychology 90, no. 4 (2006): 597–612, https://www.apa.org/pubs/journals/releases/psp-904597.pdf.

16. Sheen S. Levine et al., "Ethnic Diversity Deflates Price Bubbles," *PNAS* 111, no. 52 (2014): 18524–18529, https://doi.org/10.1073/pnas.1407301111.

17. Alexis Krivkovich, Rachel Thomas, and Lareina Yee et al., "Women in the Workplace Report 2022," McKinsey & Company and LeanIn.org, 2022, https://www.mckinsey.com/featured-insights/diversity-and-inclusion/women-in-the-workplace.

18. Benjamin Artz, Amanda Goodall, and Andrew J. Oswald, "If Your Boss Could Do Your Job, You're More Likely to Be Happy at Work," hbr.org, December 29, 2016, https://hbr.org/2016/12/if-your-boss-could-do-your-job-youre-more-likely-to-be-happy-at-work.

19. Ruth Umoh, "Survey: When Considering a New Job, Men and Women Prioritize Different Things," CNBC, August 9, 2018, https://www.cnbc.com/2018/08/09/glassdoor-what-men-and-woman-look-for-in-a-new-job.html; André Dua et al., "How Does Gen Z See Its Place in the Working World? With Trepidation," McKinsey & Company, October 19, 2022, https://www.mckinsey.com/featured-insights/sustainable-inclusive-growth/future-of-america/how-does-gen-z-see-its-place-in-the-working-world-with-trepidation.

Chapter 4

1. Associated Press, "Here's Why Your Parents Stayed at the Same Job for 20 Years," *Fortune*, May 10, 2016, https://fortune.com/2016/05/10/baby-boomers-millennials-jobs/; "How Long Do Millennials Stay at a Job?" Zippia, June 29, 2022, https://www.zippia.com/answers/how-long-do-millennials-stay-at-a-job/.

2. Paul Davidson, "Millennials, Gen Xers to Baby Boomers: Can You Retire So I Can Get a Job Promotion?" *USA Today*, November 7, 2019, https://www.usatoday.com/story/money/2019/11/07/jobs-baby-boomers-older-workers-may-block-millennials-careers/4170836002/.

3. "Job Openings and Labor Turnover Survey," US Bureau of Labor Statistics, https://www.bls.gov/jlt/data.htm.

4. Adam Allington, "Poll: Age, Income Factors in Staying with Single Employer," Associated Press, May 11, 2016, https://apnews.com/article/29d99446a0e04120af539a2d911684e6.

5. "Stress in America: One Year Later, a New Wave of Pandemic Health Concerns," American Psychological Association, March 2021, https://www.apa.org/news/press/releases/stress/2021/sia-pandemic-report.pdf.

6. Peter Lauria, "5 Reasons People Are Changing Careers More Than Ever Before," US Chamber of Commerce, December 14, 2021, https://www.uschamber.com/workforce/5-reasons-people-are-changing-careers-more-than-ever-before.

7. Anu Madgavkar et al., "Human Capital at Work: The Value of Experience," McKinsey Global Institute, June 2, 2022, https://www.mckinsey.com/capabilities/people-and-organizational-performance/our-insights/human-capital-at-work-the-value-of-experience.

8. Anu Madgavkar et al., "Human Capital at Work."

9. Tara Sophia Mohr, "Why Women Don't Apply for Jobs Unless They're 100% Qualified," hbr.org, August 25, 2014, https://hbr.org/2014/08/why-women-dont-apply-for-jobs-unless-theyre-100-qualified.

10. Tara Sophia Mohr, "Why Women Don't Apply for Jobs Unless They're 100% Qualified."

11. Estera Barbarasa, Jacqueline Barrett, and Nicole Goldin, "Skills Gap or Signaling Gap? Insights from LinkedIn in Emerging Markets of Brazil, India, Indonesia, and South Africa," LinkedIn and Solutions for Youth Employment, 2017, https://economicgraph.linkedin.com/content/dam/me/economicgraph/en-us/download /Skills_Gap_or_Signalling_Gap.pdf.

Chapter 5

1. Stefanie O'Connell Rodriguez, "Stop Punishing Women for Being Ambitious," *Bloomberg*, May 24, 2021, https://www.bloomberg.com/opinion/articles/2021-05-24 /gender-equality-how-the-ambition-penalty-keeps-women-from-building-wealth.

2. "New DDI Research: 57 Percent of Employees Quit Because of Their Boss," PR Newswire, December 9, 2019, https://www.prnewswire.com/news-releases/new -ddi-research-57-percent-of-employees-quit-because-of-their-boss-300971506.html.

3. Asaf Levanon, Paula England, and Paul Allison, "Occupational Feminization and Pay: Assessing Causal Dynamics Using 1950–2000 US Census Data," *Social Forces* 88, no. 2 (December 2009): 865–891, https://doi.org/10.1353/sof.0.0264.

4. Alexis Krivkovich, Rachel Thomas, and Lareina Yee et al., "Women in the Workplace Report 2022," McKinsey & Company and LeanIn.org, 2022, https://www .mckinsey.com/featured-insights/diversity-and-inclusion/women-in-the-workplace-arc hive#section-header-2022.

5. Alexander Eser, "Female Breadwinner Statistics: Women Lead Household Finances Across Nations," ZipDo, July 25, 2024, https://zipdo.co/female-breadwinner -statistics/.

6. Richard Fry, Carolina Aragão, Kiley Hurst, and Kim Parker, "In a Growing Share of U.S. Marriages, Husbands and Wives Earn About the Same," *Pew Research Center*, April 13, 2023, https://www.pewresearch.org/social-trends/2023/04/13/in-a -growing-share-of-u-s-marriages-husbands-and-wives-earn-about-the-same.

7. Alexis Krivkovich, Rachel Thomas, and Lareina Yee et al., "Women in the Workplace 2022."

8. Alexis Krivkovich, Rachel Thomas, and Lareina Yee et al., "Women in the Workplace 2023," McKinsey & Company and LeanIn.org, 2023, https://www .mckinsey.com/featured-insights/diversity-and-inclusion/women-in-the-workplace -2023.

9. Alexis Krivkovich, Rachel Thomas, and Lareina Yee et al., "Women in the Workplace 2022."

10. Herminia Ibarra, Robin J. Ely, and Deborah M. Kolb, "Women Rising: The Unseen Barriers," *Harvard Business Review*, September 2013, https://hbr.org/2013/09 /women-rising-the-unseen-barriers.

11. Alexis Krivkovich, Rachel Thomas, and Lareina Yee et al., "Women in the Workplace 2022."

12. Anu Madgavkar et al., "Human Capital at Work: The Value of Experience," McKinsey Global Institute, June 2, 2022, https://www.mckinsey.com/capabilities /people-and-organizational-performance/our-insights/human-capital-at-work-the -value-of-experience.

13. Alexis Krivkovich, Rachel Thomas, and Lareina Yee et al., "Women in the Workplace 2024: The 10th-Anniversary Report," McKinsey & Company and LeanIn

.org, September 17, 2024, https://www.mckinsey.com/featured-insights/diversity-and
-inclusion/women-in-the-workplace.

14. Alexis Krivkovich, Rachel Thomas, and Lareina Yee et al., "Women in the
Workplace 2024."

15. Alexis Krivkovich, Rachel Thomas, and Lareina Yee et al., "Women in the
Workplace 2024."

16. Tacy M. Byham and Edie Fraser, "P&L Responsibility: Why Women Don't
Get to the C-Suite," DDI, November 18, 2020, https://www.ddiworld.com/blog/p-l
-responsibility-how-women-get-held-back-from-the-c-suite.

Chapter 6

1. Kweilin Ellingrud et al., "Generative AI and the Future of Work in America,"
McKinsey Global Institute, July 26, 2023, https://www.mckinsey.com/mgi/our
-research/generative-ai-and-the-future-of-work-in-america; Susan Lund et al., "The
Future of Work after Covid-19," McKinsey Global Institute, February 18, 2021,
https://www.mckinsey.com/featured-insights/future-of-work/the-future-of-work-after
-covid-19.

2. Lareina Yee et al., "The Economic Potential of Generative AI: The Next
Productivity Frontier," McKinsey & Company, June 14, 2023, https://www.mckinsey
.com/capabilities/mckinsey-digital/our-insights/the-economic-potential-of-generative
-ai-the-next-productivity-frontier.

3. Eric Hazan et al., "A New Future of Work: The Race to Deploy AI and Raise
Skills in Europe and Beyond," McKinsey Global Institute, May 21, 2024, https://www
.mckinsey.com/mgi/our-research/a-new-future-of-work-the-race-to-deploy-ai-and
-raise-skills-in-europe-and-beyond.

4. Kweilin Ellingrud et al., "Generative AI and the Future of Work in America."

5. World Bank, "Databank Gender Statistics," World Bank Group, n.d.,
https://databank.worldbank.org/source/gender-statistics/Series/SP.POP.DPND,
accessed September 4, 2024.

6. Heather McMullen and Katharine Dow, "Ringing the Existential Alarm:
Exploring BirthStrike for Climate," *Medical Anthropology* 41, no. 6–7 (2022):
659–673, doi:10.1080/01459740.2022.2083510.

7. Kweilin Ellingrud et al., "Generative AI and the Future of Work in America."

8. Kweilin Ellingrud et al., "Generative AI and the Future of Work in America."

9. James Manyika et al., "Jobs Lost, Jobs Gained: What the Future of Work Will
Mean for Jobs, Skills, and Wages," McKinsey Global Institute, November 28, 2017,
https://www.mckinsey.com/featured-insights/future-of-work/jobs-lost-jobs-gained
-what-the-future-of-work-will-mean-for-jobs-skills-and-wages.

10. "Weinreb Group Presents Its CSO Findings for 2018," Weinreb Group, 2018,
https://weinrebgroup.com/cso-update-december-2018/.

11. Kweilin Ellingrud et al., "Generative AI and the Future of Work in America."

12. Alexis Krivkovich, Rachel Thomas, and Lareina Yee et al., "Women in the
Workplace 2024: The 10th-Anniversary Report," McKinsey & Company and LeanIn
.org, September 17, 2024, https://www.mckinsey.com/featured-insights/diversity-and
-inclusion/women-in-the-workplace..

13. Clifford Chen et al., "Supporting Employees in the Work-Life Balancing Act,"
McKinsey & Company, February 14, 2022, https://www.mckinsey.com/featured
-insights/diversity-and-inclusion/supporting-employees-in-the-work-life-balancing-act.

Chapter 7

1. "Eighty Percent of Professionals Consider Networking Important to Career Success," LinkedIn, June 22, 2017, https://news.linkedin.com/2017/6/eighty-percent -of-professionals-consider-networking-important-to-career-success.

2. Gina Belli, "At Least 70% of Jobs Are Not Even Listed—Here's How to Up Your Chances of Getting a Great New Gig," *Business Insider*, April 10, 2017, https://www.businessinsider.com/at-least-70-of-jobs-are-not-even-listed-heres-how-to -up-your-chances-of-getting-a-great-new-gig-2017-4; Meg Garlinghouse, "Closing the Network Gap," LinkedIn, September 26, 2019, https://www.linkedin.com/blog /member/impact/closing-the-network-gap.

3. Alexis Krivkovich, Rachel Thomas, and Lareina Yee et al., "Women in the Workplace Report 2022," McKinsey & Company and LeanIn.org, 2022, https://www .mckinsey.com/featured-insights/diversity-and-inclusion/women-in-the-workplace-arc hive#section-header-2022.

4. Alexis Krivkovich, Rachel Thomas, and Lareina Yee et al., "Women in the Workplace 2017," McKinsey & Company and LeanIn.org, October 2017, https:// www.mckinsey.com/featured-insights/diversity-and-inclusion/women-in-the-workplace -archive#section-header-2017.

5. Kate den Houter and Ellyn Maese, "Mentors and Sponsors Make the Difference," Gallup, April 13, 2023, https://www.gallup.com/workplace/473999/mentors -sponsors-difference.aspx.

6. Michael Simmons, "How Big Should Your Network Be?" *Forbes*, March 20, 2014, https://www.forbes.com/sites/michaelsimmons/2014/01/02/how-big-should -your-network-be.

7. Alexis Krivkovich, Rachel Thomas, and Lareina Yee et al., "Women in the Workplace Report 2021," McKinsey & Company and LeanIn.org https://www .mckinsey.com/featured-insights/diversity-and-inclusion/women-in-the-workplace-arc hive#section-header-2021.

8. Lareina Yee et al., "Race in the Workplace: The Frontline Experience," McKinsey & Company, July 2022, https://www.mckinsey.com/featured-insights /diversity-and-inclusion/race-in-the-workplace-the-frontline-experience.

9. "Workforce Report December 2020," LinkedIn, December 3, 2020, https:// economicgraph.linkedin.com/resources/linkedin-workforce-report-december-2020.

10. Herminia Ibarra and Otilia Obodaru, "Women and the Vision Thing," hbr .org, January 2009, https://hbr.org/2009/01/women-and-the-vision-thing.

11. Zoë Ziani, "The Hurdles Women Face When Networking," Organizational Plumber, July 26, 2023, https://www.theorgplumber.com/posts/women-and -networking/.

12. Elena Greguletz, Marjo-Riitta Diehl, and Karin Kreutzer, "Why Women Build Less Effective Networks Than Men: The Role of Structural Exclusion and Personal Hesitation," *Human Relations* 72, no. 7 (2019): 1234–1261, https://doi.org /10.1177/0018726718804303.

13. Alexis Krivkovich, Rachel Thomas, and Lareina Yee et al., "Women in the Workplace 2024: The 10th-Anniversary Report," McKinsey & Company and LeanIn .org, September 17, 2024, https://www.mckinsey.com/featured-insights/diversity-and -inclusion/women-in-the-workplace.

14. Taylor Lauricella et al., "Network Effects: How to Rebuild Social Capital and Improve Corporate Performance," McKinsey & Company, August 2, 2022,

https://www.mckinsey.com/capabilities/people-and-organizational-performance/our
-insights/network-effects-how-to-rebuild-social-capital-and-improve-corporate
-performance.

15. Lareina Yee et al., "Race in the Workplace."

16. Alexis Krivkovich, Rachel Thomas, and Lareina Yee et al., "Women in the
Workplace Report 2022."

17. Sylvia Ann Hewlett, "Make Yourself Safe for Sponsorship," hbr.org, October 7, 2013, https://hbr.org/2013/10/make-yourself-safe-for-sponsorship.

Chapter 8

1. Sapana Agrawal, "Beyond Hiring: How Companies Are Reskilling to Address
Talent Gaps," McKinsey & Company, January 2020, https://www.mckinsey.com/~
/media/McKinsey/Business%20Functions/Organization/Our%20Insights/Beyond%20
hiring%20How%20companies%20are%20reskilling%20to%20address%20talent
%20gaps/Beyond-hiring-How-companies-are-reskilling.pdf.

2. Lareina Yee et al., "The Economic Potential of Generative AI: The Next
Productivity Frontier," McKinsey & Company, June 14, 2023, https://www.mckinsey
.com/capabilities/mckinsey-digital/our-insights/the-economic-potential-of-generative
-ai-the-next-productivity-frontier/.

3. Kweilin Ellingrud et al., "Generative AI and the Future of Work in America,"
McKinsey Global Institute, July 26, 2023, https://www.mckinsey.com/mgi/our
-research/generative-ai-and-the-future-of-work-in-america; Yee et al., "The Economic
Potential of Generative AI."

4. "Stanford Professor Erik Brynjolfsson on How AI Will Transform Productivity," *Microsoft WorkLab* podcast, March 22, 2023, https://www.microsoft.com/en-us
/worklab/podcast/stanford-professor-erik-brynjolfsson-on-how-ai-will-transform
-productivity.

5. Lareina Yee et al., "McKinsey Technology Trends Outlook 2024," McKinsey
& Company, July 16, 2024, https://www.mckinsey.com/capabilities/mckinsey-digital
/our-insights/the-top-trends-in-tech.

6. "Employed Persons by Detailed Occupation, Sex, Race, and Hispanic or
Latino Ethnicity," US Bureau of Labor Statistics, 2017–2023, https://www.bls.gov/cps
/cpsaat11.htm.

7. "Girls Are Now Performing the Same as Boys in Mathematics," UNESCO,
April 27, 2022, https://world-education-blog.org/2022/04/27/girls-are-now
-performing-the-same-as-boys-in-mathematics/.

8. Penelope Espinoza, Ana B. Arêas da Luz Fontes, and Clarissa J. Arms-Chavez,
"Attributional Gender Bias: Teachers' Ability and Effort Explanations for Students'
Math Performance," *Social Psychology Education* 17 (2014): 105–126, https://doi.org
/10.1007/s11218-013-9226-6.

9. "Tenure/Tenure-Track Faculty Levels," Society of Women Engineers, n.d.,
https://swe.org/research/2024/tenure-tenure-track-faculty-levels/, accessed September 9, 2024.

10. Sven Blumberg et al., "Women in Tech: The Best Bet to Solve Europe's Talent
Shortage," McKinsey & Company, January 24, 2023, https://www.mckinsey.com
/capabilities/mckinsey-digital/our-insights/women-in-tech-the-best-bet-to-solve
-europes-talent-shortage.

11. Adriana Gascoigne et al., "Repairing the Broken Rung on the Career Ladder
for Women in Technical Roles," McKinsey & Company, March 1, 2022, https://www

.mckinsey.com/industries/technology-media-and-telecommunications/our-insights
/repairing-the-broken-rung-on-the-career-ladder-for-women-in-technical-roles.

12. Alexis Krivkovich, Rachel Thomas, and Lareina Yee et al., "Women in the Workplace Report 2022," McKinsey & Company and LeanIn.org, 2022, https://www
.mckinsey.com/featured-insights/diversity-and-inclusion/women-in-the-workplace-arc
hive#section-header-2022.

13. Jacques Bughin et al., "Skill Shift: Automation and the Future of the Work-force," McKinsey & Company, May 23, 2018, https://www.mckinsey.com/featured
-insights/future-of-work/skill-shift-automation-and-the-future-of-the-workforce.

14. Rachel Thomas, "The Real Reason Women Quit Tech (and How to Address It)," Medium, October 3, 2016, https://medium.com/tech-diversity-files/the-real
-reason-women-quit-tech-and-how-to-address-it-6dfb606929fd.

15. Rik Kirkland, "How Google.org Is Helping Workers Prepare for a Digital Skill Shift," McKinsey & Company, November 16, 2018, https://www.mckinsey.com
/featured-insights/future-of-work/how-google-dot-org-is-helping-workers-prepare-for
-a-digital-skill-shift.

Chapter 9

1. Jennifer Parlamis and Matthew J. Monnot, "Getting to the CORE: Putting an End to the Term 'Soft Skills,'" *Journal of Management Inquiry* 28, no. 2 (2019): 225–227, https://doi.org/10.1177/1056492618818023.

2. Renyi Hong, "Soft Skills and Hard Numbers: Gender Discourse in Hu-man Resources," *Big Data and Society* 3, no. 2 (2016), https://doi.org/10.1177
/2053951716674237.

3. Julie Avrane-Chopard and Jaime Potter, "Are Hard and Soft Skills Rewarded Equally?" McKinsey & Company, November 4, 2019, https://www.mckinsey.com
/capabilities/people-and-organizational-performance/our-insights/the-organization
-blog/are-hard-and-soft-skills-rewarded-equally.

4. Philip Moss and Chris Tilly, "'Soft' Skills and Race: An Investigation of Black Men's Employment Problems," *Work and Occupations* 23, no. 3 (1996): 252–276, https://doi.org/10.1177/0730888496023003002.

5. Margaret M. Zamudio and Michael I. Lichter, "Bad Attitudes and Good Soldiers: Soft Skills as a Code for Tractability in the Hiring of Immigrant Latina/os over Native Blacks in the Hotel Industry," *Social Problems* 55, no. 4 (Novem-ber 2008): 573–589, https://doi.org/10.1525/sp.2008.55.4.573.

6. Jacques Bughin et al., "Skill Shift: Automation and the Future of the Work-force," McKinsey & Company, May 23, 2018, https://www.mckinsey.com/featured
-insights/future-of-work/skill-shift-automation-and-the-future-of-the-workforce.

7. Marco Dondi et al., "Defining the Skills Citizens Will Need in the Future World of Work," McKinsey & Company, June 25, 2021, https://www.mckinsey.com
/industries/public-sector/our-insights/defining-the-skills-citizens-will-need-in-the
-future-world-of-work.

8. James Manyika et al., "Jobs Lost, Jobs Gained: What the Future of Work Will Mean for Jobs, Skills, and Wages," McKinsey Global Institute, November 28, 2017, https://www.mckinsey.com/featured-insights/future-of-work/jobs-lost-jobs-gained
-what-the-future-of-work-will-mean-for-jobs-skills-and-wages.

9. Pablo Illanes et al., "Retraining and Reskilling Workers in the Age of Automa-tion," McKinsey & Company, January 22, 2018, https://www.mckinsey.com/featured
-insights/future-of-work/retraining-and-reskilling-workers-in-the-age-of-automation.

10. Aaron De Smet et al., "The Great Attrition Is Making Hiring Harder. Are You Searching the Right Talent Pools?" McKinsey & Company, July 13, 2022, https://www.mckinsey.com/capabilities/people-and-organizational-performance/our-insights/the-great-attrition-is-making-hiring-harder-are-you-searching-the-right-talent-pools.

Chapter 10

1. Gonzalo Charro, "American Opportunity Survey: Inflation-Weary Americans Are Increasingly Pessimistic about the Economy," McKinsey & Company, December 13, 2022, https://www.mckinsey.com/featured-insights/sustainable-inclusive-growth/future-of-america/american-opportunity-survey.

2. Matthew Smith et al., "Capitalists in the Twenty-First Century," *Quarterly Journal of Economics* 134, no. 4 (2019): 1675–1745.

3. Amanda Elam, Karen D. Hughes, and Mahsa Samsami, "GEM 2022/23 Women's Entrepreneurship Report: Challenging Bias and Stereotypes," Global Entrepreneurship Monitor, 2023, https://www.gemconsortium.org/report/gem-20222023-womens-entrepreneurship-challenging-bias-and-stereotypes-2.

4. Victoria Masterson, "Here's What Women's Entrepreneurship Looks Like Around the World," World Economic Forum, July 20, 2022, https://www.weforum.org/agenda/2022/07/women-entrepreneurs-gusto-gender.

5. Amanda Elam, "GEM 2022/23 Women's Entrepreneurship Report."

6. Pino G. Audia and Christopher I. Rider, "Entrepreneurs as Organizational Products Revisited," in J. Robert Baum, Michael Frese, and Robert A. Baron (Eds.), *The Psychology of Entrepreneurship* (New York: Psychology Press, 2014).

7. January Ventures, "Jane VC Founder Survey Reveals Inequities in Tech Start Early," Medium, March 21, 2019, https://medium.com/janeventurecapital/jane-vc-founder-survey-reveals-inequities-in-tech-start-early-bb55a443d703; Dana Kanze et al., "Male and Female Entrepreneurs Get Asked Different Questions by VCs—and It Affects How Much Funding They Get," hbr.org, June 27, 2017, https://hbr.org/2017/06/male-and-female-entrepreneurs-get-asked-different-questions-by-vcs-and-it-affects-how-much-funding-they-get.

8. Ned Desmond, "The First Comprehensive Study on Women in Venture Capital and Their Impact on Female Founders," TechCrunch, April 19, 2016, https://techcrunch.com/2016/04/19/the-first-comprehensive-study-on-women-in-venture-capital/; Barbara Orser, Allan Riding, and Kathryn Manley, "Women Entrepreneurs and Financial Capital," *Entrepreneurship Theory and Practice* 30 (2006): 643–665.

9. Alexander Kersten and Gabrielle Athanasia, "Addressing the Gender Imbalance in Venture Capital and Entrepreneurship," CSIS, October 20, 2022, https://www.csis.org/analysis/addressing-gender-imbalance-venture-capital-and-entrepreneurship.

10. Pontus Alverstad et al., "The State of Diversity in Global Private Markets: 2022," McKinsey & Company, November 1, 2022, https://www.mckinsey.com/industries/private-capital/our-insights/the-state-of-diversity-in-global-private-markets-2022.

11. Surya Fackelmann and Alessandro De Concini, "Funding Women Entrepreneurs: How to Empower Growth," European Investment Bank, June 2020, https://www.eib.org/attachments/thematic/why_are_women_entrepreneurs_missing_out_on_funding_en.pdf.

12. Katie Abouzahr et al., "Why Women-Owned Startups Are a Better Bet," Boston Consulting Group, June 6, 2018, https://www.bcg.com/publications/2018/why-women-owned-startups-are-better-bet.

13. "Women Entrepreneur Series," Citigroup, n.d., https://www.citigroup.com /global/insights/citigps/women-entrepreneurs-series, accessed June 2024.

14. Adam Hayes, "Entrepreneur: What It Means to Be One and How to Get Started," Investopedia, updated July 29, 2024, https://www.investopedia.com/terms/e /entrepreneur.asp.

Chapter 11

1. Alexis Krivkovich, Rachel Thomas, and Lareina Yee et al., "Women in the Workplace 2024: The 10th-Anniversary Report," McKinsey & Company and LeanIn .org, September 17, 2024, https://www.mckinsey.com/featured-insights/diversity-and -inclusion/women-in-the-workplace.

2. M. José González, Clara Cortina, and Jorge Rodríguez, "The Role of Gender Stereotypes in Hiring: A Field Experiment," *European Sociological Review* 35, no. 2 (April 2019): 187–204, https://doi.org/10.1093/esr/jcy055.

3. Patrick M. Kline, Evan K. Rose, and Christopher R. Walters, "Systemic Discrimination among Large U.S. Employers," NBER working paper 29053, https:// www.nber.org/system/files/working_papers/w29053/revisions/w29053.rev2.pdf.

4. Sonia Kang et al., "Whitened Résumés: Race and Self-Presentation in the Labor Market," Rotman School of Management, January 22, 2016, https://www-2 .rotman.utoronto.ca/facbios/file/Whitening%20MS%20R2%20Accepted.pdf.

5. Amy Diehl, Amber L. Stephenson, and Leanne M. Dzubinski, "Research: How Bias Against Women Persists in Female-Dominated Workplaces," hbr.org, March 2, 2022, https://hbr.org/2022/03/research-how-bias-against-women-persists-in-female -dominated-workplaces.

6. Alexis Krivkovich, Rachel Thomas, and Lareina Yee et al., "Women in the Workplace 2024."

7. Dina Gerdeman, "Why Employers Favor Men," HBS Working Knowledge, September 11, 2017, https://hbswk.hbs.edu/item/why-employers-favor-men.

8. Alice H. Eagly and Steven J. Karau, "Role Congruity Theory of Prejudice toward Female Leaders," *Psychological Review* 109, no. 3 (2002): 573–598, https:// doi.org/10.1037//0033-295X.109.3.573.

9. Iris Bohnet, *What Works: Gender Equality by Design* (Cambridge, MA: Harvard University Press, 2016).

10. Hannah Riley Bowles, Linda Babcock, and Lei Lai, "Social Incentives for Gender Differences in the Propensity to Initiate Negotiations: Sometimes It Does Hurt to Ask," *Organizational Behavior and Human Decision Processes* 103, no. 1 (2007): 84–103, https://doi.org/10.1016/j.obhdp.2006.09.001.

11. Donna Chrobot-Mason, Jenny M. Hoobler, and Jasmine Burno, "*Lean In* Versus the Literature: An Evidence-Based Examination," *Academy of Management Perspectives* 33, no. 1 (2019): 110–130, https://doi.org/10.5465/amp.2016.0156.

12. Raina A. Brands and Isabel Fernandez-Mateo, "Leaning Out: How Negative Recruitment Experiences Shape Women's Decisions to Compete for Executive Roles," *Administrative Science Quarterly* 62, no. 3 (2017): 405–442, https://doi.org/10.1177 /0001839216682728.

13. Lean In, "50 Ways to Fight Bias," LeanIn.org, n.d., https://leanin.org/50-ways -to-fight-gender-bias, accessed September 9, 2024.

14. Kevin Donahue et al., "The Infuriating Journey from Pet to Threat: How Bias Undermines Black Women at Work," *Forbes*, March 3, 2022, https://www.forbes.com

/sites/forbeseq/2021/06/29/the-infuriating-journey-from-pet-to-threat-how-bias
-undermines-black-women-at-work/.

15. Bright Horizons, "Modern Family Index Shows Real Motherhood Penalty in American Workplace," Bright Horizons press release, January 28, 2019, https:// investors.brighthorizons.com/node/11401/pdf.

16. Fernanda Staniscuaski et al., "Bias Against Parents in Science Hits Women Harder," *Humanities and Social Sciences Communications* 10 (2023), https://doi.org /10.1057/s41599-023-01722-x.

17. Raviv Murciano-Goroff, "Missing Women in Tech: The Labor Market for Highly Skilled Software Engineers," *Management Science* 68, no. 5 (2022): 3262–3281.

18. Christine L. Exley and Judd B. Kessler, "The Gender Gap in Self-Promotion," NBER working paper 26345, October 2019, https://www.nber.org/system/files /working_papers/w26345/w26345.pdf.

19. Georges Desvaux, Sandrine Devillard-Hoellinger, and Pascal Baumgarten, "Women Matter: Gender Diversity, a Corporate Performance Driver," McKinsey & Company, 2007, https://www.mckinsey.com/~/media/mckinsey/dotcom/client_service /organization/pdfs/women_matter_oct2007_english.ashx.

20. "Why Women Are Less Confident and What We Need to Do to Change That," Bright Network, n.d., https://www.brightnetwork.co.uk/equal-opportunities-menu/why -women-are-less-confident-and-what-we-need-do-change/, accessed September 9, 2024.

21. Alexis Krivkovich, Rachel Thomas, and Lareina Yee et al., "Women in the Workplace 2023," McKinsey & Company and LeanIn.org, https://www.mckinsey .com/featured-insights/diversity-and-inclusion/women-in-the-workplace-2023.

22. Alexis Krivkovich, Rachel Thomas, and Lareina Yee et al., "Women in the Workplace Report 2022," McKinsey & Company and LeanIn.org, 2022, https://www .mckinsey.com/featured-insights/diversity-and-inclusion/women-in-the-workplace-arc hive#section-header-2022; Alexis Krivkovich, Rachel Thomas, and Lareina Yee et al., "Women in the Workplace Report 2024."

23. Alexis Krivkovich, Rachel Thomas, and Lareina Yee et al., "Women in the Workplace Report 2023."

24. Gregg A. Muragishi et al., "Microinclusions: Treating Women as Respected Work Partners Increases a Sense of Fit in Technology Companies," *Journal of Personality and Social Psychology* 126, no. 3 (2024): 431–460, https://psycnet.apa.org/doi/10.1037 /pspi0000430.

25. Shelley J. Correll and Caroline Simard, "Research: Vague Feedback Is Holding Women Back," hbr.org, April 29, 2016, https://hbr.org/2016/04/research-vague -feedback-is-holding-women-back.

26. Melanie Sanders et al., "Advancing Women in Australia: Eliminating Bias in Feedback and Promotions," Bain & Company, March 1, 2017, https://www.bain.com /insights/advancing-women-in-australia-eliminating-bias-in-feedback/.

27. "What Is Likability Bias and What to Do About It," Drive, n.d., https://www .enterprisedrive.co.uk/iwd-2022-what-is-likability-bias-and-what-to-do-about-it/, accessed June 2024.

28. Alexis Krivkovich, Rachel Thomas, and Lareina Yee et al., "Women in the Workplace Report 2022."

29. Erin Eatough, "Defining the Gender Gap in Coaching: What It Is and How to Fix It," BetterUp, April 6, 2021, https://www.betterup.com/blog/coaching-gender -gap.

30. Elizabeth Weingarten, "Coaching Underrepresented Women: How Coaches Create a Ripple Effect of Inclusion," Torch, March 29, 2023, https://torch.io/blog/coaching-underrepresented-women-how-coaches-create-a-ripple-effect-of-inclusion/.

31. Lean In, "50 Ways to Fight Bias."

Chapter 12

1. Shelley J. Correll, Stephen Benard, and In Paik, "Getting a Job: Is There a Motherhood Penalty?" *American Journal of Sociology* 112, no. 5 (2007), https://doi.org/10.1086/511799.

2. Marianne Bertrand, Claudia Goldin, and Lawrence F. Katz, "Dynamics of the Gender Gap for Young Professionals in the Financial and Corporate Sectors," *American Economic Journal: Applied Economics* 2, no. 3 (July 2010): 228–255, https://www.aeaweb.org/articles.php?doi=10.1257/app.2.3.228.

3. Shelley J. Correll et al., "Getting a Job: Is There a Motherhood Penalty?"

4. "How Big Is the Wage Penalty for Mothers?," *Economist*, January 28, 2019, https://www.economist.com/graphic-detail/2019/01/28/how-big-is-the-wage-penalty-for-mothers.

5. Joan C. Williams, "How to Deal with Bias Against Working Moms," LeanIn.org, video, 08:32, https://leanin.org/education/what-works-for-women-at-work-part-3-maternal-wall.

6. "Employment Characteristics of Families—2023," US Department of Labor, Bureau of Labor Statistics, press release, April 24, 2024, https://www.bls.gov/news.release/pdf/famee.pdf.

7. "LMF1.2 Maternal Employment," in the OECD Family Database, OECD, June 21, 2024, https://web-archive.oecd.org/temp/2024-06-21/69263-database.htm.

8. Susan Harkness, Magda Borkowska, and Alina Pelikh, "Employment Pathways and Occupational Change After Childbirth," UK Government Equalities Office, October 22, 2019, https://www.gov.uk/government/publications/employment-pathways-and-occupational-change-after-childbirth.

9. "How Women's Employment Changes After Having a Child," Understanding Society: The UK Household Longitudinal Study, October 22, 2019, https://www.understandingsociety.ac.uk/news/2019/10/22/how-womens-employment-changes-after-having-a-child/.

10. Ashley Stahl, "New Study: Millennial Women Are Delaying Having Children Due to Their Careers," *Forbes*, updated December 10, 2021, https://www.forbes.com/sites/ashleystahl/2020/05/01/new-study-millennial-women-are-delaying-having-children-due-to-their-careers/.

11. Lorraine Hariton, "5 Challenges Women Face in the New, Uncertain Workplace," Catalyst, August 25, 2021, https://www.catalyst.org/2021/08/25/women-workplace-challenges-covid/.

Chapter 13

1. "Menopause in the Workplace," Carrot, n.d., https://content.get-carrot.com/rs/418-PQJ-171/images/Carrot%20-%20Menopause%20in%20the%20workplace.pdf, accessed September 9, 2024.

2. The next two sections draw data from Kweilin Ellingrud et al., "Closing the Women's Health Gap: A $1 Trillion Opportunity to Improve Lives and Economies,"

McKinsey & Company, January 17, 2024, https://www.mckinsey.com/mhi/our-insights/closing-the-womens-health-gap-a-1-trillion-dollar-opportunity-to-improve-lives-and-economies.

3. "2021 NSDUH Detailed Tables," Substance Abuse and Mental Health Services Administration, January 4, 2023, https://www.samhsa.gov/data/report/2021-nsduh-detailed-tables.

4. Jessica A. Mong and Danielle M. Cusmano, "Sex Differences in Sleep: Impact of Biological Sex and Sex Steroids," *Philosophical Transactions of the Royal Society of London, Series B, Biological Sciences* 371, no. 1688 (2016): 20150110, doi:10.1098/rstb.2015.0110; Chiara Baglioni et al., "Insomnia as a Predictor of Depression: A Meta-Analytic Evaluation of Longitudinal Epidemiological Studies," *Journal of Affective Disorders* 135, no. 1–3 (December 2011): 10–19, https://doi.org/10.1016/j.jad.2011.01.011; Elisabeth Hertenstein et al., "Insomnia as a Predictor of Mental Disorders: A Systematic Review and Meta-Analysis," *Sleep Medicine Reviews* 43 (2019): 96–105, https://doi.org/10.1016/j.smrv.2018.10.006.

5. Catherine Cote, "Growth Mindset vs. Fixed Mindset: What's the Difference?" Harvard Business School Online Business Insights, March 10, 2022, https://online.hbs.edu/blog/post/growth-mindset-vs-fixed-mindset.

6. Lauren A. Wise et al., "Leisure Time Physical Activity in Relation to Depressive Symptoms in the Black Women's Health Study," *Annals of Behavioral Medicine: A Publication of the Society of Behavioral Medicine* 32, no. 1 (2006): 68–76.

7. Ben Singh et al., "Effectiveness of Physical Activity Interventions for Improving Depression, Anxiety, and Distress: An Overview of Systematic Reviews," *British Journal of Sports Medicine* 57, no. 18 (2023): 1203–1209.

8. Richard P. Troiano et al., "Physical Activity in the United States Measured by Accelerometer," *Medicine and Science in Sports and Exercise* 40, no. 1 (2008): 181–188; Philip R. Nader et al., "Moderate-to-Vigorous Physical Activity from Ages 9 to 15 Years," *JAMA* 300, no. 3 (2008): 295–305.

9. Aneeque Jamil et al., "Meditation and Its Mental and Physical Health Benefits in 2023," *Cureus* 15, no. 6 (2023): e40650.

10. Lurit Yugusuk, "The $100-Trillion Gender Wealth Gap Is an Outrage: Can Davos Get Behind a Global Economy That Actually Works for Women?" *Views & Voices*, January 17, 2024, https://views-voices.oxfam.org.uk/2024/01/100-trillion-gender-wealth-gap-davos-economy-for-women/.

11. "The Gender Gap and Retirement," Fidelity, September 20, 2023, https://www.fidelity.com/learning-center/personal-finance/gender-gap-retirement.

12. Karen Bennett, "Building Financial Independence for Women through Financial Literacy," Bankrate, March 27, 2024, https://www.bankrate.com/banking/women-and-financial-literacy/.

13. Peter C. Fisk, "Gender Gap in Financial Literacy Transcends National Borders," March 2015, US Bureau of Labor Statistics, https://www.bls.gov/opub/mlr/2015/beyond-bls/gender-gap-in-financial-literacy-transcends-national-borders.htm.

14. Tabea Bucher-Koenen et al., "Fearless Woman: Financial Literacy and Stock Market Participation," Global Financial Literacy Excellence Center, March 2021, https://gflec.org/wp-content/uploads/2021/03/Fearless-Woman-Research-March-2021.pdf.

15. Sigurður Guðjónsson et al., "Knowing More Than Own Mother, Yet Not Enough: Secondary School Students' Experience of Financial Literacy Education," *Pedagogika* 145, no. 1 (2022): 5–21.

16. Ludovic Subran et al., "Playing with a Squared Ball: The Financial Literacy Gender Gap," Allianz, July 23, 2023, https://www.allianz.com/content/dam /onemarketing/azcom/Allianz_com/economic-research/publications/specials/en/2023 /july/2023-07-27-Financial-Literacy.pdf.

17. Johan Almenberga and Anna Dreber, "Gender, Stock Market Participation, and Financial Literacy," *SSRN Electronic Journal* 137 (2012): 140–142.

18. Sigurður Guðjónsson et al., "Financial Literacy and Gender Differences: Women Choose People While Men Choose Things?" *Administrative Sciences* 12, no. 4 (2022): 179.

19. Meghan Greene, Andrew Warren, and Jess McKay, "The Gender Gap in Financial Health," Financial Health Network, July 14, 2022, https://finhealthnetwork .org/research/gender-gap-in-financial-health/.

INDEX

ACKNOWLEDGMENTS

We are deeply grateful for our family, friends, and colleagues who helped create this book, which is an expression of what we have learned collectively over our lives. Jodi Lipper was our incredible writing partner who shared our vision of making something unique for women to harness their power in the workplace. She brought immense talent, experience, and personal passion to our project—as the mother of two fabulous daughters and as an entrepreneur herself. She also had an amazing ability to hear leaders' stories and draw out the unique insights.

Our work is the result of the research we led with many brilliant friends and colleagues. We would like to thank Alexis Krivkovich for her bold leadership as the cofounder of McKinsey's Women in the Workplace research initiative and a driving force behind many of the insights shared in this book. She leads by example and has helped countless women improve their odds of success.

The Women in the Workplace team has been shaped by remarkable leaders over the years, including Kelsey Robinson, Marie-Claude Nadeau, Jess Huang, Emily Field, Megan McConnell, Monne Williams, and Nicole Robinson. Lareina and Alexis cofounded Women in the Workplace in partnership with LeanIn.org and extend our deepest gratitude to Sheryl Sandberg, Rachel Thomas, Gina Cardazone, and the LeanIn.org team.

The research to understand the role of experience capital was led by the Human Capital team at the McKinsey Global Institute. Our deepest appreciation to Anu Madgavkar and Kanmani Chockalingam in particular, who have led this work and driven the gender-specific cuts of data.

Thank you also to the broader Human Capital research team: Jeongmin Seong, Dapo Folami, Davis Carlin, Ananya Sivaraman, Bill Schaninger, Hamid Samandari, Lola Woetzel, and Sven Smit.

We also leveraged insights built upon almost two decades of global gender and leadership research initiatives that McKinsey has invested in, such as the Women Matter series, the Power of Parity reports, the Centered Leadership initiative, and beyond, and want to thank all their pioneering authors.

A number of McKinsey colleagues contributed to this book, including Isabelle Hughes, Taylor Saunders-Wood, Annie-Lou St-Amant, Brooke Harvey, Audrey Gotko, Francisca Barata Salgueiro, Leticia Gutiérrez Postigo, Veronika-Silke Kamplade, Bansri Lakhani, Diana Ellsworth, Mekala Krishnan, Sarah Gitlin, Natacha Catalino, and Tracy Nowski. We benefited from the encouragement and contributions from our senior partner colleagues—Jill Zucker, Sandra Sancier-Sultan, Lucy Pérez, Tracy Francis, Dana Maor, and Anna Hertl. We drew strength and inspiration from the Senior Partner Women's community at McKinsey (aka Wicked). A huge thank-you to Bob Sternfels, the global managing partner of McKinsey, who encouraged us to write this book together. To the women in the San Francisco, Lisbon, London, Minneapolis, and Madrid offices, thank you for being part of our focus groups and local inspiration.

To the dynamic business leaders who are our clients and friends, thank you for sharing your insights and personal journeys with us through interviews, and for paying it forward so that other women may benefit from your wisdom. You are an inspiration, and we know our connections with you will endure beyond this book.

Thank you to our publishing leadership team, who saw the potential in this book and were by our side from idea to print: Raju Narisetti, Leader, McKinsey Global Publishing, and the talented production and marketing team at McKinsey, especially Kimberly Beals; and Lynn Johnston, our terrific literary agent. Raju and Lynn shared incredible wisdom every step of the way and helped bring the book to life. We are also grateful for the entire team at Harvard Business Review Press, especially Jeff

Kehoe, Anne Starr, Joshua Olejarz, Melinda Merino, Cheyenne Paterson, Stephani Finks, Jon Shipley, Julie Devoll, Felicia Sinusas, Sally Ashworth, Lindsey Dietrich, Jordan Concannon, and Alexandra Kephart, for sharing our vision for the book and for their wonderful collaboration and thoughtful feedback. And thank you to Adrian Daub, Sylvia Jarabo, and Joelle Emerson, among others, who were early readers of this book and helped us shape it and make it better.

The authors wish to thank their families for their support of this book.

From Kweilin: Thank you to my parents and brother, who have deeply shaped who I am today and have always chosen the road less traveled. To a long family line of strong and bold women who paved the way. Thank you to my supportive and funny husband, Dave, and our three wonderful daughters—Kyla, Hana, and Alexa. You inspire me every day to do all I can to fix the broken rungs. Thank you to the sponsors and friends who have helped me grow and encouraged me to follow my passions.

From Lareina: Thank you to my strong-willed grandmother and my loving mom and dad, who came from China to the United States and taught me to lead with courage and resilience. To my husband, Bert Galleno, who is the greatest partner on the road of life, and our three extraordinary boys—Nicolas, Sebastian, and Mateo—who are my constant source of inspiration and joy. I am deeply grateful to my friends, colleagues, and clients who shaped my professional journey and encouraged me to speak up and create a more equal and inclusive workplace.

From María del Mar: Thank you to my grandparents and parents, Carmen and Martín, who raised me in an egalitarian environment in Andorra, instilled in me the belief in myself, and allowed me to forge my own path. To my husband Rafael and in-laws who have provided unwavering support, encouragement, and admiration over the years. To my three sons, Juan, Pedro, and José, as they will be champions for women in their generation. Additionally, I am deeply thankful to many sponsors and to McKinsey & Company for being the platform that unlocked my professional potential and strengthened my commitment to supporting women in the workplace.

This book has been about our own lived experiences, the stories of women who inspire us, and the data and research we have invested in together over the last twenty years. It is also about our friendship and our personal passion to help women achieve their full potential at work and beyond.

ABOUT THE AUTHORS

Kweilin, María, and Lareina have worked together for over twenty years and are friends, colleagues, and passionate advocates for advancing women in business and society. They each support clients in different industries and geographies, and each has served at different times as McKinsey's chief diversity and inclusion officer.

KWEILIN ELLINGRUD is a senior partner at McKinsey & Company. As a director of the McKinsey Global Institute (MGI), she leads McKinsey's research on the future of work and the impact of automation, as well as on human capital, gender equality, and racial equity. She is also a leader in McKinsey's Operations and Insurance practices, implementing global performance transformations. In addition, she is the current chief diversity and inclusion officer for McKinsey globally.

Kweilin instigated and coauthored "The Power of Parity," MGI's research on unlocking the potential of women to drive greater economic growth. She frequently writes and speaks about the untapped potential of women globally and strategies to achieve gender parity. Her writing has appeared in *Forbes* and *Time* magazines, and she has spoken at the United Nations, the Council on Foreign Relations, and the US Treasury.

Prior to rejoining McKinsey in 2005, Kweilin spent two years at the Center for Women & Enterprise (CWE), a nonprofit that helps women entrepreneurs start and grow their businesses. At CWE she created a microloan program for low-income women.

As a child, Kweilin spent several years in China, Japan, Ecuador, and France, living with local families, going to local schools, and learning the language. Constantly adapting to different cultures and learning new languages taught her to be more flexible, empathetic, and grateful. It also instilled in her a great curiosity about the world and the different roles women play across cultures and countries.

Kweilin earned her MBA from Harvard Business School, where she was copresident of the Women's Student Association. She attended both Harvard University and Wellesley College and graduated magna cum laude with a degree in economics and political science. She lives in Minneapolis with her husband and three daughters.

LAREINA YEE is a senior partner at McKinsey & Company, where she leads McKinsey's alliances and ecosystems. She is a director of technology research at McKinsey's Global Institute (MGI), and a member of the global management team. She is an expert in frontier technologies, including AI, and advises companies on growth and transformation.

Lareina has been on the forefront of gender and diversity research for over a decade, and is a passionate champion of seeing underrepresented talent reach its full potential in the workplace and helping business leaders create a level playing field. Lareina served as McKinsey's first chief diversity and inclusion officer and cofounded Women in the Workplace, an annual research partnership with LeanIn.org that is the largest study of women in corporate America.

In 2023, she was named as one of *Forbes* magazine's Future of Work 50, and she has published perspectives in the *Wall Street Journal, Fortune*, and *Fast Company*. She has coauthored a significant body of research on diversity, including "Race in the Workplace: The Frontline Experience." In her role in MGI, she recently authored "McKinsey's Annual Technology Trends Outlook," "The Economic Potential of Generative AI," and "The CEO's Guide to Generative AI." Each of these publications examines long-term technology shifts and their implications for different industries.

In addition to her work with McKinsey, Lareina serves on the board of the San Francisco Ballet and on the advisory councils of the Clayman Institute for Gender Research at Stanford University and the Beyond

Barnard program at Columbia University. She received a bachelor's degree from Barnard College and a master's degree from Columbia University's School of International and Public Affairs, where she was a Javitz Fellow and graduated magna cum laude. She was born and raised in San Francisco, where she currently lives with her husband and three sons.

MARÍA DEL MAR MARTÍNEZ is a senior partner at McKinsey & Company. She has more than twenty-five years of experience serving organizations on risk and resilience, transformation, and growth. In addition to serving her clients, she has held a variety of key roles at McKinsey, such as serving on the global executive team, being a core leader in McKinsey's Global Banking practice, leading the Global Risk and Resilience Practice, and chairing the global senior partner nomination committee.

María del Mar was the first woman elected partner in her office. She is committed to making a difference for women by leading diversity research in Spain, other parts of Europe, and globally, including collaborations with the World Economic Forum. She also served as McKinsey's chief diversity and inclusion officer, where she brought new rigor and accountability to diversity efforts internally and with clients.

In addition to her work at McKinsey, María del Mar serves on the board of trustees at Esade Business School in Barcelona and is a member of the board of Plan International Spain, an NGO that defends children's rights and girls' equality. María del Mar earned her bachelor's degree in business and an MBA from Esade in Barcelona, a master's in finance from the Stern School of Business at New York University, and a master's in international management from HEC Paris Business School. María del Mar is originally from Andorra and now lives in Madrid with her husband and three sons.